Carrier Observer

Carrier Observer
A Back-Seat Aviator's Story

Gordon Wallace

Airlife

Dedicated to all those young men
who were not granted my nine lives.

Copyright © Gordon Wallace 1993

First published in the UK in 1993
by Airlife Publishing Ltd

British Cataloguing in Publication Data
   A catalogue record for this book
   is available from the British Library

ISBN 1 85310 307 1

Printed by Livesey Ltd, Shrewsbury

Airlife Publishing Ltd

101 Longden Road, Shrewsbury SY3 9EB, England

Contents

Acknowledgements

The writing of this book has given me many happy hours since I retired, and brought me into contact with many of the wartime characters who flit through its pages. It has been like living it all again, with all the excitement but without the anguish.

With no diaries, and my original flying log book a casualty in 1942, I have had to rely on memory and the help of many kind folk who responded to my pleas for help through the Fleet Air Arm Officers' Association. My sincere thanks are due to the following FAA and RAF personnel: Wing Cdr E. J. Holloway, Sq Ldr A. W. Eller, and M. A. Butterworth of 18 Squadron RAF: Lt Cdr T. W. May and Lt G. C. Marley of 831 Squadron: Lt A. P. N. Ward of 800 Squadron: Rear Admiral J. A. Ievers and Cdr A. F. Paterson of 814 Squadron: J. P. Du Cane of 820 Squadron: Cdr C. R. Coxon (dec'd), Lt J. Dickson, and Sub Lt D. V. Brook of 812 Ssquadron: Vice Admiral Sir Roy Halliday and Lt Cdr V. M. Langman of 703 Squadron: Lt R. V. Hinton of 803 Squadron: Lt Cdr M. Hordern of 806 Squadron: TAGs D. Sweet and G. Dixon of 827 Squadron.

Details of Cdr Coxon's wartime career are based on his grand-daughter's (Sophie Stewart) well researched school 'project'.

I am also grateful for technical and historical information from: Captain Isaimi Kyoda, Embassy of Japan: David Brown, RN Historical Branch, MOD: Staff of the Fleet Air Arm Museum: The Public Records Office.

Janis Eagle's patience in typing my original hand-written manuscript into the word-processor is greatly appreciated.

Finally I must thank my wife and family for their encouragement and, in particular, my elder son, Kenneth, who prepared the draft typescript, and introduced me to the magic of the word-processor.

Chapter 1
Seeing the Joke

He was very young, the Army Captain, encased in plaster from waist to feet like some weird chrysalis, and lying opposite me across one side of the compartment of an old French corridor train which was slowly winding its way back to Algiers, with a full load of wounded, from a hospital near the First Army's front line at Beja, in Tunisia.

I never knew his name. I have never been good with names and, in spite of all I had been through in two years of war, I was still, at 22, ridiculously shy. I can't even tell you how he was wounded, we somehow managed to avoid the subject. His face had a grey pallor and I saw him wince every time the train lurched on ill-kept tracks.

'My God, I need a pee! Orderly! Orderly!' he shouted.

There was silence but for the rattling of the train.

I joined in, 'Orderly! Orderly!'

Nothing doing.

I dropped my legs down to the floor and, keeping my bandaged hands raised to my shoulders to avoid the throbbing surge of blood, staggered out into the corridor, fending myself from the sides with my elbows.

'Orderly! Orderly!'

'Fat chance you have chum!' came a Cockney voice from the next compartment.

In December, darkness sets in rapidly in Tunisia once the sun sets, and it gets quite cold with a frost in the early morning.

The cold got to me and I too began to experience the dreaded urge for a pee. With both hands out of commission, I had already had to suffer the indignity of having someone undo my fly buttons and manhandle me. But now what? The simple solution of peeing in my trousers never crossed my mind. I had done it once as a boy returning from school to find neither of my parents at home, and the shame had left an indelible mark.

We lay in ever-increasing misery. Time passed and the Captain began to cry in pain and distress. I had never seen a man cry, being brought up to be ashamed of tears, and taught from an early age to hold them back. The mental shock and anguish drove me to action.

'If you put your arms around my neck I think I can get you onto your feet and down the corridor,' I suggested. He agreed and I managed to pull him upright and then drag him along the corridor behind me until we reached the open gangway between the coaches, where I propped him up against the iron railing. With a whoop of joy he sprayed the tracks. I tried to brace my feet against the lurching and rocking as he undid my flies and extracted the no longer private part with a cold hand. What exquisite happiness.

We struggled back along the swaying corridor to our compartment and laughed and laughed and laughed.

'If you can't see the joke you shouldn't have joined!' So they all said.

I was beginning to grow up. War is a bad joke. At least I had seen the joke this time, it was not to be so easy three years later.

I never saw the young Captain again after we arrived some days later in Algiers, where I was to continue my education in the more sanguinary facts of life.

Chapter 2
A Phoney War

It all began as a bit of a joke. When war broke out Jack Moon and I were two years into our apprenticeship at the de Havilland Aeronautical Technical School at Hatfield in Hertfordshire. Budding aeronautical engineers, mad keen on aeroplanes, which we loved more than women, and at nineteen more unworldly than today's young men.

On Monday 4 September 1939, we set off early in Jack's Austin Seven open tourer, named *The Jeep,* to join the Fleet Air Arm. Why that particular service you may enquire? It just seemed to be a good idea at the time, perhaps we fancied the uniform. And where did we go to join? Nothing less than the main Admiralty Building in Whitehall. Jack even parked the car right outside the imposing gates — there was no one to say no in those far off days of simple motoring.

We approached an elderly commissionaire standing at the entrance of a small wooden hut to one side of the gates.

'And what can I do for you young gentlemen?' he enquired gravely.

'We would like to join the Fleet Air Arm,' we replied.

'Well that's a new one. I've never had anyone ask me that before, you'd better go up them steps and speak to the man at the desk — and when you come back, let me know how you got on.'

Behind the high Victorian counter was a nondescript young clerk.

'We want to join the Fleet Air Arm as aircrew!'

'The Navy has no requirement in that area,' was the bland reply.

'I thought there was a war on!' I said.

'Well, If you want to join the Navy, there is a recruiting office around the corner. I suggest you go there.'

After reporting events to the commissionaire, we located the recruiting office in a typical London tobacconist-sized cubby-hole close by the Admiralty Arch, and inhabited, behind a desk at the back, by what I later identified as a Petty Officer of the old school, a mixture of fearsome kindliness, to whom we repeated our enquiry.

'You need special good eyes if you are thinking of flying — stand on that there line and read the bottom two lines on this 'ere chart' — which we did without hesitation.

'Ah well! That's very good, but we don't seem to have any requirement for the Fleet Air Arm.'

Jack and I looked at each other, shrugged our shoulders and set off in the car up the Edgware Road back to Hatfield.

Halfway up the Edgware Road we saw a large RAF recruiting centre.

'Let's have a go there,' Jack said, and in we went. Here, at least, we were given a short medical, pronounced fit and told to await events.

Back at the de Havilland works I returned to my work assisting in the assembly of wooden wings for the Airspeed Oxford twin-engined trainer aircraft.

I think it was sometime in November when I got instructions to report to RAF Cardington for a full flying medical. This nerve racking affair took place in various screened-off cubicles in one of the huge black airship sheds. Draughty and cold, particularly when standing naked for unmentionable indignities. I had a very bad cold that day and they weren't impressed with my hearing. I failed. Rejecting their offer to join as ground crew, I returned to my digs in Hatfield and cold bloodedly sat in a chair and knocked back six pints of beer. It was the worst day of my life so far.

Jack was impatient and in October joined the Army as a private, being posted to the Hampshire's in the Isle of Wight. He was considered too young to go with the regiment overseas and was sent to the Officer Cadet Training Unit at Bulford where he was commissioned. Early in 1942 he transferred to the RAF and during the first stage of pilot training he accidentally shot himself in the foot with a shotgun, had a toe amputated, and was sent back to the Army. Through the intervention of a pragmatic doctor he managed to get back to the RAF and ended up flying Spitfires.

I felt thoroughly miserable and drank too much. If this was war it was nothing like I expected. There were no air raids by either side and no action between the armies in France. The only drama seemed to be taking place at sea. U-boats and pocket battleships were roaming the seas and sinking our shipping; they even got into Scapa Flow and sank the old battleship *Royal Oak*. There was the excitement of our success in the Battle of the River Plate when the Navy forced the German pocket battleship *Graf Spee* to scuttle.

Many of the older Tech School apprentices were already in the RAF Reserve and flew Hawker Harts from Hatfield aerodrome at the weekends. By the end of the year they had all left to begin operational training. They were a wild, flamboyant bunch and mostly went to fighter squadrons. Very few were to survive the war.

In the early months of 1940 I was working in the Structural Test Laboratory where we were torsion testing the wooden fuselage of the future Mosquito. This was a test to destruction and I can still hear the bang when it finally failed. Little did I, or any of us, realise what an important part this aircraft was to play in the future, and not by any stretch of the imagination that I would fly in one in the final year of the war.

At the time of the Dunkirk catastrophe I had moved on to the Stress Office and became responsible for the calculations to fit a bomb rack on the Tiger Moth designed, believe it or not, to carry a 250lb bomb, which was to be used in a death and glory attempt to attack the expected German invasion. Geoffrey de Havilland, test pilot and eldest son of the pioneer, dropped a dummy bomb on the Hatfield aerodrome and I watched the little biplane leap several hundred feet up as the bomb left the rack.

With the threat of a German invasion, I joined the Local Defence Volunteers, which later became the Home Guard. It occupied my evenings and kept me off the booze.

In late May 1940 the Admiralty advertised in the press for applicants between the age of 19 and 21 to join the Fleet Air Arm as aircrew. My application went off that same day. A letter came directing me to report for a medical to HMS *St Vincent* at Gosport. *St Vincent* turned out to be a barracks, not a ship. Mention of its name will bring a faraway look and a wry smile to the face of any old Naval Aviator.

Fortunately I was free from cold and the doctor who tested my hearing was in his dotage. By now I had learnt a trick or two about flying medicals and kept my eyes partly open when the old boy moved the tuning fork from side to side behind me; I could just see the sun glinting on it. So the fact that I was, and still am, slightly deaf in my right ear went undetected. At the end I was selected for training as an Observer. I really wanted to be a Pilot but I have a suspicion that my reflexes were never up to it. My father was an Observer in the Royal Flying Corps in 1917/18 and I felt the honour of the family was satisfied. At least I was going to fly.

At this time apprentices at de Havillands were considered to be in a 'reserved' occupation and were not supposed to join the forces. The Navy never asked and back at Hatfield they grumbled but accepted a *fait accompli.* And so in July I joined the ill-fated 43rd Observer course at HMS *St Vincent,* a shy, immature youth, without the slightest idea of what I had let myself in for, but romantically keen to do and die.

The Navy tried their best to effect the dying part of it.

Chapter 3
Bell Bottoms

All aircrew started their life in the Fleet Air Arm with the unique and never to be forgotten experience of two months at HMS *St Vincent* as Naval Airmen 2nd Class, there being no rank lower in the Navy. So much has already been written, with more wit than I possess, about how this brief time changed all our young lives that all I can do to fill this part of my tale is to recall my own special memories.

That we were destined to fly had nothing to do with the job in hand as was soon impressed on us by Chief Petty Officer Willmot and Petty Officer Oliver, both 'Gunners' with crossed guns on their sleeves and gaiters at their ankles. Stamped from head to toe with traditions going back to Nelson, it was their, probably unsought, role in life to inculcate these traditions in us miserable sinners joining straight from the fleshpots of civvy life or, more likely, straight from school or university. It was a love/hate relationship at the time, but of love alone in hindsight.

To enter the *St Vincent* gates, beneath the high arched portico, was to enter a new world with a new language. On the left side one reported to the 'regulating' office. Ahead, dominating the wide expanse of the parade ground, was a frighteningly tall, white painted mast. Suffering from vertigo I hoped that I would never be expected to climb it. Some hope. We had to go up it one day, en masse and wearing gas masks. The gas masks proved an advantage, all I could see were the heels of those above me and there was the dubious comfort of dozens more below me. Thank God, we were only expected to go half way up and down the other side. In an evening some brave or idiotic souls climbed right to the top and stood on the button. It made me sick to think about it.

Beyond the parade ground stretched a line of forbidding brick barrack blocks, rising several stories, in which we spent little more than sleeping time, and not always that. At the corner of each flight of stairs were the brown tiled 'heads', the Navyspeak for toilets. In Nelson's time the Jack Tars sat with their bottoms over the edge of the bows or 'heads' of the ship. Or so they told me. To my sensitive nature they were a bit of a shock, at that time I hadn't been to Algeria.

No sooner had we arrived, some fifty of us, than the war I expected finally arrived. Out of clear summer skies came the scream of dive-bombing Stukas amidst a thunder of gun fire. We even became a target and had our first taste of death when one of the air raid shelters was hit. The casualties didn't belong to our observer course, so that was all right. Chief Willmot, perched on top of one of the barrack blocks with a machine gun, claimed to have shot one down. He went up in everyone's estimation.

If learning to tie rope knots or rowing a naval cutter in the harbour was good 'boy scout' stuff, night duty was far from fun. Falling in to the call of volunteers — you, you and you — we might be detailed for the 'pick and shovel' party whose fearsome task was to go down to the nearby oil storage tanks should they be bombed, and dig a trench to drain away the burning fuel. Or was this one of Willmot's little jokes?

On Sunday mornings we had 'Divisions', a strange name for a rather grand church parade with full Marine band. The highlight for me was the Commander's echoing cry, 'Fall out Roman Catholics!' his resonant voice falling away on the last syllable of 'Catholics'. What terrible fate awaited them had they stayed? What fun it was to double off the parade ground to the tune of 'Wings over the Navy'.

As the weeks sped by with little to indicate our future role other than some elementary ship navigation, and many exhausting hours of Morse code, we fell more easily into playing at the role of a bell-bottomed sailor, spending hours in the ablutions scrubbing our collars to give a bleached appearance, ironing our trousers inside out to give the desired figure of eight shape and, quite against regulations, splitting our navy jumpers about two inches at the midriff to expose a greater expanse of white seaman's vest — an early version of the T shirt. After four weeks, for reasons unknown, we were promoted to Acting Leading Airmen and hastened to sew gold anchors on our left sleeves. Most of us now had 'Oppos', or special friends on the course; on one of my 'shore' leaves my Oppo and I had our photos taken in the dusty back room of a shop in Gosport, the result was stiff and Victorian but no doubt our families felt some pride when they received them. On 22 August we celebrated my twentieth birthday at a rather up-market restaurant in Portsmouth and talked of our imminent departure from St Vincent, unaware that the Gods of War were throwing dice with all our young lives.

I spent that night on duty in a cold, damp trench, armed with a Lee-Enfield rifle, guarding the creek behind the barracks against the expected arrival of German paratroops. The following night I woke up in the early hours with a fever and the shakes, and was carted off the following morning to the sick bay, which was outside the barracks on the opposite side of the main road. Little good can be said of my treatment there for, with a temperature of 103 degrees I was required to polish the lino floor on my hands and knees. Later, during a night air raid, when, clad in pyjamas and dressing gown, we attempted to sleep on the benches, we were aroused by the arrival of the Surgeon Commander: 'Patients will sit to attention while in the shelter!' I sat to attention and after a while fainted and awoke to find myself in an ambulance on the way to Haslar hospital — still without being told what was wrong with me.

At Haslar there were nurses. They even told me that I had double pneumonia. Did anyone on the 43rd 'O' Course know where I was? Would they leave *St Vincent* without me? There was no one to ask and no one came to visit me. The following night there was a heavy air raid and all the patients were taken down in the lifts to the cellars. Here my breathing became so bad that they moved me back up to the ward and a dear young nurse sat with me and held my hand, just the two of us in a darkened ward as a crescendo of ack-ack and bombs surrounded us. The next day I was moved by ambulance to an old country mansion some 10 miles north of Portsmouth, near Horndean. They told me it was a convalescent home but I wasn't exactly feeling like convalescence and was only breathing with difficulty. After a sleepless night in a large L-shaped room with about ten beds I was moved again into a bed at one end of a large oak panelled library, at the other end of which were two Free-French sailors who seemed to be perpetually asleep. In the evening a nurse wrapped my chest in Thermogene, an impregnated cotton wool, and a favourite treatment in those days for chest infections. If you perspired it burnt your skin. Matron, a small, tubby, Irene Handl character arrived by my bedside holding a small glass.

'Drink it down, boy, it's brandy. It'll do you good.'

Brandy. Brandy! Other ranks don't get brandy in hospital or anywhere else in this man's Navy. She tucked me in. Tucked me in! My God! It dawned on my fuddled brain, I'm going to die. Like Hell I was! I'd got to get back to the 43rd course or I'd miss my 'war in the air' and all that glory. I slept well for the first time. The next day one of the Frenchmen died. He had never spoken. He went out on a stretcher covered by a white sheet. Who was next? They moved me back into the L-shaped room in a bed near the large French windows looking out over the lawn. Perhaps I wasn't going to die after all.

'So you're back with us, sonny!' croaked the old, grizzled Marine in the bed next to mine. To me he looked about eighty and coughed and spat up phlegm most of the day, sometimes they raised the end of his bed up and he hung over the side and coughed up into a bowl; the smell was foul.

Nobody came to see me, where were they all? Had they left me behind? The country mansion belonged to the elderly lady and both she and Matron did a nightly round of the beds, both of them quite drunk, and clutching at the bed ends to steady themselves. This was our only entertainment.

'And how are we tonight, Sergeant?' Matron would enquire of my Marine neighbour.

'All the better for seeing you m'dear!'

'And how are you Jock?'

'Much wurrse!' was the inevitable reply of the ward's hypochondriac Scotsman. The day Jock was told he was to be discharged he stood outside in the rain for an hour hoping, without success, to catch a cold or worse.

In the cloudless skies of that September 1940, the Battle of Britain was being fought over our heads, and sitting outside the French windows I watched the cats cradle of con-trails and heard the rattle of machine guns, as remote and unreal as in a Hollywood production, and certainly not one in which I seemed likely to have a role.

At last I was free of the daily 'nightmare' of the bed pan and could sit in glorious seclusion in the 'heads'. The young night nurse seemed to have taken me under her wing and my special treat was a glass of Horlicks.

At the end of September I was returned, in the back of a transport lorry, to Haslar hospital where I had two or three days of breathing exercises during which I had a great lump of a fellow pressing down on one side of my chest while I breathed, as best I could, on the other. Breathing using the stomach and all the volume of the lungs was new to me, and greatly improved my singing voice. Finally they gave me a medical which included the dreaded 'blowing up the mercury tube and holding one's breath'. Apparently I achieved a Haslar record for this and was passed A1B (fit for aircrew).

Of course no one could tell me where I stood in the Observer stakes and I was sent off home on leave. Home was at Heddon-on-the-Wall in Northumberland and all I can remember of the month of October was an attachment to a certain red-head, a Miss Connie McGraw, who lived in Newcastle, and whose father gave me a terrible wigging when I ran out of petrol in my old man's car and she had to stay the night at our home, suitably chaperoned by my mother and father, but sinful as far as her father was concerned. How things have changed, how innocent we were — or was it just me? In November it was back to *St Vincent* to join the 45th Observer Course, in other words, back to square one. It was not until months later that I learnt of the catastrophe which struck down the old 43rd Course. After surviving being bombed while embarked on a transport ship in Liverpool docks they sailed for Trinidad to join the newly set up Observer Flying Training School. The ship was attacked and sunk in mid-Atlantic by the German pocket battleship *Admiral Scheer* out on a raiding mission. [Left Stavanger in Norway 28 October, 1940, returned to Bergen 30 March, 1941.] As far as I know, no one survived.

St Vincent was no place to dwell on the mysteries of life and death, and soon I even forgot both names and faces. Now there were sixty new ones.

'Now KG, you've got an 'ook and I'm relying on you to look after this new lot for me — keep 'em out of trouble!' barked PO Oliver. So I marched them here, there and everywhere. How different it all seemed a second time round. Once more 'Fall out Roman Catholics' echoed around the parade ground but the daylight bombing had changed to night attacks. I had all-night shore leave the night King's Road, Southsea was destroyed in a fire storm, the wind funnelling the flames like a torch down the length of the road. I had booked a room at the Salvation Army hostel, but when the raid started I attached myself to an auxiliary fire pump unit and ended up in the already blazing oil tank area of the docks on the end of a fire hose. There was a sudden whistle of falling bombs and the fireman in front of me scampered off to a nearby shelter leaving me holding a violently snaking hose under my arm. It soon pulled me down onto the river of water on the dockside where I lay until they came back. I didn't dare let go.

Later the burning roof of a building fell down on us and I felt for the first, but not last time, the searing blast of flame across my face and lost my eyelashes. I got back to the hostel well after midnight, soaking wet. The room and bed were cold but I was asleep as my head touched the pillow. The morning brought the beastly business of dressing in a soggy, damp uniform and greatcoat, and the long walk back to the ferry through smoking and debris littered streets which seemed surprisingly empty. A board on one side of the road gave the simple warning UNEXPLODED BOMB. I hesitated and walked quickly by on the other side with a racing pulse: a form of Russian roulette. Later in Algeria I was to witness the real thing.

We were given a few days leave before reporting to the infamous Naval Gunnery School on Whale Island having been warned that this was the British equivalent of Alcatraz. Why were we embryo aviators going to a Gunnery establishment you might well ask? The only answer I can find after all these years is that it was to induce in us a sense of the macabre, so essential to survive in a Navy which for the greater part of the war didn't really believe in aviation. Aircraft attacking ships of His Majesty's Navy? 'Not an 'ope in 'ell, Gentlemen, not an 'ope in 'ell! Get me? Not an 'ope in 'ell', our gunnery instructor assured us. Spotting the fall of shells from their guns might be of some use, but their gunnery was so good they could manage nicely thank you, without any of us poncing about in the air and getting ourselves mixed up between which battle line was which, and so on.

We had lectures on types of shell — 'Two green bands, three yellow. What's that boy? A Haitch E or a Harmour Piercing? You don't know do you — well I'll tell yer!'

And gun drill. Standing in line, rigidly to attention, not moving an eyelid until the command rasped out to grasp and turn the appropriate brass knob.

Compared with other courses, the 45th suffered little of the punishments meted out to all those who chose to buck the system. We chose to do what we were told and even derived pleasure from the rule that one proceeded everywhere at the double during working hours and cheerfully accepted that to volunteer to return the breakfast 'pots' to the cook house would inevitably make one late falling in for parade and be 'booked!'.The main punishment was to run a specified number of times around the parade ground with rifle and back pack, and this applied equally to the officers on gunnery courses.

As we marched for the last time over the short bridge which links the island to the shore the water looked black and cold; it was January 1941 and we were off on a few days' leave. It was early evening when I arrived in London on my way home to Newcastle-upon-Tyne, the tube stations were just beginning to fill up with all the hundreds taking shelter from the nightly blitz. Poor souls of all ages packed like sardines almost up to the edge of the platform. I felt a sense of guilt stepping over outstretched legs; how could they possibly sleep with the lights on, with the intermittent rumble of approaching trains, the screech of brakes and the discomfort of a rock hard bed. Arriving in a grim, blacked out King's Cross Station I cabled my family to say that I was on my way and when we did eventually pull out of the station it was to the chilling accompaniment of London's ack-ack barrage. I always felt an increased feeling of vulnerability in the confines of a train during an air raid, as though the enemy could see us more clearly: it was two years later when I came face to face with how it felt to be up there in the dark with my hand on the bomb switch. One was lucky to see a town, never mind a train.

I arrived at dawn to find Newcastle immobilised by snow and the telephones out of order. So I set out to walk the seven miles to Heddon-on-the-Wall, lugging my regulation green case in a primaeval urge to return to the nest, only to find it empty. Mother and father had taken the train to Newcastle the night before and were staying at the Station Hotel where eventually we made telephone contact and, after a 'sportif' drive in the family car I met up with them at the Station Hotel. It all seemed worthwhile as my red-headed Connie was there with them. The following day saw me back on my way down to 'Pompey' barracks where the 45th was to report for a course at the Signals School.

Signals School! What in Hell's name were we doing there? Shouldn't we have been up there in the sky doing battle with the enemy after all this time? Or so it seemed to all of us — we couldn't have understood that no one had foreseen such an expansion of flying training programmes and the logistics of slotting human beings into them. And what should we have been taught, what experience was there to build on? Fleet Air Arm aircraft (apart from fighters) communicated by means of wireless telegraphy so perhaps it made sense to send us to signal school. It would have made more sense if we had learnt something useful during the weeks we spent in this old barracks. If *St Vincent* had seemed grim, Pompey was grisly. All sixty of us had to sleep in hammocks slung only two feet apart in one small room, as would have been typical in Nelson's day. I dare say that one can learn to sleep comfortably in a naval hammock. When strung up it resembles a banana slit down the concave side so there is no alternative to sleeping on one's back conforming to the curved shape. The slinging hooks were about five feet high so the business of getting into the damn thing was nothing short of acrobatic. The early morning call of 'Wakey, Wakey. Rise and shine. Lash up and stow,' required another acrobatic performance with numbed arms and a stiff back. The 'lashing and stowing' to the approved manner was a skill some found beyond them and resulted in much tongue lashing from our Petty Officer instructor. For a few days we saw the funny side of it, but for some of us it was one joke too many.

My two 'oppos' at this time were Brian Walsh-Atkins and Tommy Thompson. Brian was very much a top drawer type having been at the Foreign Office before joining. The slightly supercilious curl to his lip hid an engaging personality and meticulous application to any problem, even that of joining the Navy. He found us a flat in Granada Road, Southsea and invited us to share it. We were granted permission to live out and apart from the disruption of almost nightly air raids we enjoyed some comfort in the dark February evenings after long days in dismal classrooms where a rather bitter and twisted little Petty Officer attempted to teach us the basic principles of radio theory. I still don't know how a radio works.

The bombing restricted our social life to the quick visit to a pub and we led a monastic life. The only excitement was when we had to deal with the odd incendiary bomb.

At last we had reached the end of the beginning and the real business lay ahead. We were off to fly. The 45th course was now split into two groups. One half was to go to Trinidad and the other to Arbroath, in Scotland. There was no choice, I was down to go to Arbroath. I was quite pleased. To have gone to Trinidad might have been tempting fate.

Chapter 4
Airborne at Last

Slow rail journeys north-bound on the LNER had grown to be part of life. This time it was in the boisterous company of bell-bottomed friends, linked by the shared experience of surviving the Navy's obstacle course and elated by the prospect of facing the real test. At every stop we piled out onto the platform to grab a bun and a cup of tea. Brian would hold back to dissociate himself from the rabble.

Crossing the vertiginous Forth Bridge for the first time was exciting. I looked for the painters who it was said no sooner finished one end than they started again at the other. And then on to Dundee across the Tay bridge, long, low and gently curving. It had been a long day and was already dark when we reached Arbroath station and clambered into the back of a truck with our ubiquitous green cases and kit bags. At least we were expected.

HMS *Condor* was in darkness as we entered its gates; if there was an airfield we couldn't see it. The 'regulating' office Petty Officer booked us in with the customary dead pan lack of interest and soon we were choosing our beds in a featureless wooden hut with its inevitable highly polished brown lino floor calling out for many hours of elbow grease.

No 2 Observer School lives happily in my memory, I was to spend more time there than most. The huts were comfortable by previous standards and not too crowded. The food was ghastly and I survived on bread and Marmite. Discipline was firm but fair, without silly games. We were lucky to have two first rate course officers, Lieutenants Roe and Hutchinson, both regular navy, but quietly spoken and approachable. Our paths were destined to cross in a later year in bizarre circumstances.

The excitement of those first days! Kitting up with flying gear; bulky green Sidcot suits, helmets, goggles, fur-lined boots, white silk gloves, long leather gloves and, of course, the Mae West which needs no description. We were issued with that most vital item of Observer equipment, the Bigsworth Board in its green canvas case: a quite sophisticated parallel arm drawing board about 20 inches square on which a navigation chart could be attached with clips. And finally a strange device known as a Course Setting Calculator (CSC).

At the first noise of an aircraft engine all our eager eyes would lift up and there would be a lone Fairey Swordfish stooging slowly around looking like some leftover from the First World War. Could this really be the aircraft which had wreaked such havoc on the Italian fleet at Taranto? I began to wonder what had attracted me to join this service in the first place; perhaps I thought that by the time I took to the air something more exciting would have arrived. No matter, there was no turning back and we proceeded to get an introduction to the parachute and donned its cumbersome harness which we were told had to be attached to the 'G' string, a strap bolted to the floor of both rear cockpits to prevent Observer and Air Gunner falling out in a violent manoeuvre. The cockpits of Swordfish and Shark were open to the elements just as Nelson would have wished so that he could use his telescope; no other reason was ever forthcoming.

My first flight was in a Blackburn Shark; they called it 'flight experience'. All zipped up and feeling rather like the Michelin man in my Sidcot suit I climbed into the air gunner's section of the long rear cockpit, it was rather like being in an open boat. Two characters in blue boiler suits cranked a large handle and the Armstrong Siddeley Tiger engine coughed and rattled into life sounding like a bag of nails; we had already heard tales of ill repute concerning both aircraft and engine. We staggered into the air for our 'experience', and experience it turned out to be. Our pilot had clearly failed an operational fighter pilot's course and our tour of the green fields and hills of the attractive county of Angus comprised a mixture of steep dives, pull ups and stalled turns, all taking place over his girlfriend's rather posh looking home near Forfar. When she could be clearly seen waving in the middle of the lawn, our pilot's efforts became more enthusiastic and I had my first experience of weightlessness of 'Zero g', floating standing up in the cockpit. It was a good thing we had remembered to attach our harnesses to the 'G strings'! It was a quick way to find out that I didn't suffer from air sickness but it was foolish. How many young men must have killed themselves during the war in an attempt to impress their lady friends; at Crail, in July, 1944 I was to march behind the coffin of one of our pilots who had failed to pull out of a similar antic.

The early weeks were spent more in the class-room than in the air. It had never occurred to me to wonder how one set off from an aircraft carrier, flew in all directions, blown by unforeseen winds, and arrived back to whatever spot in the ocean the carrier might have sailed in the meantime. It certainly wasn't easy in those early days, without the assistance of radio beacons and radar, and continually blasted by cold air and noise which numbed fingers and dulled the brain. As well as navigation we were required to be proficient in operating the wireless telegraphy (W/T) radio set fitted in the third seat, later to be occupied by a Telegraphist Air Gunner (TAG) in an operational squadron. Most of our flying was in

Swordfish of 753 Squadron and we alternated between navigating and operating the W/T. Relationship with our pilots could only be described as sensitive; commissioned, and either passed over for operational flying or too old for it, they must have regarded the whole business as a mighty great bore. I don't know, I was never in a position to ask one. There was generally only silence before we were airborne and then, down the Gosport tubes (our only means of talking to each other), would come the curt query, tinged with sarcasm, 'And where would we be going today?'

'If you don't mind, Sir, could we please depart over the Seaforth Hotel swimming pool on a course of 095 degrees.'

It was always the swimming pool: an imaginary aircraft carrier would 'sail' from that point at a speed of 25 knots on a course of 030 degrees, this bringing it close to the little port of Stonehaven after an hour, by which time we would have completed a dog leg course over the sea and would attempt to arrive over, or 'intercept' the carrier at the appropriate time and place on the coast. [See Appendix 4.] These attempts brooked much sarcastic comment from our pilots as we arrived back in the Tay estuary or near Aberdeen.

'Lost again are we? And where would you suggest we go now if we're not to miss lunch?'

The art in the navigation business was to establish the direction and strength of the wind and both these are more than likely to change quite considerably during a flight, particularly when passing through a 'front'. Of course we had the 'met man' to brief us on his idea of the wind and weather before we took off — his ribald reception was invariably similar to that received by today's TV pundits, and his information certainly less reliable.

On reflection I have nothing but admiration for whoever the boffin was who invented the technique for 'finding a wind', as we called it. Officially designated the Four Point Windfinding Procedure, it is difficult to imagine what we would have done without it, stars being not much use when you can't see them. Easy it was not, requiring collaboration between pilot and observer, and precision in execution whilst flying an oval course.

'Stand by to find a wind!' I would nervously call through the tubes.

'Ready!' would be the expected reply as the pilot set the bomb switches ready to release a smoke float from the wing bomb rack while I fumbled about stowing my Bigsworth board and clasping my stopwatch in a cold hand.

'Release smoke float!' — starting the stopwatch as hopefully the green and yellow bomblet left its rack and plummeted seaward. We had a table giving the number of seconds it would take from any particular height to hit the sea.

'Stand by to turn!' the second hand reached the spot.

'Turn!' as I stopped and restarted the watch and the pilot commenced a Rate 2 turn to straighten into 180 degrees from our previous course.

'Standby to turn', as my stopwatch came up to 1½ minutes.'

'Turn', and another Rate 2 turn brought us back onto our original course while I searched to port and starboard to locate the plume of white smoke streaming over a grey, wave-flecked sea. In the highly unlikely even that there was a zero wind, and if the pilot had flown the racetrack course accurately, the aircraft would be directly over the smoke float at 3 minutes on the stopwatch. The effect of a wind was to cause the aircraft to drift to one side of the smoke float, and a compass bearing on it taken at 3 minutes would give the direction of the wind. To establish the wind speed I would note the times when the smoke float was on the beam and on the quarter — easier said than done with the pilot taking the occasion for some flippant chat, or you dropped your stopwatch, or your goggles blew out of position in the ever-present slipstream and there were tears in your eyes and you couldn't see anything.

As you sat down again to start the calculation to establish the wind speed and, if necessary, correct your plot, through the Gosport tubes would come the enquiry:

'How soon to the first turn?'

'I'm working out the wind!'

'The weather's clamping in — I think we ought to go back now!'

'I'm working out the wind!'

'Well hurry up!'

And then you'd drop your pencil, an almost fatal event. An observer without his pencil is like a woman without a — well you all know.

There was plenty of opportunity to get it all wrong. Could one be sure the pilot was flying the course and speed you thought he was?

And had you given your W/T operator your position to send back to the control tower? At the worst, if you had made a cock-up, you could set a course of 270 degrees which should hit Scotland. But what would it be like in the middle of the Atlantic? Fortunately the trials of the moment obliterated such fears, there was the course to calculate to meet 'our carrier' along the Angus coast using the 'wind' we had found. But was it right? Had it changed? Should we do another 'wind find'?

'Well, boy! What about that bloody course for home?'

'Not quite ready yet!' Cold hands clumsily setting course, air speed and wind data into the CSC.

'Well for God's sake, hurry up!'

Even when the coast loomed through the mist, which bit of the coast was it? One's pilot usually had his own opinion, but he too could be misled.

Why hadn't someone told me this was what it was to be like; week after week of Navexs, as they were called, interspersed with sitting in the TAG's seat, cold and miserable, trying to keep tuned in to the right point of the dial, missing it and only just catching one's call sign, then struggling to write down the dots and dashes with the stub of a pencil. I have some mental block which produces something like ORTYOURPOSITIONIMMEDIA. Time passes before I solve this problem and scribble a note to my observer, whose response is a wild glare and a shrug. I am bound to have a radio failure and when we land and I report to the Signals Petty Officer in the control tower there is the regular castigation.

'And where was you, Wallace, this lovely morning? Or was you too busy looking at the scenery to let us know?'

My abiding memory is of the noise, cold, vibration and general discomfort of an open cockpit; did the designers at the Fairey Aviation Company never look at photographs of American or Japanese naval aircraft, or were they looking forward to times, long after the war, when observer and TAG would stand to attention and salute during each airshow flypast? And fly an ensign from the cockpit.

Some light relief was occasioned by visits to Broughty Ferry on the river Tay where we carried out similar exercises in the Supermarine Walrus amphibian aircraft of 751 Squadron. An aircraft affectionately known as the 'Shagbat'. The discomfort of an open cockpit was replaced by the odd odours emanating from its 'bilges' and the pungent smoke from the cigar which one of the 'aged' pilots would light up as soon as we were airborne, or should I say if we managed to get airborne. On a calm day we would waddle through the water, turn towards the Tay bridge and, with the throttle wide open, plough through some half mile of water and then, after the control column was pulled right back, the nose would lift, only to sink back again as we approached ominously close to the bridge. Back again down river for another try. With rougher water progress was of a bucking variety, but more likely to result in our being bumped up into the air. The Walrus had a camera hatch in the bottom of the hull, which, on one occasion, had been removed. We rolled down the slipway into the water and sank slowly to the bottom, with cheers from all ashore and a wetting for all aboard.

My first 'prang' occurred in a Walrus, the engine cutting out just as we crossed the coast near Montrose after completing a Navex. The sudden silence and the whistling of the air through the bracing wires between the wings was broken only by a brief call 'Strap yourselves in!' A glimpse of trees, an almighty thump, a juddering, bone shaking progression over field and ditches, through hedges and then only the sound of birdsong. No time for fear. What did we innocents know of fear? Fear only grows in the soil of imagination and experience.

When the weather cancelled flying we carried out our Navexs in the peace of a classroom or gathered on a remote circle of concrete to attempt the swinging of an aircraft's compass. With the coming of summer the back seat seemed less daunting and the countryside so pleasing to look down upon as we circled to land. Interludes of bomb aiming, firing the Lewis gun at a towed target and a brief, bewildering introduction to the early airborne radar (ASV), fitted to a Swordfish filled our time between the seemingly endless Navexs.

It so happened that it was the ASV Swordfish in which I had my second 'prang'. We were returning from Macrihanish at the southern end of the Mull of Kintyre where we had been sent on an exercise to 'spot' the fall of shells from a cruiser firing against a towed target in the Firth of Clyde. It was a lovely summer day and the late afternoon sun felt quite warm on my back as we flew down the Forth valley at about 2000 feet, the Fintry Hills rising up nearly level with us on our starboard side. No need to navigate, just sit back and enjoy the wonderful scenery. The engine coughed, rattled to a stop, and once again that sudden silence broken only by the sound of rushing air. Just missing the roof tops of a village, we banked towards the hills. A grassy slope seemed to come up and hit us. There was a prolonged grinding and tearing noise and I was thrown against the radar set. Then absolute silence, not one of us spoke or moved.

Looking down the hill behind us I could see that we had ploughed a furrow through a very green field and spread either side of it there was a scattering of wheels, struts and bomb racks. Led by small boys every single villager seemed to be approaching at the run as though they were following the Pied Piper. We still hadn't spoken a word and, when they arrived, neither did they. I think they expected us to be corpses; in fact none of us was even scratched. I think they were disappointed. Eventually what must have been the whole of the village of Kippen surrounded us and a buxom Scottish lady approached carrying a large tray of tea. We were having our cups of tea in our cockpits when I noticed that some of the boys were marching off down the hill with bomb racks on their shoulders. The Army arrived about then and we sent them off to retrieve our property. We then asked if they could place a guard on the wreck as it contained some very secret equipment (the ASV).We were kindly entertained in one of the villager's homes and, without cause, felt heroes. Late in the evening, transport arrived to take us back to Arbroath, a rather uncomfortable journey through the night in the back of a covered truck.

At the end of August my twenty-first birthday was celebrated with a party at the Glencoe Hotel in Carnoustie; my mother and father travelling up by train. I don't know who had arranged for the attendance of some local lasses, my interests in this direction had been lacking while I retained an unrequited affection for Connie McGraw to whom I wrote once a week. We all attempted Scottish dances. I have never been fond of this jigging about or the type of music which goes with it. Beer was more to my taste and we all had plenty of that before struggling aboard the train back to Arbroath.

The end of our course was now drawing close. After all this time the fear of failure to pass out as observers dominated every waking hour. I felt sick as the day approached, I knew my Navex record was not too good. What on earth would I do if I failed?

But we needn't have worried. I think they suddenly needed aircrew so badly that they passed the whole lot of us. We were, of course, unaware of the mounting losses among aircrew, seeing only the briefest mention of naval air activities in the press. The RAF got what little glory was going. The crippling of a significant part of the Italian fleet at Taranto by Swordfish from HMS *Illustrious* was soon forgotten and few appreciated the role *Ark Royal*'s Swordfish had taken in sinking the *Bismarck*. And you didn't have to be flying in action on an aircraft carrier to die easily.

There was almost no time to say goodbye to each other before we were off on leave to our various homes, taking with us a formidable list of the items of uniform and equipment recommended for an officer.

My feelings of elation were somewhat deflated when my Connie showed little interest in my return. She had found someone else. Now all I wanted to do was to get up there in the air. My wish was granted much sooner than I expected.

Chapter 5
To Sea in a Fleet Carrier

I received my commission as a Temporary Acting Sub Lt (A) RNVR on 20 September, 1941. When I stood for the first time in front of the mirror with all the 'gear' on 'Acting' was truly the definitive word; I had got so used to the peculiar, corset-like feel of bell bottoms and heavy boots. A solar topee was one of the items on the list so I tried on this monstrosity without knowing that it was a joke from a previous age; it went with me, laced into the top of my kitbag but never again saw the light of the sun.

We had all expected to be sent first to the famous naval establishment at Greenwich, where we would be turned into officers and gentlemen, taught which knife and fork to use, and which way round to pass the port. Instead of this skylark I received a letter from Their Lordships instructing me to report on board HMS *Indomitable* at Greenock on 11 October where I was to join 831 Squadron. So it was not until I met my wife that I found out all about those knives and forks and it is arguable as to whether I ever learnt how to behave as an officer and gentleman.

Arriving at Glasgow I took the local train to Greenock. It was in no hurry and I was alone in the compartment and feeling cold in spite of being enveloped in my spanking new greatcoat. I stood looking out of a rain flecked window at the grey expanse of the Clyde feeling butterflies in my stomach. How would I find the *Indomitable*? Then suddenly I saw the silhouette of a large aircraft carrier anchored about half a mile off shore, camouflaged in grey and blue, it dwarfed all the shipping lying nearby. My anxiety increased.

How was I going to get on board with all my gear which now comprised a large trunk, and two kitbags? Greenock station was almost empty so I left my pile on the platform and sought out the Military Transport Office; wartime stations always had an MTO. I presented my dilemma to the PO in charge and transport was found to take me down to a small office facing onto the quay. The carrier now looked even bigger than it had from the train and without sign of life at this distance. The Petty Officer in the office examined my papers without comment and passed them to a Warrant Officer who examined me with a baleful eye. I probably looked what I was, just out of the shell, gold braid crisp and shiny.

'Yer for the *Indom* are yer? Well hang around, there's a tender due from 'er in 'alf an hour!'

My kit was taken round to the opposite side of the quay in a handcart. It seemed a long way down to the water and I wondered how I was going to get myself and baggage down into a boat. When it arrived, the boat, or more correctly ship's tender, proved to be much bigger than I had expected, rising up and down on the swell. I climbed clumsily down the iron ladder and scrambled onto the wet deck by the side of the cabin, and then along to the cockpit into which my trunk was being lowered on a rope. I was happy to be totally ignored by all aboard as we pulled away into the gloom of a late afternoon. Once out into the estuary the sea was quite choppy and broke over the unhappy seaman perched on the bows with his boathook. I could see the first sign of life on the quarterdeck as we circled the stern, and headed towards a long gangway sloping down the starboard side. It ended in a perforated platform just above the swell of the water. I realised that I would have to get myself onto it. What if I fell in the water in my No.1 uniform? Nobody had warned me about this in all those months of seamanship.

We had to make two passes before we came alongside the gangway, which now rose and fell several feet as the tender crew held onto it with the dubious grip of boathooks. There was no escape for me. I slithered along the wet deck, leapt blindly and arrived safely, to my considerable surprise.

I dimly remembered that when arriving on board one must salute the Officer of the Watch. What was I supposed to do after that? There seemed to be no end to the problems of this first day of being an officer. I felt there ought to have been a rehearsal, I wasn't ready for going on stage.

'Sub Lt Wallace reporting on board Sir,' I mumbled to the young RN officer who returned my salute and said:

'We'll just get your gear stowed out of the way and then I'll have someone to take you to the wardroom where you should be able to find the First Lieutenant'.

What, I wondered, did a First Lieutenant do?

Trunk and kitbags were moved into a corridor, and then I followed a matelot through what seemed like miles of passages, dominated by the smell of new white paint. I was yet to learn that *Indomitable* had only just been commissioned. We went through watertight door after watertight door, each with its numerous clamps to be undone and done up after we passed through. Up and down companionways and eventually to the broad passage between the wardroom and the anteroom, with rows of hooks on either side, many of them draped with officers' caps. A knock on the polished mahogany door of the anteroom, a whispered discussion and I was ushered inside and led towards an elderly but kindly looking two and a half ringer. Lt Cdr Pennyfather held out a welcoming hand.

'Well young man, are you joining us?'

'Yes Sir, in 831 Squadron. Here are my papers.'

'Ah yes! Well, we'll have to find you a cabin — we haven't got things sorted out yet so it will have to be temporary — what's your seniority?'

'Pardon Sir?'

'When were you commissioned lad?'

'20 September, Sir.'

Little did I realize the long term effects of this simple reply. He didn't believe that I could have been commissioned and be joining a ship in as short a time as three weeks, so he put down 20 September 1940, giving me a full year's seniority.

'I expect you'll want to get settled in before dinner so I'll have someone take you to your cabin. Get the steward there to collect your gear!'

Back through the corridors, back through the clamped doors, up and down, left and right. Direction ceased to have meaning in this maze. The cabin was sheer luxury, varnished mahogany in all directions, washbasin, desk, comfortable bed on which I stretched out until a perky faced matelot put his head round the door and announced in an effeminate voice, 'I'm yer steward, Sir, 'ave yer got yer kit?'

'Just off the quarterdeck somewhere.'

'That's just up a deck or two, Sir, I'll fetch it.'

So I was in the stern somewhere, that was news. Trunk and kitbags were dragged in.

'Yer can't go into dinner with shoes like that Sir — let me 'ave 'em.'

'What time is dinner?'

'Haight o'clock Sir, and I'll see yer pyjamas is looked out.'

The days' trials were far from over, how did I find my way back to the wardroom? Too shy to ask, I set off towards what I thought was the sharp end of the ship, soon to find myself facing one of those multi-clamped doors. There was nothing for it but to have a go — clang, clang, clang — and I stepped into what was clearly the aircraft hangar (at this time I didn't even know that *Indomitable* had hangars on two levels). Bright lights and steel decks stretched out into the distance, no aircraft and at this time of the evening, not a soul in sight. Feeling that the wardroom should be somewhere about the middle of this vast space I wandered down and selected a hatchway on the starboard side only to emerge before some dozen matelots sitting around a mess table. They stopped talking and all eyes focused on the intruder. I looked around, as though carrying out an inspection, and then retreated back through the door into the hangar. I had better luck at the next attempt, arriving at the foot of a series of stairways and opted to go upwards. Wherever was everybody? Halfway up a rather superior looking RN Lieutenant came down a passageway. I paused and nonchalantly followed him at a few paces. What relief to see all those caps on their pegs. The anteroom, like a large hotel lounge, was now a forest of straight ringed gold braid. Lt Cdr Pennyfather came over and offered me a sherry which saved me from further embarrassment.

Having survived at HMS *Condor* on a diet of bread and Marmite, that first dinner in the wardroom aboard *Indom* was a gastronomic delight. Stewards served at rows of long tables, partly empty as the aircrew were not yet on board. After coffee I managed to get some guidance back to the luxury of my cabin. This was certainly the life. Nobody, of course, had told me that I was occupying my future Commanding Officer's cabin; I never dared to tell him.

The following day the ship seemed to be full of civilian workmen — I hadn't realized how new *Indom* was and the flash and sparks of welding illuminated every corridor as I wandered about exploring. I eventually found my way up to the long grey expanse of the flight deck. There was activity everywhere with warning bells clanging continuously whenever the huge aircraft lifts were in operation. Stores and aircraft spares were being taken down into the hangars. The aft lift was rectangular and served both upper and lower hangars, the for'd lift was square (I found out later that this was to accommodate the Hawker Sea Hurricane which was not designed to have folding wings) and served only the upper hangar. Swinging from a bow anchor, the cold autumn wind blew straight down the length of the deck as I moved to one side of the open chasm and then passed the almost flush turrets of the twin 4.5 inch anti-aircraft guns, to stand, with an acute sense of vertigo, where the deck curves downwards to blend into the bows. A sudden shower rushed across the deck driving me back to the warmth and comfort of the anteroom where I was pleased to see a wavy navy Air Branch Sub Lt who turned out to be an observer in 827 Squadron equipped with the Fairey Albacore. He told me that 831 Squadron also had Albacores and the further exciting news that we were the first carrier to have a squadron of Sea Hurricanes and to complete the aircraft complement, a squadron of Fairey Fulmar two-seat fighter aircraft. They were all at Macrihanish and would be landing on the carrier during the next few days.

Fortified by a large number of sherries I began to feel some confidence in navigating the honeycomb of passages and lost the feeling of being the central miserable character in a Bateman cartoon: 'One of those volunteer flying types'.

The following day the ship weighed anchor early in the morning. I was now moved into quite a large double berthed cabin directly under the flight deck on the starboard side aft. The sheaves of the 4th arrestor wire passed through it's top corner producing a tortured screaming noise every time

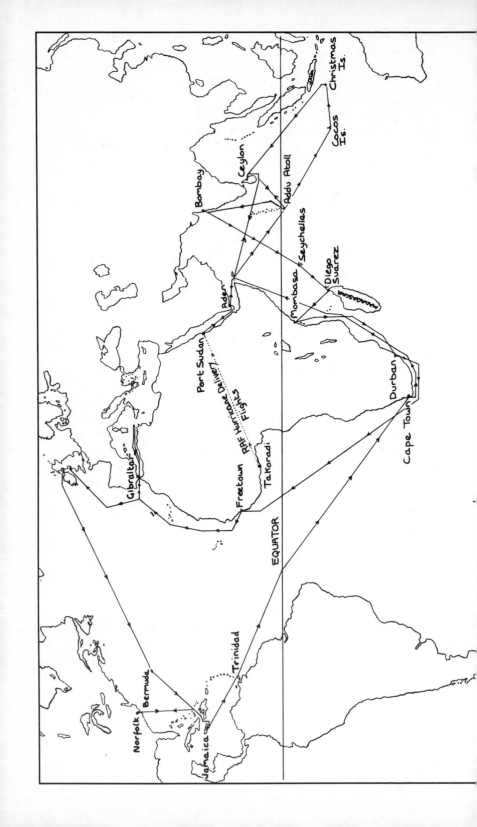

this wire caught an aircraft, and this proved to be a fairly popular wire out of a total of eight. The cabin even had the bonus of a porthole and was only a few yards away from a short companionway up to the flight deck. Of course I didn't deserve all this with my almost total lack of seniority, but it was to last some nine months before I was rumbled.

The ship became alive with noise and vibration overlaid with a continuous stream of orders assailing the ears from trumpet mouthed Tannoy speakers. By mid morning we were clearing the islands at the entrance to the Firth of Clyde and the vibration increased as the ship put on speed.

'D'ye'hear there! D'ye'hear there! Stand by to receive aircraft!' With mounting excitement I followed the few officers left in the anteroom up to the 'island' and then on to the pom-pom gun position at its aft end, later to be known always as 'the goofer's gallery'. After boozing and sleeping, the macabre activity of 'goofing' at the frequently spectacular and oft times disastrous attempts to land on a small length of steel deck surrounded by water, was by far the most popular leisure occupation of the majority of the crew of any carrier. In time, many a pundit would assess the form of the individual pilot and the likelihood of his ending up either over the side or, more likely, in the clutches of the steel mesh barrier, two of which were raised up across the deck before each landing, and only lowered when an aircraft had caught one of the arrestor wires and been brought to a stop.

The ship heeled over sharply, shuddering in spasms as she turned into wind. And there overhead were the Albacores in the customary flights of three aircraft, silhouetted against a stormy grey sky. Below me, peering around an opening from the island onto the deck, was the macabre bulk of the crash rescue man, clad from head to feet in an asbestos suit. Down aft, on the port side, the stocky figure of Lt Cdr Pares, our 'Batsman', struggled to stand against the gale now blowing straight down the length of the deck; the plume of steam from an orifice in the bow signalling that we were steaming directly into wind. One after another the Albacores of 827 Squadron broke their formation and spread out into a long line astern from which the first flew downwind past the port side, some quarter mile away, and then banked sharply to line up with the flight deck. With 50 knots of wind now blowing down the deck, its approach seemed surprisingly slow and as unsteady as a butterfly in a breeze. With a nose up attitude the pilot struggled to follow the signals from the waving, outstretched arms of the Batsman; one minute too high, the next too low, then suddenly it seemed to loom large with its engine noise topping that of the wind as it rushed high over the aft end and thumped down onto the deck. The arrestor hook bounced on the steel deck, bounced again over the second wire and caught the third; the tail lifted as the hook dragged the wire from the shock absorbers at either side bringing the aircraft to an abrupt halt. The flight deck crew, one from each side, ran to the tail of the aircraft, crouching low as the pilot released the aircraft's brakes to allow the wind to push it back far enough for the crew to unhitch the hook from the cable with their gloved hands. As soon as it was clear, the cable was drawn back to its operating position, the barriers were lowered, and the pilot got the signal to open up the throttle and taxi the aircraft forward to park it near the bows. I thought how the movements of Batsman and deck crew had the formalised grace of a ballet.

The next aircraft was approaching quickly and the barriers had not yet been raised. The Batsman waived one of the bats around his head and with its engine at full throttle the Albacore banked and slowly climbed away to take another place in the circling gaggle. After twenty minutes all aircraft were safely on board and ground crews were busy folding their wings before manhandling them back down the deck to the aft lift.

With all 827s Albacores aboard, *Indom* turned back to the Clyde and anchored in Gourock Bay for the night. The wardroom took on new life, the majority of the newly arrived aviators were RNVR, full of noisy chatter and much banter about their prowess, or lack of, in landing for the first time on the Navy's newest and largest carrier. The ship's officers, mostly RN, looked upon this with total disdain or even distaste: the Air Arm was clearly of a lower caste. I wondered what Nelson would have made of it all? As for me, I was very much a totally ignored bystander, but infected with the pervading sense of excitement.

The following day stores were loaded onto the ship from lighters, huge raft like affairs clinging like leaches to the ship's side. I occupied much of the day exploring the aircraft hangars, almost empty of humanity, but their sides and ceilings stocked, like a fantastic museum, with spare propellers, wings, wheels and almost any of the larger spares we might need; a carrier must operate as a fully self-contained floating airfield with no possibility to 'phone anyone to send two 3/4 inch castellated nuts for an engine mounting or a can of beans. Soaring up two decks high, every step echoed in this steel coffin. When an aircraft lift came down the sound of tortured metal, combined with the continuous clamour of the warning bell, would have fitted well into an Edgar Allan Poe horror film. The ultimate horror to be crushed beneath it. Or to slip on the wet flight deck and fall down it.

I threaded my way through the serried ranks of 827's Albacores, packed in the aft end of the upper hangar so close that their folded wings nearly touched. I tripped over the cables which lashed them to eyebolts on the steel decking; a hazard one never seemed to overcome. How robust their metal-clad fuselages looked after the fabric covered Swordfish, and oh, those lovely, lovely Perspex covered cockpits with the luxury of a door for entry into the observer's domain; tall enough to stand fully upright when the seat was folded to one side. Sliding windows gave comfortable access to the compasses mounted on each side, and narrow Perspex shutters could be opened to deflect the airstream, making it possible to lean well out to look ahead; the view otherwise was entirely blocked by the large petrol tank reaching from floor to the upper wing which separated pilot and observer by some six feet. The rear of the tank had a sloping cutaway from halfway down to the floor level giving access to a bomb aiming hatch. An aluminium cover, shaped like a jumbo sized baking tin and hinged at its front end, protected a Perspex roller shutter mounted flush with the aircraft's belly. This little used feature was later to save one of my many lives.

The pilot sat high up with his back to the tank and level with the leading edge of the upper wing giving probably the best view over the engine of any naval aircraft of the day. The 1130 hp Bristol Taurus sleeve valve radial engine seemed dwarfed by the bulk of the aircraft. I had, and still have, a great affection for the Albacore, though its performance offered little improvement on that of the Swordfish: both were sitting ducks to an enemy fighter.

Waking the next morning, the vibration and slight roll proclaimed that we were underway again, which a quick peep out of the porthole confirmed. All the three remaining squadrons were due to embark from Macrihanish; it was to be a long day with much of the time spent in the goofers gallery with many a camera to hand in morbid anticipation of a prang.The grey silhouette of Arran loomed off to starboard and rain squalls swept across the deck as the twelve Albacores of my squadron, 831, droned overhead and the ship turned into wind to receive them. One by one they approached, arrestor hooks and lower wing flaps down, noses high, and with a final engine cut, their hooks caught wires and they were safely down. Wings were folded and they were pushed back to the aft lift and stowed in the lower hangar. The Fulmar Mk IIs of 800 Squadron now approached. The landings of these heavyweight, underpowered two-seat fighters were more theatrical than the Albacores and the efforts of the batsman became increasingly balletic, waving both yellow bats above his head with demonic frenzy when a pilot's approach was perilously low; with larger bats he might well have taken to the air himself. When the deck wasn't clear and the pilot was given the signal to go round again, then you could really see the effect of lack of engine power; the Fulmar would seem to stagger drunkenly, then banking to clear the ship it would lose height before climbing back to regain its place in the circuit for another attempt.

The arrival of the nine Sea Hurricane Mk IBs of 880 Squadron brought everyone on deck. They certainly came in fast and hit the deck hard, but all got down safely. We were all impressed. The CO, Lt Cdr 'Butch' Judd, was a barnstorming, larger-than-life character, tall, red bearded and of fearsome countenance. After being first to land (who dared land before him?) he pulled off his flying helmet and dashed down the deck to a position opposite the batsman where he stood, beard blowing in the gale, and shook his fist at any pilot whose landing was not to his liking. This became his custom.

With well over 100 officers now on board out of a total ships complement of some 1,500, I sought out my CO, Lt Cdr Peter Mortimer RN, amongst the forest of gold braid in the anteroom. Whether by natural selection or design the pecking order had already been established, with flying types occupying the aft end, and sea going types the for'd part. I found him sitting in an arm chair, reading a newspaper, with a silver tipped cigarette holder dangling from one corner of his mouth. An ascetic face, aquiline nose, and somewhat older than I had expected.

'Excuse me, Sir,' I began deferentially. He glanced up and surveyed me with cool eyes and a slight smile (he never laughed).

'Wallace, Sir.'

'Ah yes, you must be our new observer. Been at sea before?'

'No Sir.'

'You'd better come and meet our senior observer and, by the way, you'll be flying with Fisher — I'll fix for you to get airborne tomorrow.'

The senior 'O', Lt David Buchanan-Dunlop RN, proved to be a most kindly and considerate gentleman, far too senior in years for any of us to call him David. I think he and the CO must have been about thirty which to us seemed really ancient. They both kept aloof from the young and wilder generation.

With every take off and landing on a carrier an observer's life depended entirely on the skill of his pilot. Through all the years I had the greatest good fortune to have the very best of pilots. Jack Fisher was slightly older than myself, slender with dark, curly hair, a long, slightly bent nose rather like my father's and somewhat bow legged (only discernible in shorts). Apart from the CO, I think he was the only married man in the squadron, except possibly Lt 'Uncle' Wilkinson who was an RANR observer of very advanced years, forty I guess. How did these old characters manage to climb into their aircraft?

I met our TAG, 'Oscar' Halhead, the following day when we reported to the Operations Room to be briefed by the senior 'O' for a Navex laid on especially for my benefit. The chart I clipped onto my Bigsworth board showed an area covering the Mull of Kintyre, Galloway and Northern

Island. The blackboard displayed the position of the carrier and its forecast course and speed over the next three hours, nothing 'imaginary' this time. The Met Officer forecast a 25 knot south westerly wind.

'Do you know how to tune in to the ship's beacon?' asked the senior 'O'.

'No I don't, I'm afraid,' I replied.

'Well, never mind, you shouldn't find any difficulty getting back to us with all this land around, but you'd better get yourself genned up on the beacon as soon as possible.'

By the time I had taken note of the dog leg track we were to fly, Jack came in from reporting to Commander Flying, Cdr C. R. V. Pugh RN.

'Just to give you a bit more excitement they're going to boost us off,' he announced with a grin.

I hadn't realised what it would be like walking down a slippery wet steel deck in a blustering gale, with a Bigsworth board under one arm and binoculars and a lead weighted code book clasped in the other hand. The board took on the behaviour of a square-rigged sail and the leather sole of a flying boot didn't have the best of grip. What a lot of things they hadn't told us back at Observer School. Albacore 4C stood alone, wings spread and rocking slightly in the wind; its fat tyres straining against the chocks, being all that prevented it being swept back over the stern.

Thankfully, Oscar opens the door; I don't seem to have any hands available. He climbs in and takes my board off me which makes it a bit easier to get my foot in the stirrup-like step and clamber in. Seat up. Plug in Gosport tubes — no, we still don't have proper intercom — stow all gear. I can just see Jack's parachute shoulder straps between the tank and the canopy. I fasten my seat belt.

'You OK in the back?'

'Yes thanks.'

The deck crewman gives a thumbs up and the Coffman cartridge starter fires with a loud bang; the three black blades of the propeller rotate jerkily, the engine coughs and then bursts into life and is gradually brought up to nearly maximum revs to warm it up. There isn't enough time to calculate my first compass course before the chocks are waved away and we taxi up the deck past the island where, from his eyrie, Commander Flying looks down upon us. We veer over to the port side to where the catapult crew are waiting, crouched down on the deck or in the catwalks alongside. The crew chief guides Jack with hand signals until with a lurch we come to a stop against the raised steel plates, which act as chocks. The catapult cradle mates with the four spools in the fuselage and we are raised into a flying attitude. .

'Ready in the back? Strapped in?'

'Yes!'

'Here we go!'

The crew chief waves his hand in a circle as though stirring a pudding upside down; the wind tears at his coloured waistcoat and helmet. The aircraft shudders as the engine comes up to full power. I can just see Jack's left hand raised and the crew chief bringing his arm sharply down before being pressed with a mighty hand back into my seat. We are over the bows, the pressure has gone, it is as though we are floating; the aircraft wallows for a second as though the air is too difficult to grasp and then we are in a slow left hand climbing turn.

'OK in the back?'

'OK!'

'I'll climb up to 2000 feet — let me know what course you want when you're ready.'

I undo my seat belt and look down for the first time on our strange grey home, only just distinguishable against a grey sea by the white vee from its stern. Goofing time over, get your board out and get on with the job.

Using the met officers' wind I quickly work out my first course using my CSC.

'Could we depart over the ship on course 085?' I call nervously. Enclosed in a perspex canopy, engine noise still fogs the mind but what a relief not to have the cold wind tearing at ones hands. We bank steeply and fly over the ship on the compass setting for our first leg. This is not the swimming pool of the Seaforth Hotel at Arbroath. This is for real.

I check the time of departure, fix the position of the ship at that time and from there start my plot marking my estimated position at six minute intervals. [At 95 knots ground speed we travel 9.5 miles in six minutes — it is easy to make one minute sub-divisions by eye.]

I check the air speed, then the course on one of my compasses. I glance behind and there is no sign of the ship we have just left. Too late to take a back bearing to check our track. It is time to find a wind.

'Er, could we find a wind please?'

'Ready when you are,' comes the friendly, efficient sounding reply.

So we go smoothly through the procedure; the answer seems reasonably close to the met wind, speed a bit higher. I correct my plot, glance at my watch and note our position, then call for a small course alteration to ensure that we reach our first turn point. Time to look around: nothing but grey sea and sky joined without a clear horizon, the sea flecked with the white broken wave tops which begin to appear when the wind exceeds about twenty knots. Nearly time to turn onto the next leg, I check the figures and pass them to Jack. As we turn, the Ayrshire coast is dimly visible, but not in sufficient detail to allow me to fix my position. Time to work out a course to intercept the carrier. A scrabble to find a dropped pencil.

'How are you doing in the back — when do we turn for home?'

'In about 10 minutes.'

Should I find another wind? Not really time before we turn. As we turn onto the final leg a rain squall blanks out everything, multitudes of tiny rivulets of water have a brief life on the Perspex canopy. We'll never see the carrier in this.

'What's our ETA?' asks Jack in a voice devoid of the anxiety which engulfs me.

'Um, 1216,' I reply without conviction.

At 1210 I can't see a damn thing ahead on either side, just a blank greyness. The minutes rush by and I feel a cold sweat. Still nothing at 1216. Where the Hell is it?

'Not too bad!' comes the laconic voice from the front.

'What?'

'Not too bad! Do you see her — about 3 miles starboard beam.'

Not even then do I see her; bows on to us she is almost invisible even this close. Not until we are diving down does the lop sided grey shape catch my inexperienced eye. And its not over yet, we still have the landing to get over. But at least now I can pack up my board and gear, stand up and enjoy the view. Oscar grins at me and holds up his thumbs; I hadn't had time to remember that he was there behind me all this time.

I can see flitting glimpses of other aircraft on the deck so there is some delay before we get the signal to land on. Diving down past the port side, a steep bank, flaps down, arrestor hook down, and we level up over the turbulent wake overhauling the ship at a relative speed of no more than 55 knots. With my head against the left hand side of the canopy I can just see the batsman, his yellow bats outstretched, now slowly waving to an upward vee. I tighten my seat belt and quite suddenly the downward curve of the deck flashes below, a glimpse of the batsman, knees bent, briskly sweeping the bats in a low scissors motion. A quick bounce and then a jerk forward hard against the seat belt as the hook engages: figures rush to either side as the tail sits firmly down on the deck. The engine revs up and we are moving forward; I glance up as we pass the island, there are a few goofers and further forward Commander (F) looks down from his perch. It all seems so exciting and I feel unjustifiably pleased with myself and life in general. The aircraft stops and is surrounded by a melee of deck crew. Inside the cockpit only a slight rocking motion disturbs the peace and quiet. Once outside the gale plucks at me and my board. I wait for Oscar and Jack, and the wind buffets us down the deck until we enter the island and climb up to the Ops room. This is the domain of Commander Operations, Commander B. E. W. Logan RN, always known by all aircrew as 'Lofty', for obvious reasons; I was to serve happily under him long after my time in

Indom. He asked how I felt about my first carrier borne Navex — there was not a lot one could say — we had returned safely. What else mattered?

Jack and I went down for a quick drink before lunch. No one showed the slightest interest in our flying saga, everyone was talking about the announcement that the ship was going to the Caribbean via Bermuda to 'work-up'. There we would be exercising and coordinating all the complex routines essential to make a carrier battleworthy, and would be assured of good flying weather and little threat of submarines. There were, however, hidden dangers lying in wait.

We sailed on 18 October 1941, with a small fast convoy which included the ex-French luxury liner *Pasteur,* now a grey painted troopship. Our escort was a motley collection of ageing destroyers. No sooner had we rounded the northern tip of Ireland than we plunged straight into a full south-westerly gale. Flying was out of the question as we pitched into massive waves; these even broke over the flight deck in spite of its height, and the ship shuddered each time its propellers broke the surface. My only duty was a submarine watch, standing at a remote corner of the bridge with my binoculars. The boredom was relieved by the spectacular view of the old destroyer *Verity* (launched 1919) almost disappearing as its bows dipped and cut into a wall of water, and close by a narrow beamed lend-lease ex-American destroyer, rolling to such a degree that from my height I could look down into the four long funnels which gave them such a distinctive appearance.

Down in the hangar a forest of swaying Albacores strained against their lashings, lurching at you menacingly as you weaved your way between them, not a soul in sight. Nothing to do but read old papers to see what 'Jane' was getting up to — or getting out of — in the *Mirror.* I lacked the imagination to do something more useful.

Whether or not I had shown someone my pen and ink drawings, the CO put me in charge of the squadron 'line book' — a huge leather bound tome with screwed brass clamps in which I was instructed to record any bizarre squadron event, word or deed. In some squadrons the line book took the form of a diary. I chose to use mainly colour washed pen and ink cartoons.[1]

Four days passed, and with the worst of the gale over, two Fulmars were hastily flown off into a grey, overcast afternoon sky — there had been a report of a German long-range Focke-Wulf Condor in the area — the observer in one of them had been on our course at St Vincent. Neither had returned at nightfall, and we had to face the fact that, by now, they must be out of fuel and down somewhere in the sea; a chilling thought which dampened our spirits. At first light Fulmars and Albacores were flown off to search for them; I was not amongst the chosen, being probably

---

[1] The book itself can be found in the records of the Fleet Air Arm Museum.

considered too much of an additional risk. One of 831's Albacores sent a W/T report that it had sighted a dinghy and the ship lost no time in making for the spot; there was no shortage of lookouts at all points of vantage throughout a long day. At last three yellow dots, rising and falling in the swell, signalled the launch of a whaler as *Indom* stopped dead in the water. Now we could all see the main aircraft dinghy and the two aircrew personal dinghies tied together (the Fulmar observer had a pilots type parachute and personal dinghy). As the whaler came up alongside two blanket wrapped figures could be seen crouched in the stern, the observer was Sub Lt Lucas; they had been 22 hours adrift and were mighty lucky. It was presumed that the crew of the other Fulmar did not survive the ditching, which was not surprising in such a rough sea. With visibility of less than a mile, they had been unable to find the carrier; a reminder of the observer's perennial problem, that someone was always actually moving his airfield.

We left the convoy making its 14 knot progress to the USA and made for Bermuda at nearly double that speed. With the weather improving and the temperature in the seventies we changed into tropical rig, fastening epaulettes to white or khaki shirts, and displaying bony knees beneath shorts which today look so uncomfortably long. Jack could now be seen to be slightly bow-legged and some of the older officers to have a girth not observable in their blues.

Now entirely on our own, regular anti-submarine patrols were flown throughout the day ahead of the ship. During one of these I was instructed to familiarise myself with the ship's radio beacon, this being the only means of finding the ship should a navigational catastrophe occur; although *Indom* had the best available radar of the day and could detect aircraft at a line of sight distance of up to 100 miles, she would only break radio silence in a situation affecting her own safety and certainly not to guide back a wayward Albacore. The British beacon system was somewhat bizarre and is best likened to a radio lighthouse; the ship transmitted a narrow high frequency radio beam which rotated precisely once every 60 seconds with the start of each 360 degree sweep occurring at a due North heading. This was displayed on a master beacon chronometer in the Ops Room from which each observer would set his own chronometer. This signal could be picked up by the retractable rod aerial of a beacon receiver in the aircraft during the brief period when the radio beam 'illuminated' the aircraft; the observer would note the heading on his chronometer when he heard the signal and would know that the carrier was on a reciprocal bearing and that if he called for such a course he would eventually arrive 'home', even allowing for the fact that the ship was also moving. That was the theory. In practice it was more of an art than a science; it was essential to have the receiver accurately tuned to the signal — no crystals in those days — and if you tried to tune it while on the carrier's deck the transmitted signal was so strong that all you got was a continuous noise all round the clock. The only thing to do was to wait until you were airborne and some miles from the carrier before attempting to tune, and even this could be a bit of a hit or miss affair. Assuming that you remembered to do it at all, you only had one chance every minute and when there was nothing but silence all you could do was twiddle the dial and wait, and wait, and wait. Like all radio gadgets it didn't take kindly to the all pervading salty atmosphere. It was to be nine months before I needed it in anger.

I had never set foot outside the UK, so the first sight of Bermuda from the air seemed a romantic vision; a jewelled brooch on a blue setting. Little green islands scattered at random, each edged with a white band of surf. All the roofs of the houses were painted in white, pale blue or pink; from these I learnt that they collected the scanty rainfall.

For the first time I felt glad that I had joined the Navy.

The ship edged into Hamilton harbour through 'Two Rock' passage where the rocks either side came within feet of the hull. Standing on the boat deck I could easily have jumped onto them. It seemed very risky but we tied up safely alongside the dockyard.

On our first run ashore Jack and I sampled the many bars along the 'Front' and nearly got embroiled in a fight between our matelots and those of the American cruiser USS *Brooklyn* which was moored in the Sound. We beat a rapid retreat from the scene. For one glorious day we explored the main island's narrow lanes on hired bicycles. With no cars being allowed on the island and only donkey carts, it was like moving back in time. On reaching one of the scores of beaches we were disappointed to find the sea much too rough for swimming and had to resort to paddling in the surf like a couple of children.

We sailed early on 31 October, and for the first time the whole of 831 was ranged on deck for a dive-bombing exercise, the aircraft loaded with a 250lb bomb under each lower wing . Although the take off can be made in very rapid succession, forming up into a formation of four groups of three was a slow struggle due to the Albacore not having the reserve engine power to catch up those ahead. Flying close on the CO's port side, in the No 3 position, we could all see each other clearly but the only way we could communicate was by pre-arranged hand signal or, between observers, by the use of a small blackboard and a piece of chalk. Nelson would have expected us to hoist flags.

This was my first experience of dive-bombing and I was excited at the prospect. Not that I was expected to take any part in the activity, but the words conjured up memories of the fearsome impression made by the

German Stukas when we were at *St Vincent*. We climbed slowly to 6000 feet and moved into line astern before peeling off one by one into a steep dive throughout which I seemed to be floating and only restrained by my seat belt. I dimly heard somebody say something, but I couldn't hear it for the pain in my ears, and gravity was now trying to push me through the floor. I could just see that we were pulling out of the dive with the sea looking ominously close. We banked steeply and I could see the shipwreck target ringed by bomb bursts, but I had no idea which were ours. One by one the squadron formed up again and began to circle the carrier. Now began the first round of a never ending competition between squadrons to see which could land on the deck in the quickest time. A carrier is at its most vulnerable from air or submarine attack when committed to steaming into wind and Commander (F) was prepared to shed blood to achieve an interval of ten seconds between aircraft. This required feats of judgement between pilot, batsman and flight deck crew if the barrier was to be raised just before the next aircraft caught an arrestor wire. It was to be some time and a number of bent aircraft before we reached this target during the working up period.

By the time I was back in the ante-room the pain in my right ear had become excruciating and drove me to putting up the first major black of my career. The only doctor in the room was the portly, red faced Surgeon Commander Patrick RN whom I rashly chose to approach.

'Excuse me, Sir, I've got very bad ear-ache after this morning's dive-bombing and I wondered . . .'

I immediately became the central character of a Bateman cartoon.

'You can't come and speak to me in the mess about medical problems — you should know that there are proper consulting times and this is certainly not one of them!'

I blushed and muttered that I was sorry and turned away.

'Wait boy!' he called after me.

After a pause he growled,'Report to my cabin in one hour.'

And a miserable hour it was. I had to locate his cabin in the first place and when the time came I still got it all wrong.

'Which ear is it?'

'The right one.'

'Stand to attention, boy, while I'm examining your ear — and call me 'Sir' when you speak to me'.

'Yes Sir, I'm sorry, Sir.'

I clearly wasn't a very well brought up boy — perhaps it was due to missing my spell at Greenwich Naval College.

'You got a cold boy?'

'Yes Sir.'

'Shouldn't be flying with a bad cold.'

'No Sir.'

'Can't do anything for you — take some aspirins and tell your CO you're off flying until it's cleared up.'

Many months and a lot of sea were to pass before our paths crossed again.

Meanwhile we enjoyed ever more tropical weather as we passed through the Windward Passage between Cuba and Haiti and entered the Caribbean. Knees and arms bore painful witness to the strength of the sun.

For the first time the whole ship's company fell in on the deck for Sunday Divisions, drawn up behind the perforated windbreak in serried rows of khaki, whites and blues with the ships chaplain booming over a portable tannoy, and Cuba an outline of mountains brushed on the horizon. Nobody mentioned Roman Catholics, no doubt in the immensity of our ship they had their own appointed nook.

And so to our fateful arrival on 3 November at Kingston, Jamaica, which was to be the base for our working-up activities. The description by Hugh Popham in *Sea Flight* of our running aground onto a reef at the convoluted entrance to the harbour has a tragicomic element beyond my ability to improve upon. Whilst he was in his cabin changing, I was enjoying a pleasant cup of afternoon tea in the wardroom when we came to a shuddering stop, chair and cup sliding several feet along floor and table. And then for a time absolute silence, with the startling absence of any of the motions or vibrations which had been the background to our waking hours. The wardroom emptied and we joined an ever increasing stream of bodies climbing up to the flight deck; rumour was soon dispelled by the all too visible tips of coral reef, rising just clear of the water around the bows of the ship. We flying types had been given the impression that the gentlemen who were in charge of driving the ship were infallible, so some pretty ribald comments flew around, overlaid with some real concern as to what would happen next. As the afternoon wore on, two tugs arrived and struggled to pull us off without having the slightest effect. To this day I laugh every time I think back to the circus act which followed. Whose idea can it have been? Was there a precedent in Nelson's time? The whole ships company, apart from a few engineers, was mustered in one huge group at the stern end of the flight deck where we were instructed to jump up and down in time to the ship's Marine band. At the same time the two tugs gave all they'd had got. Portly commanders, seamen, airmen, jumping shoulder to shoulder and roaring with laughter — I wish I could remember the tune. Gilbert and Sullivan could not have improved on the scene.

The whole glorious affair was stopped when a ship's engineer rushed up from below to announce that we were damaging the structure below deck (through two inches of armoured deck?). And we hadn't moved an inch. Night came shrouded in speculation. Who had boobed and what were they all going to do about it? I was glad I wasn't the navigator. We awoke to find, as if by magic, that the ship was peacefully lying at anchor only a few hundred yards from the cluster of white painted buildings which formed the water frontage of Kingston, with dark green hills rising up behind into a tropical sky. Tide and tugs had released our bows while we all slept. All day the wardroom buzzed with rumour, divers were said to have been down to inspect our damaged bows but no one seemed to know how bad it was or how it would affect our future. Nothing was achieved by peering over the edge of the flight deck apart from my usual vertigo.

All was revealed after we set sail on the 6th, our Captain, H. E. Morse RN, came on the Tannoy to tell us that we were on our way to the American Navy Yard at Norfolk, in Virginia, where the ship would be docked for repairs. It so happened that *Illustrious* was there completing the very extensive repairs necessary after the repeated bombing attacks she had endured whilst at Malta in the January of 1941. With their considerable ability in these matters, the Americans pre-fabricated a new bows for *Indom* by taking measurements from *Illustrious* which saved some of the time lost, but this loss was to prove one of the greater calamities of the war. We didn't know it at the time, but it had been planned that after working-up in the Caribbean, we were to have joined the *Prince of Wales* and *Repulse* at Cape Town and then on to Singapore, where it was hoped that such a force, would deter the Japanese from making any warlike moves in the Far East. Not knowing how long we would be out of action, the Admiralty decided to send them on without delay, and they arrived at Singapore on 2 December 1941.

The Japanese carried out their surprise attack on Pearl Harbor on the 7th with a technical efficiency far beyond our own. It was followed by a seaborne landing in Malaya on the 8th, in which *Prince of Wales* and *Repulse* attempted to intervene without air cover. The disaster which befell them on the 10th is only too well known. Had *Indom* not run aground, it seems likely that we would have completed our working-up by 15 November, and by sailing at 25 knots we might well have been with them about that date, or they might have waited for us at Colombo which would have delayed any action at Singapore until about a week later. Although we were only equipped with one squadron of Hurricanes and one of Fulmars, the Japanese land-based aircraft were slow twin-engined aircraft operating from bases 400 miles from Singapore with no fighter cover and in daylight — an attractive target. With *Indom*'s effective radar and efficient fighter direction section it is unlikely that *Prince of Wales* and *Repulse* would have been sunk at this important stage, and the reinforcement of Singapore might have been possible, particularly its air defence. It will be remembered how successfully Malta had been defended by relatively few Hurricanes. *Indom* would not have been able to survive an attack by Admiral Nagumo's well equipped modern carriers but, at worst, the abject surrender at Singapore need not have taken place and any delay in its capture would have given the USA time to organise its vast military resources. But that is not how it was to be.

Back in *Indom* we were changing back to blues as we sped north. Nowhere in the world does the temperature change so rapidly with such a small change in latitude — within two days we went from basking in tropical sunshine to shivering in flurries of snow sweeping across the flight deck as we approached the Eastern seaboard of the USA. An exciting prospect, particularly as we were to fly off all our aircraft to the large US naval air station at Norfolk and carry out flying exercises there. This was a surprise as America was not yet in the war, and it was probably the first time that British operational aircraft had operated from neutral soil. It was certainly a surprise and a source of amazement to the US Navy aircrew to watch 24 seemingly antique, camouflaged biplanes descend onto their enormously long and wide runway and park on the spotless white concrete apron alongside their Devastator, Dauntless and Wildcat monoplanes, ranged in immaculate rows and reflecting the light from their polished aluminium wings and bodies like silver fish. At least we could feel proud of our Hurricanes and Fulmars. To add to our sense of inferiority our Albacores were unable to communicate by voice radio (R/T) with the control tower to ask permission to take off or land — they just couldn't believe this. There was a valiant, but only partially successful attempt by *Indom*'s radio mechanics to modify our W/T radio sets, and we all got special call signs. The whole situation was exacerbated by our normal procedure of taking off and landing in loose formation which the station flying control considered sheer irresponsibility and I believe a lot of harsh words were passed between Senior Officers. We were, of course, guests and probably not especially welcome. Our Albacores left black pools of engine oil wherever we parked on the immaculate concrete and I could even see our despoiled nesting area as we flew round the circuit — still vainly attempting to get permission to land as our wheels settled on the runway. Most of our days were spent in practising formation flying over the sea with the occasional interception by our Hurricanes.

We lived in huts on the station in reasonable comfort. There was remarkably little fraternising with the American airmen. Jack once suggested that one of their pilots came out with us for a drink — the station, like all American ships, was dry — it was difficult not to laugh at his earnest response.

'No thank you, Sir, I guess I'm down to fly tomorrow.'

'So are we, so what?' replied Jack with a grin. They seemed so much older than us and much taller. In the communal showers there was no difficulty in telling us apart, the British with short stocky figures and unruly, school-boyish behaviour.

We found the town of Norfolk a rather grim place, a typical naval port reminiscent of Portsmouth. The bars proved depressing, the beer equally so, but by a lucky chance we chose to dine in the 'Starlight Room', its name taken from a very fine dome shaped ceiling, blue painted and lit with dozens of small light bulbs. At the next table a very nice married couple in their forties asked us to join them and thus we had our first experience of whole-hearted, engulfing American hospitality which began with filling up our glasses to the brim with neat whisky because that was the way they had heard we liked it. They thought we were very young, which we were, and heroes, which we weren't. We avoided mentioning that we had yet to be in action and that our ship had run aground. It was a good thing that we were driven back to base, I doubt if we would have made it under our own steam. They collected us the following evening to join their family in their Thanksgiving Day turkey dinner of which the highlight was my first experience of the uniquely American ice cream gateau.

Back on board it was difficult to believe the tales told by those who had visited the 'Burlesque' show in town.

'Makes the Windmill or Prince of Wales look like a vicar's tea party!' announced 'Buster' May, with a leer. We didn't believe a word of it, but Jack and I thought we had better go and see for ourselves. They were quite right, the performance of what I found were called 'Bump and Grind Queens' — and these were apparently some of the best — put me into a state of erotic shock. You can see as much any week on TV but the sight of bare boobs bouncing and 'G' strings gyrating for two solid hours left us emotionally, if not physically, exhausted. Join the Navy and see the world.

It was equally hard to believe that the American dockyard completed the welding of a completely new stem to *Indom*'s bows in ten days, and off she sailed, heading back south. All the squadrons flew on board and I think everyone was glad to be back and keen to get on with the job. Ships officers were noticeably more subdued and had to put up with remarks like 'Have you seen any rocks ahead?' By the end of November we were back in Kingston harbour and back in tropical kit.

We put to sea almost every day in a concentrated effort to catch up on our working-up flying programme. For nearly three weeks we flew almost night and day with Commander (F) imposing ever stricter landing-on disciplines. This resulted in a number of spectacular prangs, fortunately no one was injured but there were a lot of bent aircraft. Cameras were much in evidence in Goofer's Gallery. 800 Squadron went through a particularly bad patch; their CO, Lt Cdr 'Willy' Wroughton looked miserable; 'Butch' Judd looked almost benign. While practising night deck landings without me in the back, Jack went into the barrier and our Taurus engine ended up on the deck. Pilots bore the brunt of the working-up period which involved numerous dummy torpedo attacks on the carrier as well as dive-bombing a target towed behind it. 'F' was none too pleased when 831 managed to put one or two bombs closer to the ship than to the target. When we anchored off Kingston for a few days we operated from Pallisadoes, a small airstrip on an isthmus at the entrance to the harbour. On shore leave Jack and I spent lazy afternoons sitting in the shade of the palm trees around the Myrtle Bank Hotel's swimming pool, and in the evenings acquiring heavy hangovers from Planters Punch, a rum concoction which seemed to slip down all too easily, the word punch having real meaning; I awoke in my bunk one morning and couldn't seem to move my head. Our attempts to be more adventurous were usually a disaster, wherever we asked the taxi driver to take us we seemed to end up at a brothel, which was not always obvious until we got inside. It always surprised me how many of our matelots were keen to dip their wicks in dark pools.

Towards the end of this exotic interlude the real war intruded sharply with the news of the Japanese attack on Pearl Harbor on 7 December 1941. It was some time before we learnt of its success or grasped its implications. What little I knew of their aircraft was that they were somewhat inferior copies of American aircraft, and as for their carriers, with their strange names, *Akagi, Zuikaku, Shokaku,* they were somewhat vague outlines on a ship recognition chart. We were to learn the hard way how much we underestimated them. At least America was now in the war: I wondered how they all felt about it back at Navy Norfolk? Were they still polishing their aircraft and parking them in neat but vulnerable rows?

Illustrious arrived at Kingston, spic and span after her six months of repairs at Norfolk and embarked some of her Swordfish before returning to the UK. We sailed for Cape Town, calling in at Trinidad for two days where we were joined by an escort of three new Australian destroyers [*Napier, Nizam* and *Nestor*]. The whole tone of the ship changed, there was no doubt that we were off to the Far East, and with the sinking of the *Prince of Wales* and *Repulse* on 10 December, it was made clear that we were to be ready for action at all times. Our Albacores flew reconnaissance and anti-submarine (A/S) patrols from dawn until dusk throughout the passage across the South Atlantic, and I suppose these could be counted my first operational flights.

During this period I particularly remember my first 'dawn patrol'; it had a romantic ring to it, probably childhood memories of the First World War film. Woken at 0400, damp with sweat, no need to shave, just clamber into underpants, shirt and shorts, in a half dark cabin; then wind my way down through deserted passageways to the wardroom for a mug of long stewed cocoa (maybe my taste buds have deteriorated, but cocoa has never since had such a rich flavour). Jack arrives and it is time to climb up to the island to collect our flying kit from the crew room, don our Mae Wests and report to the Ops Room: there was no greater aircrew crime on a carrier than to be late for a briefing. Oscar checks with the radio room, I set my beacon watch and note down the carriers course and speed, the wind and weather from the duty met man. A sleepy looking Lofty Logan arrives and gives the soon familiar instruction to patrol at 2000 feet, fifteen miles ahead and ten miles either side of the ship's mean course and return after three hours. He gives me details of shipping that might be in the area and the interrogating code to flash at them with my Aldis lamp should any be sighted. Helmets on, down the stairs and out onto the deck where we have to pause to get used to the darkness at this pre-dawn hour.

I shiver as the ever present wind tugs at my shirt and shorts and dries off the last remnants of sweat. I can feel the slight rise, fall and roll of the deck as we approach the dim outline of 4C, its engine already idling, shadowy figures lurking either side. This is always a dangerous moment because the Taurus is a quiet engine and you don't hear it with a helmet on, so one has to remember to keep well clear of the propeller as you approach. As Jack climbs up to his cockpit Oscar and I follow the lower mainplane around until we reach our door. A pair of Hurricanes on fighter stand-by are ranged just behind our tails, their pilots whiling away their duty time in the ready room. In the dim cockpit light I stow my gear, clipping the top of my chartboard to the cross bar at the front of the cockpit as had now become the accepted custom. I can't see a thing outside but I feel the Albacore lurch sideways and rock slowly as the ship begins to turn into wind.

'OK boys, here we go,' calls Jack over increasing engine noise and vibration. A brief glimpse of blue light over to the left as the flight deck officer gives the take-off signal with his torch and we are trundling down the deck. No effort has been taken to effect any streamlining of the two depth charges we carry on the wing racks, so their weight and very considerable drag, combined with a light wind, require every bit of the deck to get airborne. But from the back I might as well have had my eyes closed; all I can see behind is the ship's curving white wake, slightly luminous, as she turns back onto course. As we slowly climb away and set course, a faint wash of light defines the eastern horizon on our port bow. Behind us the ship has already merged into the darkness. There's a bit of work to be done on my chart and the beacon to be tuned in — just in case

— and quite suddenly each little detail of the cockpit lights up as the first crescent of sun peeps over the horizon. Time to turn onto the first leg of the zig-zag, to maintain a patrol 15 miles ahead of the carrier.

As we level up, the canopy glows with orange light and it becomes warm enough to slide open the side windows and settle down to some 'observing'. The horizon now looks like the rim of a large blue saucer. We seem to float above its centre and with a calm sea and only the faintest hatching of swell there is no real feeling of motion. It's not worth finding a wind but I check the beacon and get a rough bearing. Every time we 'cross the T' ahead of where the ship should be I do a quick scan with my binoculars getting used to the fact that she would appear to be well below the saucer's rim, and with her effective camouflage, quite difficult to see with the naked eye. The hours pass slowly with nothing to relieve the monotony. Gosport tubes and engine noise totally inhibit any conversation between the three of us. With our time up I could enjoy that never to be forgotten thrill of returning to our floating nest. It is still early in the morning with little life to be seen, the aircraft replacing us sits on the aft end of the flight deck with the Hurricanes behind it. The first sign of the ship turning into wind is the curving of her foaming wake. The Albacore seems to crawl along the deck to be silhouetted against the sea as it moves over the bows, but we have to keep circling whilst the Hurricanes are pushed down the deck ahead of the barrier. Jack has it judged beautifully as we begin our turn in to land. I am already packed up and my stomach is calling for its breakfast. One of our destroyers passes just below us, the boiling water spreads either side of us and thump we are down.

It so happened that we were flying anti-sub patrols and missed out on both the main events of this part of the voyage: Crossing-the-line and Christmas Day lunch. From photographs of the event the former was a lucky miss; the latter was somewhat dried up when we got it and the bar was closed. It proved impossible to capture any of the spirit of the occasion.

With the good weather, both fighter squadrons put in some concentrated flying and kept us all entertained with their rivalry in the landing-on stakes. The most spectacular event was the occasion when one of the Fulmars opened up to full throttle to go round again without realising that his hook had caught one of the arrestor wires. As he roared over the barrier it was as though a hand had clutched him and stopped him in mid flight, and then slammed him down on top of several of the Fulmars parked by the for'd lift. The anti-sub patrol had a long wait that day and the CO of the Hurricanes showed an unaccustomed bonhomie to all his boys.

Moving further into the South Atlantic we met the south east trade winds and an associated swell with such a long pitch between peaks as to cause the extremities of the flight deck to rise and fall some forty feet. The Albacores kept up their patrols, but landing-on in these conditions was an alarming experience with the deck either coming up to hit you or disappearing just when you expected the wheels to touch; the accepted technique was to aim for a wire well amidships, where the pitching effort was reduced at the expense of slamming into the barrier. We survived in 4C, others were less lucky and bent their aircraft. The fighters didn't fly but were still ranged as stand-by. Early one morning a Hurricane got loose when the ship rolled and ended up hanging over the side. Willy Wroughton cheered up considerably. All in all the enemy could hardly have done worse in wrecking our aircraft.

Jack and I were lucky to be given shore leave the day we arrived in Cape Town — it was New Year's Eve — and we were off down the gangway in our best blue uniforms, with white cap covers, as soon as *Indom*'s towering hull had been carefully edged into the dockside: quite a feat of seamanship. Strolling up the main street it seemed so familiar that it was just like being at home on one of our better summer days. We were a bit surprised to be approached by a boy of about fifteen who asked whether we were from the aircraft carrier and would we like to go to a New Year's Eve party his parents were giving. Unused to this direct approach it was with some misgiving that we agreed and he gave us an address. It turned out to be quite a sophisticated affair, held at an excellent restaurant part of the way up Table Mountain. Our hosts were most kind and had provided dancing, and eating, and girls, and everything. I had a rather romantic idyll with a young lady, sitting on a flight of steps after midnight looking down on the lights of the town and harbour. It was their summer and the air was balmy. It was 1942, a fateful year for all of us and me in particular.

We had leave again the following day and Jack and I, together with one of our RN observers called Shaddick, enjoyed a further experience of the incomparable South African hospitality when we found ourselves 'picked up' on the dockside by a South African Air Force pilot and his most attractive wife. They drove us up and around Table Mountain and along the coast where my old camera took some quite spectacular photographs. We ended up choosing our steaks from the grill at the Del Monico (they were very tough).

As soon as much needed aircraft spares, including complete aircraft, had been transferred from HMS *Engadine*, *Indom* edged out of the harbour and headed east at twenty six knots. There were few doubts that we were on our way to the Far East to take on the slit-eyed Japs, and this seemed to be confirmed when the back of the loo doors had pinned onto them the black silhouettes of Japanese aircraft — Mitsubishis, Aichis, Nakajimas. They didn't seem to favour biplanes.

Our progress eastwards was assisted by a following wind of gale force, so on the 3rd, Commander (F) decided that this was an opportunity to attempt a landing-on from the bows, this being generally considered to be a dodgy affair as the ship only had two wires ahead of the for'd lift. 'Buster' May, a South African pilot in 831, arriving back from a patrol, had the dubious honour and received great acclaim from the critical assembly of goofers by making a perfect landing. Even the CO lifted himself out of the loneliness of his special arm chair and bought him a drink.

It soon became clear that our course was taking us up the east coast of Africa, and that we must be in a hurry . For once it was a relief to get up in the air for a few hours to get away from the heat of the ship which had became a monstrous oven; it was discovered some weeks later that the ship's ventilation intakes and exhausts were positioned so that recirculation took place. Like almost everyone else I was suffering the constant irritation of 'prickly heat' on my chest for which there seemed to be no cure. The ship's crew, with little occasion to get up on deck, suffered dreadfully and were to be seen in shorts and plimsolls with their sweating bodies painted all over, like ancient Britons, with Gentian Violet which was said to give some relief from this torture. Up in the air it was sheer joy to open all the canopy windows, untie the Mae West tapes, open one's shirt and let the raw flesh chill in the buffeting, but wonderfully cool air, as we dived down on yet another dummy torpedo attack (ALT).

Drinking and fitfully sleeping was all we seemed to have energy for. Jack and I persuaded one of the engineer lieutenants to take us on a tour of the ship's engine rooms one evening, down dozens of steep metal stairs into a cats cradle of pipes, pregnant with blankets of insulation but giving off such waves of heat that the average temperature was about 130 degrees, drying mouth, tongue and eyes as though we were in some level of Dante's Inferno. The hottest spot was where a massive plant converted sea water to fresh water, a luxury we had taken for granted in our wanton use of bath and shower. There was little to excite the eye in the boilers, steam turbines or gearboxes, but the propeller shafts were another matter for they could be seen rotating in all their massive glory, with intermittent periods of a resonating vibration which could be detected all over the ship and which rose to a shuddering peak when our speed got up to 30 knots. Except for the control room, with its row upon row of dials, the whole system seemed to run with very few matelots or maybe, being evening, they were trying to find some cool air on the boat decks. Emerging back into the wardroom area was like a magical return to winter, such was the effect of a drop of some 20 degrees in one short step.

Seven days and 4000 miles after leaving Cape Town the jagged outline of the Aden's old crater could be seen shimmering in the horizon. The aircrew and ground staff of both 800 and 827 Squadrons had been given instructions to pack up their kit and gear ready to go ashore to the RAF base at Khormaksar. Nobody seemed to know why. After an impressive range on the deck they flew off into a coppery, dust filled sky and it was the last we were to see of them for six weeks.

I always think of Aden as the back of beyond, always hot, always humid, always smelly. Seen from the ship it didn't look very inviting, everything looked so barren, the drab town lying at the foot of dirt brown hills, devoid of vegetation. The only greenery to be seen was a small cluster of trees — reported to be gardens — on the foreshore of the town. To the left the hills fell away to extensive flats where salt pans were made by pumping sea water onto the land.

We anchored for the night to disembark the squadron ground crews and stores onto lighters manned by scruffy Arabs. Jack and I made a brief trip ashore, pursued almost the whole time by ragged Arab urchins seeking baksheesh and offering to take us to their 'very pretty sisters'. They clutched at our clothes and nothing except a vigorous f... off seemed to get rid of them. Nearly every building seemed to be a shop or some sort or a bazaar. In one of these I bought the colourful Japanese photograph album which survived the war together with its now fading memories. Sadly my VPK [Vest Pocket Kodak,1913 Model] after going through World War I with my father, became a war casualty later that year.

A memorable event was the night I was given the duty of Second Officer of the Watch assigned to the midships gangway where my *raison d'etre* was to receive back on board the ORs from shore leave. Thank God I was supported by the Master at Arms as I had had no briefing on my duties. Before the first Liberty boat loomed into sight in the moonlight I had grasped the idea that it was a matter of how best to handle a boatload of paralytic drunks with the minimum of incident and within the terms of KR and AI [Kings Regulations and Admiralty Instructions]; the criterion seemed to revolve around the man's ability to climb unaided up the gangway, salute me and proceed inboard without falling flat on his face. Only a Gilroy cartoon could do justice to the individual performance of our gallant crew: the eyes-shut dash and stumble; the glassy-eyed, one foot at a time, with salute in the wrong direction; or the time serving PO, white faced, trouser flies wide open, urged up from behind, whose heavily breathed 'Reporting on board, Sir' nearly asphyxiated me. To my relief none was judged to be drunk and incapable, or putting it another way, none had passed out.

After a days sailing up the Red Sea we tied up alongside at Port Sudan, wondering whether we were now going to the Mediterranean. Captain H. E. Morse, together with the ship's navigator, departed for the fate due, we presumed, for those who run the Navy's capital ships aground. He was a dour man who had seemed to have no interest in naval aviation. By good fortune Captain T. H. (Tom) Troubridge RN took over command. A man of entirely different character and calibre, much liked and respected in the months to come.

The dusty dockside was an amazing sight, packed with row upon row of Hurricanes which had been stripped of their wings. We counted 48 of them, a mixture of II As and II Bs, and they had all been flown by their RAF pilots all the way across Africa in stages from Takoradi in the Gold Coast (near Ghana) nearly 3000 miles over inhospitable territory. A considerable feat.

I was duty air officer that day, and without the slightest experience of crane handling, I found myself in charge of the party hoisting them all up onto the flight deck. Fortunately there was a Petty Officer to give the orders, but I knew who would be to blame if one fell off the hook. I kept out of the way and hoped for the best. It was a long hot day before wings and fuselages were packed like sardines in the upper hanger.

A small piece of the jig-saw had fallen into place but the picture was still a mystery.

The next day Jack and I had a run ashore to experience the sights and smells of an Arab market. The many varied eatables looked interesting but the flies thought so too. Unlike Aden no one was offering their sister for our delight. Like most, we ended up in the lounge of the Red Sea Hotel, a veritable colonial picture book of a place with large, slow moving, ceiling fans, waiters with red fezs, and, best of all, cold beer.

That evening RAF pilots almost outnumbered us in the anteroom; an invasion of moustaches in an unfamiliar setting. There was much speculation as to where we were going to take them. One thing was certain; we were not going into action with this lot aboard. What a let down for the Navy's latest fleet carrier to be relegated to being a fast transport for the RAF.

It was a relief to put to sea and feel cooler air flowing through the ship. After anchoring in Aden for one night we left on 18 January. We soon cleared the Horn of Africa and headed south east at 26 knots with our destroyers cleaving the water ahead.

Anti-submarine patrols were carried out from dawn to dusk, so with only the one Albacore squadron on board we were flying every other day. Our new Captain had ruled that observers must report to him before take-off. The first occasion for me was before a dawn sortie. Having found my way to his sea cabin in the island and knocked on the door several times without getting any response I gingerly opened the door, and there was the Captain's portly figure lying on his bunk, fully dressed, with his back to me. With some trepidation I put out a hand and shook the shoulder of God. It needed more than one shake before he awoke and swung his legs down to a sitting position.

'Just about to take off for the first A/S patrol, Sir.'

'What's your name young man?'

'Wallace, Sir.'

'Well Wallace, tell me what you plan to do on this patrol.'

So I told him the routine and he questioned me about what we would do if we sighted any vessel. He conveyed a warm interest in everything, which we all appreciated even if he wasn't a flying type.

It was some days later that we did see smoke on the horizon and dashed off towards it in great excitement. It turned out to be a merchant ship of some 5000 tons. I flashed the appropriate interrogating signal with my Aldis light with a prayer that it wouldn't flash a long signal back to me, as receiving flash had never been my forte. We were totally ignored.

'Better go down and see if we can read its name,' I suggested. We dived to sea level and passed close alongside her. She was flying the Red Duster and I could read her name on a white board alongside her bridge.

'What are those bods doing with that gun on the stern,' shouted Jack as we made our second pass.

'Might be thinking of shooting at us!' I replied, giving them a rather unsteady once-over through my binoculars. There was a large puff of smoke and Jack veered away and climbed.

'Silly buggers — I don't think we'll hang around here, let's get back on the job.'

With a flash of fear I realised that I didn't know our position. I had neither recorded the time nor the course we had taken in the excitement of closing the vessel — nothing had been mentioned about this sort of situation back at 'O' School. My eyes prickled with sweat. Jack asked me for a course. I asked him to circle around while I sorted myself out, not wanting to tell him about the pickle I was in. I decided to try the beacon first and switched it on. Never had sixty seconds seemed so long. At last I heard a faint bleep at about 145 degrees — 'Course 325, Jack,' I croaked. Checking the time and laying off the bearing from the ship's forecast position I reckoned that she should be bows on to us. I got another bleep around 148 degrees and leaning out into the slipstream I peered through my binoculars into the featureless heat haze ahead. Suddenly happiness took the form of a lop sided grey shape. I kept its sighting to myself and altered course back onto our patrol track feeling weak at the knees but a much wiser navigator.

Our Sea Hurricanes were maintained at stand-by with occasional airborne forays to keep their hand in. Their take-offs and landings were keenly watched by the RAF pilots who, it was now clear, were going to have to fly off *Indom* at some undisclosed point in the ocean. Their justified fears were impishly fanned by 880's pilots with graphic descriptions of what happened if you failed to keep straight down the deck, or if you dropped a wing, or if the wind speed over the deck was on the low side and you didn't get your tail up quickly. There was no chance of a trial flight for them to check their aircraft after re-assembly and, of course, they had no arrestor hooks.

We continued south east with a school of dolphins speeding like grey phantoms just ahead of our bows; perhaps they knew where we were going even if we didn't. We were not much wiser when, on the afternoon of 21 January, a small palm fringed island appeared on the horizon, stirring romantic images of Dorothy Lamour, grass skirts and sarongs. We sailed slowly through a gap in a barrier reef of coral to anchor in the middle of a deep water lagoon, large enough to shelter a complete fleet. We learnt that this was Addu Atoll, a secret naval base identified as Port 'X' [Port 'T' in official records] situated almost on the Equator at the southern end of the Maldive Islands and one of a group of 2000 small coral islands stretching north for nearly 500 miles. The island part of the atoll rose only a few feet above the sea and appeared to be uninhabited, but we were soon surrounded by small lateen rigged sailing craft manned by very dark skinned natives wearing strange cone shaped hats in pink and blue. It was difficult to imagine what they must have thought of an aircraft carrier sailing into their world, and of the flying machines that came with it.

We took on fuel and stores for the next stage of our Odyssey. It was hot and very humid.

Not having an atlas I was not conscious of the enormous distances we were travelling over the globe — covering 600 miles each 24 hours. It can be appreciated why the fleet carrier had become a high speed aircraft delivery system wherever fighter reinforcement was essential. On reflection it may well have been an effective use at this critical time of what was soon to become the dominant naval weapon in the hands of the Japanese and American navies.

We sailed south east for another 2000 miles, stopping briefly at the remote Cocos Islands to refuel from an oiler before proceeding east to Christmas Island, which lies 300 miles off the coast of Java. A wild looking Australian dressed only in a battered straw hat and khaki shorts arrived on board and made an incongruous sight knocking back beers in the ante-room. It was said that he was the sole inhabitant and had brought on board gen on the Japanese situation: it is likely that he had been assigned the thankless job of operating a radio in the event of Japanese occupation.

In the upper hangar work proceeded night and day assembling the first batch of RAF Hurricanes — a difficult and exhausting business in the heat and confined space. The wings and fuselages had got muddled up and the RAF ground crew taken aboard were not familiar with the Hurricane, so the men of 880 had to shoulder most of the work as well as keeping their own planes serviceable.

We had now guessed that their destination was Singapore. It was obvious that we were now in enemy waters as the ship was at action stations throughout daylight hours. There was now little joking amongst the RAF pilots and the general feeling of tension was sharpened by two events. The ship's radar had picked up an unidentified aircraft and the two Hurricanes from 880's standing patrol were directed to intercept what turned out to be a Sunderland flying boat.

On 27 January 1942 we were about 100 miles from the coast of Java and dawn was just breaking as the first batch of 16 RAF Hurricanes of 258 Squadron was brought up on deck to have their engines tested and then be manhandled down the deck and ranged. With their large tropical oil radiators and underwing long range fuel tanks, they looked less graceful than our Sea Hurricane. I joined the macabre crowd filling every inch of goofer's gallery and watched their pilots stream out of the island and climb into their cockpits. It was much like what I imagine a crowd to be at a bullfight. Perhaps we would have been more respectful had we known how much the cards were being stacked up against these ill-fated young men. They sat sweltering in the sun as all eyes scanned the sky for the Blenheim IV which was reported to be on its way to rendezvous with us in order to navigate the fighters to an airfield at Batavia. Quite suddenly it appeared out of the haze and (F) gave the signal to start engines. The throaty roar of sixteen Merlin engines quickly dominated an otherwise peaceful scene as *Indom* swung round into wind and increased speed to 30 knots. The first Hurricane's wings were shaking and its wheels strained against the brakes as the pilot ran the engine up to full revs. His tail was up as he roared past us, his gaze rigidly ahead to keep a straight line down the deck, and he was airborne with plenty of deck to spare.

After the first few sections had flown off with apparent ease, the remaining pilots must have assumed that it was all a 'piece of cake' and took to glancing up at the island audience as they passed by, some raising a hand in farewell, an action which seemed to result in them dropping their port wing. There were one or two close shaves including one which veered off to port, bouncing on the raised edge of the catapult and only just staggering over the side. In loose formation they soon disappeared from sight. There was no blood in our bullring ; it was only in recent years that I discovered that only thirteen reached Singapore where, outnumbered by over ten to one, they were decimated by more experienced Japanese pilots, equipped with aircraft of an unforeseen agility and firepower.

On the 28th, the dawn patrol patrol failed to return; it was our Swordfish, and the only aircraft *Indom* carried which was fitted with ASV. Lt 'Bugs' Willoughby RN was the pilot with my friend Sub Lt Shaddick as observer. There was a severe tropical rainstorm in the area, and 'Buster' May and his observer 'Geordie' Marley ran into it when they flew off on a fruitless search.

Through the night the struggle had gone on to assemble the next batch of Hurricanes, and by the end of the following day, 32 more had climbed away from our floating airfield. Of the last batch, one pilot radioed that he had low oil pressure and proposed to land back on. 'F' agreed and the ship put on full speed to give him the maximum wind over the deck. What must his thoughts have been as, all alone, he circled with wheels and flaps down? Should he bale out? At least he had watched our own Sea Hurricane pilots and observed their technique — but he had no hook to catch him, only his brakes. The excitement on board was intense as he made his first approach, so low that he almost disappeared below flight deck level before pulling up and dashing across the deck just above the barrier. We held our breath as he began another approach from well astern, but this time he got it just right, touching down well aft with his tail jerking up every time he applied his brakes. (F) took the risk of lowering the barrier before he reached it, and he skidded on ominously towards the bows. As he slowed, the deck crew rushed out, grabbed his wings and stopped him only feet away from the edge. Everyone cheered. It was a brave effort.

It was a pity that such a magnificent logistical and skilful operation ended up by being a total waste of good men and aircraft. The last two batches never got further than Sumatra where rudimentary airfields, lack of ground crew, and constant enemy strafing halved their numbers within days of arrival. When joined by the few Hurricanes forced to withdraw from Singapore on 10 February they achieved a surprisingly large number of victories, but the only effect was to slow the relentless Japanese advance. None of the aircraft survived and few of the pilots.

On board *Indom* we knew nothing of these tragic events. We were now heading for Ceylon and crossing the Equator for the fourth time in six weeks. It was back to dawn to dusk A/S patrols over a seemingly empty Indian Ocean.

Lacking the imagination to consider what would happen should we be forced to ditch and take to a dinghy in these latitudes of burning sun, I had taken to stripping down to only a Mae West, shorts and plimsolls as soon as we got airborne and settled into our patrol. I had also found that a joined up safety belt formed a comfortable and cool seat somewhat higher than the normal seat and giving a better view (it was particularly good when dive-bombing due to its inherent ability to pivot in response to the dive angle). Jack got excited one day when he was sure that he had sighted a submarine, but when we got to the spot it turned out to be a large whale. Sub Lt 'Swee'pea' Morrell improved on this by dropping his depth charges before discovering that his target was also a whale.

After my earlier experience, long excursions from our scheduled flight path were no longer a navigational problem. I discovered other tricks of the trade. While scanning the horizon through binoculars from our usual height of 2000 feet I found that in these tropical ocean conditions it was possible to catch a brief glimpse of the carrier just as it came over the rim of the horizon at about forty miles distant and before it disappeared into the haze of what I have called the saucer. I could take a compass bearing at this distance which reduced the possibility of error in making an interception. Long before Jack had seen the ship on the final approach I had my Bigsworth packed up and was sitting relaxed, with just the occasional squint through the binoculars. There seemed no need to disclose this particular trick to my ever trusting driver who assumed our spot-on arrival to be due to my navigational expertise.

Apart from the flying, life was just a round of sleeping and eating. The food was always first class even when the potatoes ran out and the cook had to resort to deep fried rice balls to which I became quite addicted. There were always prunes for breakfast and, at lunch, an everlasting supply of pickled walnuts. My taste in the bar had shifted from dry sherry to creme-de-menthe frappe or whisky. Socialising was kept mainly within the squadrons and between pilots and their observers. We rather shunned our 'old' CO who was usually to be found alone in his own special chair, with his long black silver tipped cigarette holder at one side of his mouth. He would sometimes approach a group of us and suggest a game of 'Uckers' [navalese for Ludo], only too frequently to be rebuffed — the young can be very cruel. Sub Lt Brooks, one of our pilots, usually found that it was time to 'crash his swede' (which was the in-phrase for going to bed), when it was his turn to buy a round. Many plots were made in an attempt to trap him, all in vain.

What time I wasted. If only I had appreciated that I was being paid to be taken on the cruise of a lifetime in the company of an elite group of often talented young men. All the books I could have read; all the music I could have heard; all the aircraft design features I could have studied. I like to blame it on the all pervading heat, but it was really intellectual laziness; I was not what is now called a self-starter. I filled in the long hours with a few drawings and paintings, but I was more likely to be found on one of the boat decks watching the magic of the flying fish, flashing out of the sea like silver darts to glide briefly in an alien world of spray and sunlight. After dark I could be found drinking or sleeping.

As we approached Trincomalee on the east coast of Ceylon the island seemed lushly green and beautiful. All serviceable aircraft were flown off to China Bay airfield; a romantic name for what turned out to be an unromantic spot surrounded by jungle. It had belonged to the RAF and in fact they still had a squadron of Vickers Vildebeests there; an aircraft which entered service in the early thirties and looked even more of an oddity than the Swordfish also based there while their carrier, the old *Hermes,* was being repaired in South Africa.

Unaware of the impending tragedy unfolding at Singapore we enjoyed two weeks of rest and relaxation in our floating hotel, now anchored close by Sober Island to which boat trips were arranged so that we could lie in the shade of every variety of tropical tree, or swim in the clearest of water, clear enough to see the large water snakes; whether or not they were dangerous I kept my feet well up, just in case. The islands oldest inhabitant was a giant tortoise, said to be over a hundred years old so it must have peered through its lidded eyes at generations of visiting seamen. Maybe we kept sober on the island but it was not so in the mess — the only other evening entertainment was the occasional cine film shown on a big screen in the hangar. One trip to the small native town of Trincomalee was enough and the local population was not exactly friendly. Some more adventurous characters made their way in monstrously overcrowded buses up to Kandy in the hilly centre of the island.

All aircrew were given two days leave in Colombo and 831 ran an airline taxi service to the civil aerodrome at Ratmalana. When our turn came, Jack and I stowed our bags in 4C and set off due west across the flat plain at 500 feet, past the old town of Anuradhapura, almost touching the spired tops of the huge domed Buddhist shrines for which it is famous, and finally reaching the surf fringed coast. Then turning south we flew at sea level for nearly 100 miles, an exhilarating experience after all those patrols over empty ocean, but not much fun for the occupants of some native canoes who took one look at us and dived overboard. We took a taxi to the Galle Face Hotel on the coast south of Colombo and undoubtedly one of the best on the island. Signing the register we noticed that a Lt Cdr and Mrs P. Mortimer had booked in a few days previously; we didn't think he had it in him at his age. I made a not very subtle record of the event in the line book.

We shared a room and in a somewhat drunken sleep Jack managed to knock over and smash the bedside lamp which didn't seem to please the management — I rather think they had had a bellyful of *Indomitable*'s aircrew.

The next day we went into Colombo. The heat was suffocating and everywhere we went shopkeepers in their doorways pressed us to purchase precious stones; my wife has never forgiven me for missing the chance of buying a moonstone ring; but of course I hadn't yet met her. I did buy a garnet bracelet and a pair of the indigenous elephant book ends, both of which have survived the years creditably.

Back on board the terrible news reached us of the fall of Singapore. Things looked very bad — we didn't seem to be winning anywhere. We put to sea early the following day, 16 February, and both squadrons flew on board. With only half our aircraft complement we were not surprised when we rounded the southern end of Ceylon and headed west to Aden arriving at that godforsaken place on 21 February. Commander (F) was not notable for kind word or deed so we were happily surprised to see pinned up on the wardroom notice board the following memo:

> 831 Squadron will disembark on Sunday (22 February) and exchange duties with 827.
> The following are interesting figures from 831 squadron records and speak for themselves:
> ADEN to ADEN 501 hours flown = 50,000 miles.
> Daily percentage serviceability 93% including running an airline to Colombo.
> 3 engines changed.
> 3 – 180 hour inspections and two aircraft erected.
> All this with Albacores is great work.
> WELL DONE 831!

I went ashore with the baggage to the sandy, featureless RAF airfield of Khormaksar. *Indom* sailed the next day and our aircraft flew ashore and were replaced by 827 Squadron on 23 February.

While we languished in the desert, *Indom* returned to Port Sudan and Rear-Admiral D. W. Boyd RN arrived aboard to fly his flag; another piece of the jig-saw which gave no hint of the picture. Forty two Mk II B Hurricanes of 30 and 261 RAF squadrons were hoisted on board and their pilots embarked. They were destined for Java, but the situation there had reached such a sorry pass that they were diverted to Ceylon, being flown off on 6/7 March. It was one of the better decisions in view of the events which followed only a month later.

Our three weeks at Khormaksar were not memorable. The accommodation was reasonable, but the surroundings were like my imagination of a Biblical wilderness. During the mornings we lounged around the crew ready room grumbling about the intense heat and humidity which drained us of every ounce of energy or initiative. There was not even a lot of pleasure in the afternoon visits by truck to a steeply sloping pebble beach where we swam behind shark nets which had too many holes in them for comfort. In the evenings there was nothing to do but get drunk on warm beer in the RAF mess whose permanent inhabitants did not appreciate our bawdy songs and general rowdiness; posted out there with a few Blenheim IVs they had a lot to put up with and none of the action.

To impress the local natives with the might of the British Empire at a time when we seemed to be losing on all fronts, the whole squadron took to the air for a 'Balbo'; flying in impeccable formation low over Aden and the flat roofed dwellings nestling in the bottom of the old volcanic crater.

Lt 'Puppy' Kennard RN had an engine failure, and had to ditch in the harbour within sight of the Crescent Hotel. My drawing of the incident shows his observer rather pleased with himself for having retrieved his lead weighted code book from a submerged cockpit. Buster May was detailed to salvage the aircraft and wore out four tail wheels towing it back to Khormaksar.

We carried out a few patrols over the Gulf, passing close by the coast of Vichy French Somaliland and the port of Djibouti which was far from friendly territory. It was on one of these trips that I felt the onset of a dose of the endemic 'trots' and it was a long, long hour sitting doubled up on the cockpit floor before we landed. I leapt out and wasn't to be seen for a swirl of dust. A large brandy was indicated as the only treatment but, after I passed out while sitting on the loo, the dreaded dysentery was diagnosed and I was whisked off to the RAF hospital situated on a hill overlooking Aden's harbour. I joined dozens of poor souls similarly afflicted whose only compensation was the presence of a few British nurses. It is not possible to combine romance with the trots. The treatment seemed to be based on starvation, so it was ironic that I received my first and only parcel from home containing a Christmas cake and chocolates, both of which had seen better days. Jack smuggled in some brandy and appraised the nurses.

A week later, from our vantage point, I saw *Indom* anchor in the harbour. I immediately feared being left behind and pressed the doctor to discharge me. It took most of the day and an interview with the senior MO before it was agreed that I could go. It was evening before I stumbled happily up the gangway feeling very weak at the knees and with my khaki shorts nearly falling down — I had lost two stones and weighed only eight and a half. But how good it felt to be back home even if I had been banished to a smaller cabin way down in the ship's stern where the hull curved both down and back into a wedge shape. I shared it with another of our observers, young Sub Lt 'Willy' Protheroe, the son of a clergyman, a gentle character and a good companion. Had he lived I think he might well have gone into the church. We were both keen pipe smokers although by now I was also hooked on cigarettes, particularly in the crew room, where a pipe seemed too much of an effort.

On 16 March, both 831 and 800 flew on board, the latter had had to suffer nine weeks at Khormaksar and it was said that they had almost gone native. We finally sailed from Aden on the 19th with our full complement of aircraft and an Admiral. There was a general feeling of excitement as once more we headed south east. Now we had 827 to share the A/S patrols and both fighter squadrons spent more time in the air on exercises.

Tom Troubridge announced that we were on our way to Addu Atoll to form part of a new Eastern Fleet with Admiral Somerville as C in C. Since the Battle of the Java Sea on 27 February the Indian Ocean had been left open and undefended by the navy. We were about to take part in what, after the war, Sir Winston Churchill called 'the most dangerous moment of the war' but I don't think any of us realised this at the time.

Chapter 6
An Eastern Fleet Cruise

By the time we arrived back at Addu Atoll on 24 March I had put most of my weight back on. It must have been the whisky. We slipped into the lagoon to find the four old 'R' class battleships, *Royal Sovereign, Resolution, Revenge* and *Ramillies* anchored there; low squat shapes dominated by their towering tripod masts. Impressive to the eye, but hardly so as fighting ships — after all they had been launched well before I was born. They were to prove a liability.

We lay at anchor sweltering in the equatorial heat with the only diversion being beach parties for which crates of beer were shipped to white sandy beaches behind which rose low growing tropical plants, fruit trees and coconut palms. The lagoon water looked so inviting, translucent and ripple free, but too warm and shallow to make swimming a pleasure, and we had been warned of the deadly danger of cutting one's feet on the coral; I discovered just how deadly a month later. Peter Mortimer joined one of these parties but, whereas nudity or shorts was the dress of the day, he stands out in my photograph fully dressed, including cap and long stockings. 'Geoff' Smith on the other hand is to be seen holding a large piece of coral in place of a fig leaf and looking like Michaelangelo's Young David.

After a sudden rush of activity we put to sea just before midnight on 29 March. On waking the next morning a quick dash up to the flight deck revealed the four old battleships wallowing behind us in line astern and surrounding us a screen of destroyers. After rushing around this ocean at 25 knots we were now only making 15 knots which was the most that the old 'R's could manage.

Rumours were rife that a Japanese fleet was on its way to attack Ceylon. Guns were manned and A/S and fighter patrols were flown with a new alertness. Our target-towing Swordfish took to the air and the ship's pom-poms opened up as it trailed majestically (and slowly) passed us. I recalled the Gunnery Chief back at Whale Island — 'They'll never get through that lot, not never!' The noise was certainly impressive but the drogue wriggled through the air in mocking virginity.

More impressive was our rendezvous, 100 miles south of Ceylon, at teatime on 31 March with the battle proven fleet carrier *Formidable*, the light carrier *Hermes*, and battleship *Warspite* together with a number of cruisers and destroyers. It was a stirring sight with signal lights flickering in all directions as 28 ships manoeuvred to form two separate groups. A fast group, Force A, comprising *Warspite, Indomitable, Formidable,* three cruisers and six destroyers with Admiral Somerville flying his flag in *Warspite.* Force B was made up of the slower ships, *Hermes,* the four 'R's, three cruisers and eight destroyers commanded by Vice-Admiral Willis in *Resolution*; they disappeared to the westward as the sun set. [*Hermes* had only one squadron of Swordfish and no fighter aircraft, so this group was particularly vulnerable to air attack.]

Rumour was now confirmed that a Japanese carrier group was expected to be in the area the following day and there was talk of our making a night torpedo attack on them. There was a rush to study silhouettes of Japanese warships and a more prolonged study of their aircraft types while on the loo. How little we knew of this enemy was soon to be demonstrated.

April Fool's Day came and all we seemed to do was cruise slowly to and fro in the same area, flying off regular A/S patrols. We were all keyed up but not a word came from those above as to what was happening. Sub Lt Trevor Turner, our most flamboyant pilot, livened up the day by 'shooting up' *Warspite*'s tower block bridge structure after returning from a patrol. The C in C was not amused and, well before his wheels touched our deck, there was an ominous flashing of signals in our direction. Later, a pale Trevor turned up in the wardroom after a severe carpeting by (F), but in fact he enjoyed the brief fame. It was well known that he thought he should have been a fighter pilot and to demonstrate his flying talent he would, on occasion, fly alongside the carrier trailing his arrestor hook in the water. Highly strung, and with a random facial twitch, he shot himself in the head some years later after taking a night fighter course. Who knows what demons possessed him.

Formidable had three squadrons on board — 818 (9 Albacores), 820 (12 Albacores), and 888 (12 Martlet IIs). Goofers found a new interest in watching *Formidable* operating her Albacores and American Martlet fighters; especially the Martlets with their grotesque, narrow tracked, retractable undercarriages; a cats cradle of rods, cranks and levers which we had first seen at Norfolk. They looked well in the air and seemed to have no trouble getting down on the deck. As is typical in this sort of situation we aviators were told nothing about their flying missions and no doubt they knew nothing of ours. By the time the sun set just after six o'clock we knew nothing about anything.

With the imminent possibility of encountering a Japanese carrier force we guessed that Admiral Boyd, who was in command of air operations, would be having high level tactical conferences to which we were not privy. We had, however, any number of amateur tacticians, and a very few who had had experience of operations in the Mediterranean. There was at that time no precedent for conducting a battle between opposing carrier fleets. [The famous Battle of the Coral Sea took place 4/8 May, 1942.]

British and American practice was to use the multi-role approach, the carrier strike aircraft doubling in the search role; this produced a conflict with the relatively few aircraft available. If sufficient Albacores were despatched to cover a wide search area they then would not be available for any subsequent air strike. It was also highly probable that without cloud cover any Albacore making a daylight sighting of an enemy carrier would almost certainly be shot down by their fighters before the long winded enemy sighting procedure could be completed. This procedure required the observer to code up a sighting report, position, course, speed and composition, on his SYKO coding machine (an unwieldy device), which then had to be passed to his TAG who would transmit it using the 'intercept' procedure. This meant transmitting to another aircraft in the search which would then transmit the signal back — giving the fleet W/T operators a double chance of receiving it. The fleet would be maintaining strict W/T silence and under no circumstances communicate with aircraft.

Although I doubt that it was understood at the time, the Japanese had adopted a different approach, using their battleship and cruiser catapult launched seaplanes for the search role and avoiding the multi-role concept, even to the extent of having dedicated aircraft for the torpedo and dive bombing roles. Even more important they had the Mitsubishi A6M2 (Zero), a carrier fighter with enough range to accompany their strike aircraft all the way to the target.

Both sides carried more strike aircraft than fighters, not appreciating at that time the vital need to defend their carriers.

The Albacores of *Indomitable* and *Formidable* were capable, if inadequately practiced, in the execution of a night torpedo attack, but the only ones fitted with ASV were those on *Formidable*. There was a full moon on 1 April so there seemed a reasonable chance of success if we were given the chance. The Swordfish on *Hermes* [814 Squadron] were also not fitted with ASV; being part of Force B we saw little of her.

However, when the sun rose on the 2nd we were back again in the same position steaming slowly west. 'Where were all these Japanese?' was all we could say to each other.

I had often expressed the view that the Fulmar would be more effective in the search role than the Albacore; it had about the same range, but, with its higher speed, it could cover the area in a shorter time and, if intercepted, it had a better chance of defending itself. As for making sighting reports, it was capable of a rapid climb to enable it to make an

R/T report which, even if not heard correctly, would show up on *Indom*'s excellent radar, giving a bearing and distance.

Admiral Boyd must have come to this decision about this time and, as 800 Squadron did not have a full complement of observers, Geoff Smith and I were assigned to fly with them on searches. We were unduly pleased with ourselves. I was certainly excited the first time I strapped myself into the pilot's type harness and seat parachute fitted in the rear cockpit, and then to experience cruising at 145 knots instead of 95 knots. After completing the usual dog-leg search (see Appendix 4), and with our fleet in sight, my pilot, Lt Muir-Mackenzie RN, rolled the aircraft without warning me. As the sky rotated my pencils and navigation gear enjoyed a moment of free fall — not the sort of thing an Albacore observer would expect, though he might have done with Trevor Turner as pilot.

On the morning of the 3rd, word got around that we were on our way back to Addu. Albacores of 831 carried out a search ahead of the fleet to a distance of 150 miles. There was no sign of Force B and we were now making 18 knots. It was all a bit of a let down and I felt flat and dyspeptic.

We entered the tranquillity of the lagoon on 4 April as the sun beat down overhead; it was beginning to feel like our own tropical island if not exactly a home. As the sun went down that night it cast a red glow over the great gathering of ships and changed their angular features into black silhouettes. I tried to capture the scene in water colour but the result was too much like the poster for a Hollywood epic.

I had no sooner finished when the ship became alive with the shrill piping of orders. I made a quick dash up to the flight deck where all was peaceful but it was clear that we were preparing in haste to go to sea again. We sailed with Force A at midnight.

It could only mean one thing, and even at this late hour the excitement could be seen in everyone's eyes wherever small groups of aircrew gathered. Jack said that torpedos were being slung beneath our Albacores and I felt the first stirring of fear in my guts. We went down into the hangar where our long suffering armourers were struggling to manoeuvre the tin fish in the confined space, stripped down to no more than a pair of underpants and plimsolls in a temperature of 115 degrees, sweat glistening on their bodies in the dim light. Jack and I took a final stroll on the flight deck to cool off before attempting a few hours sleep.

I hardly seemed to get my head down before the chilling sound of action stations blared out from the speaker and Willy and I fell over each other in our rush to get dressed. No time to shave before climbing the long way up to the flight deck. It was four o'clock in the morning of Easter Sunday, 5 April and still dark. Fulmars were being brought up the for'd lift and ranged aft. Small groups from every squadron were wandering around like lost sheep — we had no action stations to go to but felt we ought to be up and doing something. There had never been such a crowd lining the breakfast table and never such a dearth of 'gen'.

Just before 0700, four Fulmars were flown off on a search. I was disappointed at not being asked to take part but when our CO called us to the ready room it was to explain that we were to stand-by to make a torpedo attack on a Japanese fleet which he understood had been sighted by the RAF. Torpedo depth settings were discussed in relation to various possible targets and the usual routine for an attack was reviewed. At 0750, 827's Albacores began a search ahead of the fleet and it was past midday when they returned without making any sighting.

Mid morning there was a flurry of activity around the stand-by Hurricanes - the starter trolleys were manned and the pilots strapped into their cockpits — all eyes were on the cloudless sky. Nothing happened and half an hour later they had to be moved forward to land on the returning Fulmars. It was rumoured that one of them had seen a Japanese floatplane at the extremity of his search and it was this that had caused the flap.

I had often wondered why we were told so little by those in command. By this time the C in C had been informed of the massive Japanese air attack on Colombo and that somewhere ahead we were faced with an enemy with overwhelming carrier strength.

At 1345 the Tannoy broadcast that enemy aircraft were on the radar screen at the extreme range of 84 miles. The Hurricanes prepared to take off and all ship's guns closed up. I put on my Mae West and collected the rest of my flying gear. Four of 827s Albacores were boosted off to carry out a dog-leg search — I wondered why we didn't send Fulmars. Soon after we were told that the radar echoes had faded from the screen, which seemed odd. There was no more news as the afternoon hours dragged slowly by. By now everyone had heard that Colombo had been attacked and we all knew that the Japanese fleet must be somewhere ahead. Would 827's boys find it? We hadn't long to wait for an answer.

The swollen red disc of the sun was sinking to the horizon when a change in vibration announced an increase in speed, so we all rushed up on deck to find two Albacores circling and *Indom* pulling out of line to land them on. A third arrived about fifteen minutes later with a burst tyre and, after touching down, nearly went over the side. It was piloted by Sub Lt Robin Grant-Sturgis RNVR and we all saw that his TAG, Leading Airman Gordon Dixon, had been wounded. The fourth aircraft piloted by Sub Lt Streathfield, with Sub Lt Weston as observer and L/A Porter as TAG, failed to return and the ship ominously pulled back into line as darkness fell. The decibels of rumour increased and the crews of the search aircraft were ensconced in the Ops room incommunicado. If it was true that they had made contact with the Japs and been attacked by Zeros then why weren't we doing something about it? Someone pointed out that the fleet had reversed course and the general view was that we were running away.

The Hurricanes were taken below and I saw our Albacores coming up on the lift, torpedoes slung and flares on the wing racks. The Tannoy called us to the ready room; you would have thought we were all going to a party. Peter Mortimer told us that Grant-Sturgis had made a sighting and that as soon as the enemy position was confirmed we could expect to make a night attack. Meanwhile we were all to go down to our aircraft and sit and wait in them.

Ground crew were milling around as we approached 4C, ranged in the first section on the port side, so we would be one of the first to go in to the attack. I bent down and looked at the torpedo, all 1600 pounds of death reflecting what little light was left. A voice out of the dark said 'You've got a good one there, Sir, see you put it right up one of those squint eyed bastards!'.

I climbed in after Oscar and, after switching on the little hooded light, unpacked all my gear and checked the beacon receiver. There was nothing else to do but sit and shiver in the darkness as the aircraft gently rocked on its fat tyres. From my compass I saw that the ship was now on a north westerly course which seemed strange. Acrid fumes from the ship's funnel percolated into the cockpit. I lost count of time and don't remember how long it was before there was a rap on the cockpit door and a disembodied voice said we were packing it in for the night.

The C in C's ears must have burned when we gathered in the ready room; Peter Mortimer arrived with a bottle of whisky, which lasted until about 1am. Out of a confused story it seemed that Grant-Sturgis had indeed caught a glimpse of two enemy carriers and almost immediately been attacked by a Zero. He had been torn off a strip for not staying to shadow the enemy — TAGs were obviously considered expendable and Zeros just a minor nuisance. Another of the Albacores had reported seeing wreckage in the water. It was assumed that Streathfield had been shot down. So why hadn't we been flown off for our night attack? No one knew.

Heavy hearted we returned to our bunks for a restless sleep, broken by action stations at dawn on the 6th. All our Albacores were back in the hangar and only the stand-by Hurricanes stood on an otherwise empty flight deck. Somehow we seemed to have joined up again with Force B and were sailing east at a sluggish twelve knots. There was no sense of urgency and even rumour had succumbed to a sense of defeat. There was no flying all morning. After lunch *Formidable* flew off a number of Albacores and there was a strong rumour that the cruisers *Dorsetshire* and

Cornwall had been sunk. This was confirmed in late afternoon when two of 800's Fulmars were flown off to cover the rescue of survivors. Only one found them and it was dark when he arrived back with harrowing tales of survivors clinging to wreckage and a few floats — they had been 28 hours in the open sea.

No sooner was the last Fulmar brought on board than the fleet reversed course to the north west; we aviators had no idea where we were or where we were going — the whole day had been an anti-climax. The next day was similar, there was no flying apart from the usual A/S patrols, and we heard that we were on our way back to Addu, where we arrived just before lunch on 8 April, quite unaware that the Japanese fleet was manoeuvring to make an attack on Trincomalee 900 miles away.

Chapter 7
The Most Dangerous Moment

At the time and for many years after these events I was convinced that we had simply run away from the enemy and it was a bitter feeling shared by most aircrew. Even after reading what Winston Churchill had to say in *The Second World War**, where he stated that we had narrowly avoided a major disaster, I still felt unconvinced.

It is only now that I can appreciate how little anyone understands of what actually takes place while playing some small role in the major events of history. Or even how little Admiral Somerville knew hour by hour of events in a drama taking place over thousands of square miles of ocean. His information was almost entirely second or third hand and, like all of us, he had to sleep sometime. Although I thought all Commanders and above were old men, I was not aware that our C in C was approaching 60, nor was I aware of his considerable experience in the operation of carrier aircraft gained in command of Force H in the Mediterranean.

It was when writing my impressions of events in the foregoing chapter that I began to wonder just where the Japanese fleet had been through those days and even where our fleet had been (land was too far away to show on the charts we used in the air). After studying many accounts of the operation it seemed as though some of the pieces of the jigsaw had got mixed up leaving me with a distorted picture both of events and the C in C's part in them. Part of the problem was due to both naval and RAF aircraft playing leading roles in the drama and the inevitable lack of communication imposed by the need for wireless silence.

I have come to disagree with the accepted official view that Admiral Somerville cannily avoided engagement with a vastly superior enemy force and thus preserved the Eastern Fleet. So I decided on one more attempt to tell the story of what I accept to be the most dangerous moment of the war and to express my belief that, far from running away, Admiral Somerville almost rashly stuck his neck out in an attempt to engage the enemy, and that only fate preserved us.

None of us young officers was aware of the strategic implications of a Japanese assault on Ceylon, which, if successful, would have meant loss of control over the Indian Ocean from Singapore across to the east coast of

---

* Volume IV, Chapter X

Africa. This would have resulted in closing the only supply routes to Egypt, the Middle East, India and Burma and their eventual conquest. It could well have meant our losing the war.

There is no doubt that Admiral Sir James Somerville was aware of the implications when he was appointed C in C of the Eastern Fleet, and even more painfully aware of the inadequacy of the fleet he was to command. In spite of being of an age when most men should expect to have their feet up in front of a fire, and having been retired as unfit before the war, he was probably the best man for the job, having a keen sense of humour and considerable wartime experience in the tactical operation of carrier aircraft as part of a naval force. He knew the limitations of the Swordfish, Albacore and Fulmar but he could not have known how greatly superior was the performance of the Japanese naval aircraft and their elite aircrew. Their success at Pearl Harbor had been against a virtually undefended target and most of their control over the air in Malaya and the East Indies had been achieved mainly by land-based aircraft, including their sinking of the *Prince of Wales* and *Repulse*.

Sir James realised that should the Japanese send a force into the Indian Ocean similar to that used against Pearl Harbor — and there was no reason why they should not — then his Eastern Fleet would be no match for them and could even be destroyed. Such has always been the penalty of engaging in battle with anything other than a superior force.

To add to his difficulties the fleet he had been given had been brought together from all parts of the globe and had had no time to work together to practice the procedures involved in manoeuvring such a large number of disparate ships. The four 'R' class battleships were a handicap rather than an asset, only just capable of making 18 knots and at that speed their fuel would only last three or four days. They had to be defended against both submarine and air attack which indicated that they ought to accompany *Warspite* and the fleet carriers — on the other hand their slow speed would put the fleet at risk on both counts.

If the strategic objective was to defend Ceylon against seaborne attack or invasion, then Admiral Somerville did not have a force capable of seeking out and successfully engaging a Japanese main battle fleet, although it appears that some high-ranking officers at the Admiralty, having been overly impressed with the exploits of torpedo armed Swordfish at Taranto and against the *Bismarck,* expected him to do so.

This meant that Ceylon would have to rely on shore-based aircraft for its defence, and here again, as at Singapore, they were totally inadequate, even though Admiral Sir Geoffrey Layton, C in C Ceylon, had greatly improved the position by diverting the two Hurricane squadrons from Java as reported in the previous chapter. But this only amounted to three squadrons of RAF Hurricanes and two of FAA Fulmars. For air search and A/S patrol there were only six RAF Catalinas — which were to play a vital role — and a striking force which was limited to a squadron of Blenheim IV bombers and six FAA Swordfish.

Ceylon is a big island 250 miles long and 150 miles wide and it was necessary to share the air forces between Colombo and Trincomalee which are 150 miles apart, and there was no way of knowing whether or not they would come under simultaneous attack.

Admiral Somerville probably did not even have the comfort of knowing that the Japanese ships were not yet fitted with early warning radar and were unable to direct their fighters to meet an attack.

Out of all the options open to the Japanese high command, he judged that a sortie into the Indian Ocean was the most likely, and in this event he advised the Admiralty and his staff that his strategy would be 'to keep the Eastern Fleet in being and avoid losses by attrition.' This was to be achieved 'by keeping the fleet at sea as much as possible'; to avoid its being caught in harbour; to avoid a day action whilst seeking to deliver night torpedo attacks; and not to undertake 'operations which do not give reasonable prospects of success.'

But it must all have looked a very gloomy prospect as he arrived in Colombo on 24 March 1942, having taken passage from the UK on board *Formidable*. On the 26th he transferred his flag to *Warspite* which was the only ship with suitable accommodation for his staff. Launched as far back as 1915 and a veteran of the fifth battle squadron at Jutland, she had been modernised in the mid thirties and was nominally capable of making 24 knots.

Events moved much faster than he expected. On 28 March he received a report from Admiralty Intelligence of an impending Japanese attack on Ceylon on 1 April by two or more carriers, two 6 inch cruisers and a large number of destroyers, possibly supported by battleships of the *Kongo* class. He was still in Colombo Harbour with the other units of his fleet split between Trincomalee and the secret new base at Addu Atoll.

It is typical of Somerville that he did not hesitate in making immediate plans to engage the enemy. It was essential for him to concentrate his fleet and he lost no time in arranging a rendezvous 80 miles south of Dondra Head at 1600 on 31 March. This was the soonest time the old Rs could make the 615 mile passage from Addu Atoll, being unable to make more than 15 knots (see Map 1).

Admiral Willis, flying his flag in *Resolution,* sailed just before midnight on 29 March with *Indomitable* and nine destroyers. The C in C sailed in *Warspite* from Colombo during the forenoon of 30 March with *Formidable,* the cruisers *Cornwall, Enterprise, Caledon, Dragon* and five destroyers — the cruiser *Dorsetshire* was under refit and was not ready to sail. At the same time *Hermes* sailed from Trincomalee with the cruisers *Emerald, Heemskerck* (Dutch), and the destroyer *Vampire;* the latter a survivor from the *Prince of Wales* and *Repulse* disaster.

From his experience with Force H, Somerville realised that daylight attacks with Albacores would be both suicidal and ineffective; in this he was considerably at odds with the First Sea Lord. Sir James considered the only strategy with these inadequate aircraft would be to make night torpedo attacks taking benefit of the full moon on 1 April. It appears that he had the erroneous belief that the Japanese disliked night actions and would avoid them. During daylight he hoped to be able to withdraw outside the enemy's air search area.

For this strategy to have any chance of success it was essential that the enemy fleet be located, and its position fixed, as early as possible during its approach; this was equally important to the shore-based defences. This approach could be from either of two directions; the east from the northern end of Sumatra via the Malacca Strait or south east through the Sunda Strait between Sumatra and Java.

For long range search the C in C was fortunate in having RAF Catalinas based on Koggala lagoon, just south of the old Dutch fort off Galle. At this time only three out of five were serviceable — an additional Dutch Catalina was kept as standby to maintain communications with Addu Atoll. On 30 March they commenced patrols to a distance of 420 miles from Colombo between bearings 110 degrees to 154 degrees (see Map 2).

If the enemy was indeed to make his approach from the south east and fly off his aircraft at dawn on 1 April, it can be seen that he would not enter this search area until sunset (1809) on the 31st, and so it was quite possible for him to arrive undetected under cover of darkness. An alarming prospect.

It was only two hours to sunset on this day when the outwardly impressive array of 28 warships assembled at the rendezvous. Somerville sent Willis the following signal — 'So this is the Eastern Fleet. Never mind, many a good tune is played on an old fiddle.'

There was no sighting of an enemy fleet but during the night he received a report that the Catalina patrols had sighted Japanese submarines on an arc 360 miles from Colombo between bearings 090 degrees and 140 degrees. He decided that this was the enemy's reconnaissance and became concerned that their approach might be from the east. He therefore despatched an Albacore from *Formidable* to Colombo taking a message to the Deputy C in C requesting a search between 090 degrees and 110 degrees. This was carried out the following day.

Meanwhile Somerville needed the freedom to manoeuvre at full speed with *Indomitable* and *Formidable* if he was to fly off a night strike, and to

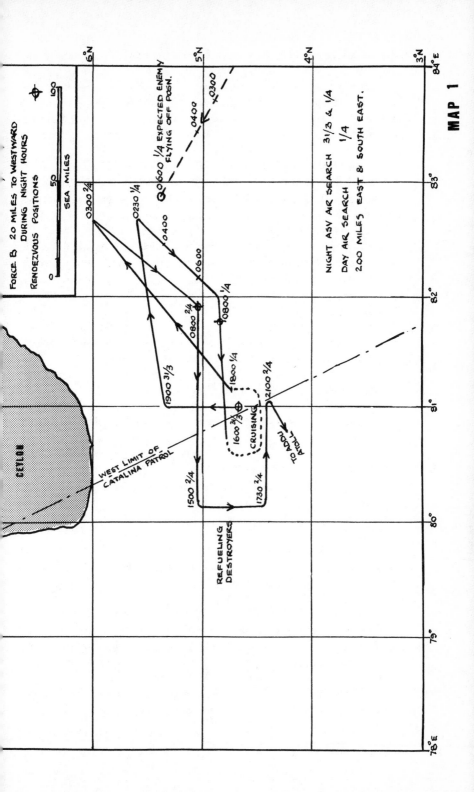

MAP 1

achieve this he split his fleet into two groups. Force A, the fast group, comprised the *Warspite, Indomitable, Formidable,* the cruisers *Cornwall, Emerald* and *Enterprise* with six destroyers. Force B consisted of the four 'R's, *Hermes,* the cruisers *Caledon, Dragon* and *Heemskerck* with eight destroyers. *Hermes* carried no fighter aircraft, so to give Force B protection against air attack he kept both forces together during daylight hours.

As soon as darkness fell he took Force A on an easterly course at 15 knots, leaving Force B to conform 20 miles to westward. Throughout the night *Formidable* flew ASV searches ahead and to the southward but there was no sign of the enemy. At 0230 the fleet altered course to the south west where a rendezvous was made with Force B at 0800 on 1 April.

He was now exposed in daylight in a very dangerous position. Should the enemy be approaching from a more southerly direction he was directly in their path and remained so as he steamed slowly east until mid-day. Formidable sent out an air search to the east and south east to a distance of 200 miles with no result.

In the afternoon he felt relaxed enough to carry out fleet manoeuvring exercises while cruising in the area 100 miles south of Dondra Head. *Dorsetshire* now arrived from Colombo to complete Force A.

Assuming that the enemy had been delayed, Somerville waited until dusk before making another sortie to the north east and *Formidable* flew off night ASV searches. Once again nothing was sighted and he reversed course at 0300 to join up with Force B at 0800 on 2 April. Some of the older destroyers were now running short of fuel, so he took the fleet 100 miles west to keep clear of any submarines which might have sighted such a large gathering of ships. The destroyers refuelled from the cruisers *Dorsetshire* and *Cornwall* and from the fleet oiler *Appleleaf.*

At this point fate decided to play the joker in the form of a signal from Willis reporting that his old battleships had only three days of fresh water left due to a water tanker having failed to arrive at Addu.

The C in C was now beginning to doubt the validity of the Admiralty intelligence report on the Japanese intentions. If submarines had reported the presence of the Eastern Fleet, it seemed unlikely that this would have deterred them — more likely the opposite.

He decided to make one final short sortie to eastward and, if there was no report of an enemy sighting, he would take his fleet to Addu Atoll to refuel. To have made for Colombo or Trincomalee, which were so much closer, would have risked another Pearl Harbor disaster. He finally shaped course for Addu at 2100 hours. During the night he received a report that the merchant ship *Glen Shiel* had been torpedoed 350 miles to the south and he despatched the destroyer *Fortune* to her assistance.

The following morning, 3 April, he made the fateful decision to send the cruisers *Dorsetshire* and *Cornwall* back to Colombo, and *Hermes,* with the destroyer *Vampire,* to Trincomalee. *Dorsetshire* was to complete her refit, *Cornwall* to be ready to escort an Australian troop convoy due to arrive on 8 April, and *Hermes* to prepare for the Madagascar operation (Ironclad). Three more Catalinas of 413 Squadron (Canadian) had arrived at Koggala and long range patrols were continuously maintained.

Force A arrived back at Addu Atoll at noon on 4 April and Force B three hours later. All ships commenced refuelling and the C in C held a conference on board *Warspite* to review events.

The curtain was now about to go up on the real drama as we focus on what the Japanese had been doing up to this time.

In mid February, after the fall of Singapore and the sinking of the *Prince of Wales* and *Repulse,* the Japanese High Command decided that the Royal Navy would move a fleet into the Indian Ocean using Ceylon as a base and they ordered a plan of attack to be prepared. Early in March, Admiral Yamamoto sent an order to carry out an attack to destroy enemy forces around Ceylon during the period from mid March to the beginning of April. This attack was to include a raid on the Bay of Bengal in order to threaten British forces in Calcutta and thereby weaken their effect on the Burma campaign.

Their plan was to attack Ceylon on 1 April, leaving a base at Kendari in the Celebes on 21 March. Their aim was to achieve a similar surprise to that at Pearl Harbor. They were not to know that the US Navy had broken their naval code and it was an outline of this plan which reached Admiral Somerville on 28 March.

However, the operation was delayed by the appearance of a US Navy carrier raiding force at Wake Island on 10 March. This put their departure back to 26 March — the day Somerville hoisted his flag on *Warspite.* The attack on Ceylon was re-scheduled for 4 April. The Allies were not aware of this change in plan and this was to have a critical effect on the outcome.

Vice-Admiral Nagumo was in command of the 1st Air Fleet comprising five of the six fleet carriers he had so successfully used at Pearl Harbor: *Akagi, Shokaku, Zuikaku, Hiryu* and *Soryu.* The sixth, *Kaga,* had been forced to return to Japan for repairs after being damaged on a reef on 15 March — so *Indomitable* was not the only victim of this hazard.

Unlike British carriers, the Japanese ships were not armoured above the water line and were thus able to accommodate more aircraft for a similar displacement. Between the five carriers Nagumo had 318 aircraft compared with only 90 in the three carriers of the Eastern Fleet. The Nakajima 97 (Kate) torpedo bomber, the Aichi 99 (Val) dive-bomber and the Mitsubishi A6M2 (Zero) fighter which formed this complement were all superior in performance to British designed naval aircraft throughout the war. The astonishing range of the Zero fighter — nearly 1400 nautical miles — made it possible for their strike aircraft to be escorted all the way to the target as well as extending the time they could operate combat air patrols over their fleet. With well trained pilots the Zero was more than a match for either the Sea Hurricane or the Wildcat in all aspects except fire power.

To complete his powerful fleet Nagumo had with him the modernised fast battleships *Kongo, Hiei, Kirishima* and *Haruna*, the cruisers *Tone, Chikuma* and *Abukama*, eleven destroyers and seven submarines.

For the co-ordinated operation in the Bay of Bengal, Vice-Admiral Ozawa had a force consisting of the light fleet carrier *Ryujo*, six cruisers and four destroyers.

If the Japanese objective was to gain control of the Indian Ocean by knocking out the Eastern Fleet (which they thought consisted of two carriers, two battleships, ten cruisers and an unspecified number of destroyers), they would have been better advised to have concentrated their ships in one force. A similar strategy was to prove fatal to them, at the Battle of Midway. Even so, Nagumo's battlefleet was vastly superior to any force he might expect to meet and it had the benefit of three weeks extensive training before sailing.

He must have felt supremely confident when he left Kendari during the early hours of 26 March and took the rather surprising passage into the Indian Ocean through the Ombai Straight between the islands of Flores and Timor (see Map 3).

At dawn on the 31st a few of his aircraft attacked the undefended Christmas Island. It seems his fleet was sighted by an allied submarine but I have found no record of events on this day being reported to Somerville.

Ozawa sailed separately through the Malacca Straight to the port of Mergui on the north west coast of the Malayan peninsula, while Nagumo was proceeding on a course heading directly for Ceylon which, if maintained, would have taken him to exactly the position Somerville had forecast. He was steaming slowly as he had decided to delay his attack on Ceylon from 4 April to Easter Sunday, 5 April, as he felt that the Eastern Fleet was more likely to be in port and the island defences less alert on a Sunday. He had adopted the same strategy with such success at Pearl Harbor.

He refuelled his fleet from an oiler during the morning of 3 April before altering to a westerly course and increasing speed to 20 knots. This was to bring him to a flying off position 160 miles to the south west of Somerville's expectation and as much as 200 miles from Colombo. As we

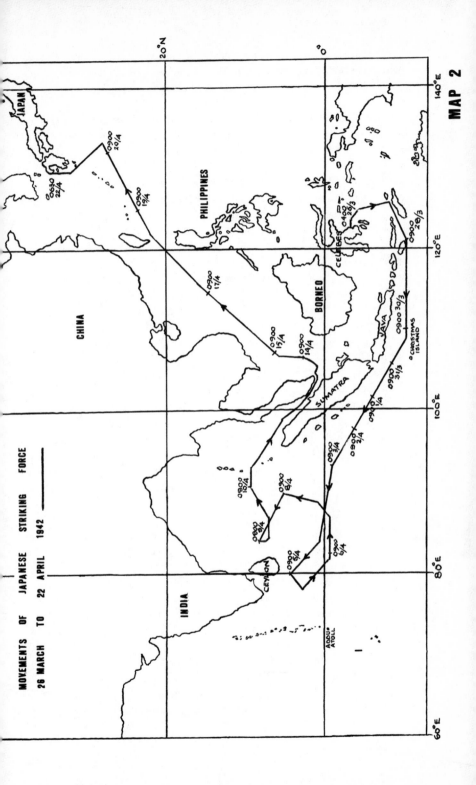

MOVEMENTS OF JAPANESE STRIKING FORCE
26 MARCH TO 22 APRIL 1942

MAP 2

have seen, the range of Japanese naval aircraft came as a surprise to both British and American naval staff. At mid-day on 4 April, at the time Force A was entering the lagoon at Addu Atoll, Nagumo was 750 miles to the east.

The critical moment for all concerned in the drama arrived at 1600 when Nagumo altered course to the north west. It was only two hours to sundown and he was still undiscovered. But his luck was not to hold for more than a few minutes. At this very moment Squadron Leader L. J. Birchall in a Catalina of 413 Squadron was at the southern extremity of his patrol and after 10 hours in the air was preparing to turn back to base when he caught sight of a small speck on the horizon. He turned south towards it and saw what no allied airman had seen before, a major enemy carrier striking force approaching at 20 knots over a wide arc. Their bow waves must have reflected the reddening light of the sun, now low down to the west. The radio operator, Sgt Phillips, sent a first sighting report giving the enemy's position at 1605 (see Map 3). Birchall turned north at full boost, but the Japanese had seen the Catalina and the carrier *Hiryu* turned quickly into wind to fly off six Zero fighters which rapidly overhauled it. Phillips was making his third transmission when his radio was hit and two of the crew killed before their aircraft, now on fire, crashed into the sea. The Japanese pilots strafed the seven survivors in the sea killing one more; the remaining six, all of them injured, were picked up by the destroyer *Isokaze* on which they were interrogated, brutally beaten and locked in the heat of a for'd locker without being given any medical attention. But their appalling plight had not been in vain — the enemy had lost the vital element of surprise and allowed the defences of Ceylon to be put on alert.

When the report reached Somerville his fleet was refuelling. It was clearly impossible for him to intercept the enemy before an attack on Ceylon, but he must have felt that he had a chance of catching them as they retired, which he expected to be to eastward. It was imperative to get Force A to sea as soon as possible but he was frustrated in this due to the cruisers *Emerald* and *Enterprise* not being able to complete their refuelling until midnight. Both his heavy cruisers, *Dorsetshire* and *Cornwall,* were now at Colombo and he sent a signal instructing them to sail with all speed towards Addu. *Hermes* and *Vampire* now at Trincomalee were ordered to clear harbour and proceed north east out of harms way.

Dorsetshire and *Cornwall* were not ready to sail until 2200 and Force A not until 0015 with Force B following seven hours later. These delays were to have a dramatic effect on the outcome.

It is difficult to know what the C in C had in mind at this stage. He had no information about the enemy's composition as Birchall had been shot down before he was able to report in detail but it was not long before he received another sighting report from a Catalina of 205 Squadron giving the position of six destroyers heading north west at 0127 (see Map 4). This aircraft piloted by F/Lt Graham never returned to base but there is no report of his being sighted by the Japanese.

Dawn on Easter Sunday found all the warriors on both sides girding themselves for battle with hundreds of miles separating their various points of vantage — or disadvantage in the case of the Eastern Fleet. At 0600 the Japanese carriers were turning south west into the wind and beginning to fly off a massive strike force of 180 planes — 90 Kates, 54 Vals and 36 Zeros. Their target was Colombo, 200 miles distant. About the same time F/Lt Bradshaw of 240 Squadron was taking off in a Catalina from Koggala; 6 Fulmars of 803 Squadron, led by Lt Basil McEwen, were carrying out a dawn patrol on a line from Ratmalana to the east coast at a height of 2,000 feet, in hindsight a strange height for a fighter patrol. Meanwhile, Lt Longsdon was leaving China Bay with 6 Swordfish of 788 Sqadron, TBR pool, carrying torpedoes, and intending to refuel at Ratmalana for what could only have been a suicide attack on the approaching enemy. Scattered cloud over the west of Ceylon and to the south was now to play its part.

At 0645, and 400 miles to the south west, *Indomitable* was flying off the first of the day's A/S patrols, followed by four Fulmars of 800 Squadron to carry out a dog-leg search 200 miles to eastward — it is difficult to see what this search was intended to achieve. At 0750, 827's Albacores were being flown off to begin a parallel track search to a depth of 200 miles.

Operating separately from their carrier force, the Japanese battleships and cruisers had launched seaplanes at dawn from their catapults, to carry out a wide ranging search to the west and south to a depth of 250 miles. Their task was to locate the Eastern Fleet if it was not at Colombo as Nagumo hoped it would be. This part of the enemy's fleet was sighted by F/Lt Bradshaw's Catalina at 0648, a few minutes after he had seen the Japanese strike force pass high overhead. The enemy carrier force was by then 20 miles to the east, having resumed a north westerly course after completing flying off the strike force. Bradshaw transmitted a report of sighting 'two battleships, two cruisers with destroyers' and continued shadowing them for the rest of the day in the classic manner, keeping low and only going in until their masts could be seen before withdrawing and skilfully avoided being seen. As luck had it he never caught sight of the carrier force so at no time was Somerville aware that he faced five enemy fleet carriers.

At 0730 the Japanese strike force crossed the coast over Galle flying at 145 knots and 8,000 feet. The warning radar failed to pick up this enormous formation, and they were not sighted by the six Fulmars of 803 Squadron on patrol at 2,000 feet, so they arrived over Ratmalana airfield at 0750, catching the Hurricanes of 30 Squadron and Fulmars of 803 and 806

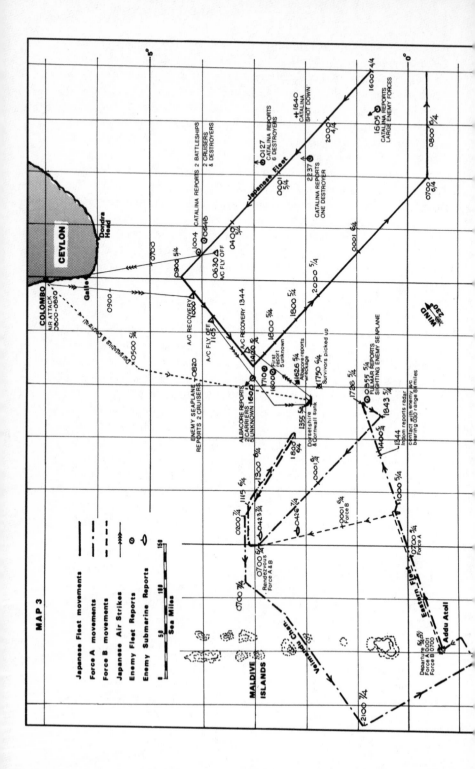

MAP 3

on the ground. One squadron of Vals dive-bombed the airfield, and escorting Zeros made strafing runs. Nineteen Hurricanes and 12 Fulmars succeeded in getting airborne. Struggling to gain height, they were easy prey for the Zeros and eight Hurricanes and four Fulmars were shot down while accounting for four Vals. Sub Lt M. Hordern recalls engaging a Zero and a Val off Mount Lavinia and Sub Lt F. Leng reported chasing a solitary bomber out to sea but, to his disgust, was unable to catch it. The Val's top speed of 210 knots was similar to the Fulmar's.

Lt Longsdon's six Swordfish had the misfortune to arrive north of Colombo at this time, and were attacked and shot down by six Zeros, which machine-gunned the survivors on the ground.

Meanwhile the main Japanese formation flew inland before turning to attack the harbour from the east. They were unaware of the racecourse airfield from which 14 Hurricanes of 258 Squadron had taken off and been able to climb unmolested to make an attack out of cloud. They shot down two Vals, but like 30 Squadron, they made the mistake of engaging the highly manoeuvrable Zeros in dogfights and lost nine aircraft.

Commander Fuchida, leading the strike force as he had done at Pearl Harbor, must have been sorely disappointed to find so little shipping and no important naval targets in the harbour after coming so far. The old destroyer *Tenedos* and the armed merchant cruiser *Hector* were sunk and the submarine depot ship *Lucia* damaged by dive-bombing Vals. The Kates bombed the port installations and oil depots but the damage was less than might have been expected — the vigorous presence of the Hurricanes probably blunted their attack. The arrival of Zeros on the scene came as a considerable surprise to the defenders as both the range and performance of this aircraft had still not been appreciated. But the real tragedy at Colombo was the failure of the early warning radar.

Nagumo had retained sufficient aircraft for a second strike but was advised by Fuchida to cancel it. In any case, Nagumo had just received a report from the cruiser *Tone*'s seaplane, searching to the west, that it had sighted two destroyers heading south at 25 knots (see Map 4). When this was corrected to read 'two cruisers' he ordered additional aircraft to the scene to continue shadowing and a dive-bombing force to be prepared to fly off as soon as all the planes had returned from the Colombo attack.

These cruisers were, of course, the *Dorsetshire* and *Cornwall* which had altered course at 0530 and increased speed to $27\frac{1}{2}$ knots to comply with a signal to rendezvous with Somerville's Force A at 1600.

At 0900 Nagumo's carrier force was 100 miles due south of Galle when he altered course south west into wind and increased speed to 26 knots ready to receive aircraft. His battleship force was now some 40 miles to the south east which seemed unwise if he was expecting a shore-based air attack; he had every right to do so as at that time ten Blenheim IVs of 11 Squadron took off from the racecourse airfield led by Wing Cdr Smyth. They were each armed with two 500 lb semi-armour piercing bombs for a high level attack. One turned back with engine trouble while the remainder flew south. It would appear that at about 1000 they must have passed between the two enemy forces without seeing either of them through thick cloud, so they returned to base. Without fighter escort, most would surely have been shot down by patrolling Zeros had they located the carriers, but the Japanese were vulnerable at this time with aircraft landing on after returning from Colombo, some of them undoubtedly damaged. By 1030 the last aircraft had landed and a new strike force of 30 Vals [80 quoted in some reports] was ranged. A fighter escort was considered unnecessary.

It is time to examine the situation from the Eastern Fleet viewpoint. At 0702 Somerville had received a report of the Catalina sighting enemy battleships and then, at 0809, a report of the large-scale attack on Colombo which gave an estimated position of enemy carriers at 0615 — they were in fact a further 35 miles to the south east which once again indicates how we underestimated their capability. At 0855 one of *Indomitable*'s searching Fulmars reported sighting an enemy seaplane in a position 150 miles dead ahead of the fleet. Somerville was now aware that the enemy was on the look out for him, but not that *Dorsetshire* and *Cornwall* were already being shadowed, as Captain Agar RN of *Dorsetshire* had decided to maintain wireless silence. Neither side was aware that they were on converging courses, Nagumo's attention being focused on *Dorsetshire* and *Cornwall* whose updated position he received at 1100 with their course and speed incorrectly reported as 240 degrees and 24 knots.

The strike force of Vals set off on a course of 237 degrees at 1105 expecting to arrive over the target at 1220 but due to the error in the target's position they were too far to the north and it was only after circling the area for an hour that they sighted the cruisers.

At 1257 the two cruisers were being shadowed by two aircraft and as they were now only 75 miles from the rendezvous, Captain Agar decided to break wireless silence to warn Somerville. But the signal was received in corrupt form and not identified as coming from *Dorsetshire* until 1400. Only *Dorsetshire* was fitted with radar but it failed to pick up the approaching Vals which were not seen until they arrived high overhead at 1340. Four minutes later they were picked up by *Indomitable*'s radar at a range of 84 miles as they manoeuvred to make their attack from dead ahead of the cruisers. As they dived on the two hapless cruisers they disappeared from the radar screen within minutes causing some confusion on *Indom*.

The Japanese dive-bombing in flights of three planes was one of the most brutally effective operations of its kind on record. Releasing their bombs sometimes from as low as 1000 feet they achieved a high percentage of direct hits over the next ten minutes. Both ships were abandoned and sank before 1400 leaving their crews, many of whom were wounded, in the midst of a sea carpeted with oil and wreckage, under a burning sun.

The most dangerous moment was now at hand. The two fleets were now only 180 miles apart with both Admirals unaware of each other's position and four hours of daylight still left. Somerville knew only that the enemy was somewhere to the north east, with probably a superior force of carriers. He called for an air search in this direction which resulted in four Albacores of 827 Squadron flying off *Indomitable* at 1400 on diverging courses to a depth of 200 miles. It might have been wiser to have used Fulmars for this search in view of the low speed and vulnerability of the Albacore, but, no doubt, he wished to conserve what few fighters he had. Meanwhile he maintained his course to rendezvous with *Dorsetshire* and *Cornwall*, unaware that they had been sunk. Sub Lt R. D. Smith of 827 Squadron, with Sub Lt L. A. Wilde as observer, was on patrol at this time and had been ordered to keep an eye open for the cruisers which were due to rendezvous at 1600; he landed back on at 1640 and reported no sighting.

If Nagumo was concerned to bring the Eastern Fleet to battle one wonders where he thought the two heavy cruisers were heading at high speed if not to join their fleet. Had he extended his air search ahead of them to the south he would undoubtedly have sighted Force A and been in an ideal position to launch an overwhelming strike force.

But at that very critical time he chose to alter course to the south east with his main force, leaving behind two carriers and escort to await the return of the strike force of Vals. These were all recovered without loss by 1600 and the ships turned south east to catch up with the main force.

This change of course was probably due to Nagumo adhering to a pre-arranged plan to rendezvous 500 miles to the south-east with an oiler and refuel before moving into position for an attack on Trincomalee. It is doubtful whether he was now seriously looking for the Eastern Fleet, but the two most northerly Albacores were rapidly approaching him.

Sub Lt Streathfield passed over a large area of oil and wreckage at 1500 and sent a report which was received at 1526 giving a position which proved to be some 25 miles in error. Fifteen minutes later he came upon the main Japanese force but was shot down before he had time to make a sighting report. Had he been able to do so it might have given Somerville the vital information that the enemy was retiring to the south east giving him an opportunity to carry out his plan for a night torpedo attack.

About the same time, Sub Lt Grant-Sturgis, with Sub Lt Jaffray as observer, was on the most westerly leg of the search, and sighted an enemy force in the distance. His TAG, Gordon Dixon, managed to transmit a report of sighting 'five unknowns' 126 miles on a bearing 026 degrees from the fleet before they were attacked by a single Zero. Dixon was wounded in the first attack but Grant-Sturgis was so successful with evasive action at sea level that the Zero broke off and the only damage to the Albacore was a burst tyre.

Due to the slowness of the intercept reporting procedure, Somerville did not receive this vital first sighting report until 1655. Five minutes later he received an equally alarming signal from the Deputy C in C, Ceylon, that the Catalina had reported enemy carriers at 1400 steering 230 degrees at 24 knots. It was only an hour to dusk and he ordered aircraft to be prepared for a night torpedo attack and recalled the destroyer sent to investigate the wreckage.

It was now past the rendezvous time with *Dorsetshire* and *Cornwall* without sight of them, and 827's Albacores were due back, so at 1726 he ordered Force A to alter course to 210 degrees which would bring the carriers into wind and increase his distance from the enemy. The first two aircraft, which had flown too far to the east to encounter the enemy, landed on at 1730. Fifteen minutes later Grant-Sturgis put his plane down successfully in spite of the burst tyre. At the debriefing he reported he had in fact seen two carriers and five other ships at 1600 steering north west in a position 25 miles further north than the one transmitted, but after reconstructing events it seemed more likely that the enemy course was south east and a revised position at 1710 was signalled to the C in C.

The southerly course was maintained for an hour awaiting the return of the fourth Albacore but when darkness fell and it failed to appear Somerville altered course to the north west at 1843, unaware that Nagumo was 150 miles on his starboard beam steering an exactly opposite course. It was an ideal time to launch a night attack and 831 Squadron on *Indomitable* and 820 Squadron on *Formidable* were ranged, armed with torpedoes and manned by their crews. But Somerville felt that the information on the enemy's position and course was inadequate and decided to send a single ASV Albacore from *Formidable* to search 170 miles to the north. It was flown off at 1930 to be followed by others at intervals throughout the night over a wide arc and an area that the Japanese had long since left.

The most dangerous moment had been passed unbeknown to all those taking part in the drama.

Force B had been following 120 miles astern and was ordered to rendezvous at 3°N 75°E at dawn on 6 April, a position considered well out of range of the enemy. During the night the C in C learnt of the sinking of the *Dorsetshire* and *Cornwall* which added to his quandary. He felt obliged to go to the rescue of the survivors but, not knowing the enemy's whereabouts, he would be putting his fleet at risk by returning in daylight.

Two Catalinas sent out during the night had failed to renew contact which seemed to have been lost at about the critical time of 1400 on the 5th.

It is interesting that on this day he chose to keep his fleet together as a combined force. By now he must have guessed that he faced a superior enemy but he was clearly still of a mind to engage them because, instead of withdrawing to the west, he steered due east at 0800 and sent off 827's Albacores on a search 200 miles ahead of the fleet. With no sighting reported, and against the advice of his staff, he altered course to the southeast, heading towards the last known position of his two cruisers whose survivors had now been clinging to the wreckage for nearly 24 hours. This was a brave, if arguably foolish, decision, particularly as at 1400 he received a signal from Admiral Layton in Ceylon warning him that in his opinion there was a strong Japanese force somewhere between Addu and Colombo.

At 1300 Somerville detached the cruiser *Enterprise* with the destroyers *Paladin* and *Panther* to move ahead at 30 knots to locate and pick up survivors. An Albacore search was flown off *Formidable* to a depth of 200 miles, one of them sighting the survivors in late afternoon and flashing a message that help was on its way. Two of *Indom*'s Fulmars was then despatched to the scene to provide cover. But *Enterprise* saw no sign of them when at 1700 it arrived at the position in which their ships were reported to have been sunk and both Albacore and Fulmars were forced to return to their carriers. *Enterprise* continued searching on the same course but it was not until the sun was setting and she was about to give up when they were seen at last. Many had died during the long night but 1,122 men were brought on board the three ships out of a total of 1,546. This is more than might have been expected and they owed their lives to Somerville's gallant gamble — many of the wounded would not have survived another night.

The fleet reversed course at sundown to retire to the north west, changing to due west at 0200 on 7 April in anticipation of a return to Addu. *Formidable* continued to fly off ASV searches through the night and two enemy submarines were picked up almost simultaneously at 0430, one at 20 and one at 60 miles south of the fleet. Sub Lt John Du Cane reported the sighting of a very large submarine but was not believed; it was almost certainly one of the 2000 ton Japanese vessels which appeared off the east coast of Africa in May. Not expecting submarines in the search area, his aircraft was not armed with depth charges. The C in C suspected that they were covering the approaches to Addu and decided to pass to the west of the Maldives through the Veimandu Channel and thereby make an unexpected approach to Addu from the north west. At dawn on 8 April the fleet was 40 miles south of Addu and an all round air search was flown to a depth of 175 miles with negative results. It arrived in the lagoon at 1100.

The C in C held a conference on board *Warspite* in the afternoon. He decided that the four 'R's were a liability and that Force B should go to Mombasa to guard the convoy route to the Middle East. Force A he proposed to base on Ceylon, but was instructed not to do so by the Admiralty and a decision was made to proceed to Bombay which was far from an ideal base but nearer than Mombasa if a presence in the Indian Ocean was to have any significance.

After refuelling, Force B left Addu at 0200 and Force A at 0600 on 9 April. Somerville intended to make a brief visit to Colombo to discuss the situation with Admiral Layton but at this very hour the curtain had already risen on the final act of the drama, one in which the Eastern Fleet was to play no part but which forced it to proceed straight to the safety of Bombay.

It was part of the Japanese plan to make a surprise attack on Trincomalee four days after that on Colombo. After his retirement to the south east on Easter Sunday, Nagumo circled around Ceylon at a 500 mile radius to keep clear of air search. He refuelled his fleet from an oiler on the 7th, then at 0900 on the 8th he turned north west to be in position to fly off his strike force before dawn on the 9th when 200 miles to the east of Trincomalee.

Once again his aim to achieve surprise was foiled by the RAF. At 1517 on 8 April, F/O Round in a Catalina of 240 Squadron made a sighting of four battleships and one carrier 500 miles east of Dondra Head. This time the Catalina was able to escape unseen into cloud to transmit an accurate position and course. The island defences were put on full alert and during the night Trincomalee Harbour was cleared of most ships; *Hermes* escorted by *Vampire,* the Fleet Auxiliary *Athelstone* with the corvette *Hollyhock* and the tanker *British Sergeant* put to sea with orders to sail south keeping close to the coast. The Swordfish from *Hermes* had already been disembarked to China Bay and, of course, she had no complement of fighters, so all these ships were without air cover — by dawn Ratmalana and China Bay airfields were each 130 miles away. At dawn the 12 Swordfish of 814 Squadron, armed with torpedos, took off and flew to the satellite airfield at Kokalai, a few miles to the north, and prepared to attack the approaching enemy. It was an old recipe for disaster.

If Nagumo had hoped to find and destroy the Eastern Fleet he was once again to be sadly disappointed. Left in harbour was only the cable ship *Hecla,* the old monitor Erebus and the merchant ship *Sagaing.* He would have saved himself a lot of effort if he had used the long range and speed of the Zero to make a quick recce before making his attack, but search and reconnaissance did not seem to rate highly in Japanese strategy.

It was 0500 on 9 April and still dark when his carriers turned south east into wind and commenced flying off 91 Kates escorted by 38 Zeros. Two Kates were detached to make a recce of Colombo harbour and a strike force of Vals was ranged ready to attack the Eastern Fleet should it be located at either base.

Three Hurricanes of 261 Squadron took off at 0635 from China Bay and twenty minutes later the radar at Trincomalee reported enemy aircraft at a range of 30 miles. Thirteen more Hurricanes were scrambled and were able to gain sufficient height to engage the Kates as they commenced their attack at 0720. Outnumbered and outclassed by the Zeros, they lost eight aircraft for a score of two Kates and one Zero shot down and ten Kates damaged. Two Zeros were shot down by AA guns at China Bay. The bombing of the harbour facilities and the airfield was carried out with practised efficiency but the results hardly justified the scale of attack. More could be said to have been achieved by Ozawa's small carrier force which sank 23 merchant ships (112,312 tons) on 6 April between Madras and Calcutta.

Meantime two significant events occurred. F/Lt Thomas, who had taken off at 0230 in a Catalina of 413 Squadron to locate and shadow the enemy, made contact at about 0630 but was shot down by Zeros before he could transmit a sighting report. He sent out an emergency signal at 0700 which was sufficient to give his approximate position. At the same time the two Kates heading for Colombo reported sighting *Hermes* and *Vampire* steering south.

Nagumo must have been alarmed by both events. Suspecting the Eastern Fleet to be not far away he ordered the launching of the second strike force. This comprised 50 Vals with an escort of 20 Zeros which flew off at 0750 led by Lt Cdr Egusa off *Hiryu*. Nagumo was now in a very vulnerable position with the return of his first strike force imminent, his carriers committed to a south easterly course into wind until they were all aboard, and expecting either shore- or carrier-based air attack (he was not aware that *Hermes* was without her aircraft). Indeed eleven Blenheims of 11 Squadron had been standing by at Colombo racecourse but, due to confusion about the enemy's position, they did not take off until 0820. Two of them had to return with engine trouble, the remaining nine, led by Sq/Ldr Ault, set off on the 300 mile flight. In daylight, and with no fighter escort, they must have known that they would be lucky to return: but Blenheim squadrons had been doing this sort of operation since the beginning of the war, and would continue to do so as I was to learn at first hand later that year.

Nagumo must have been relieved to complete the reocvery of the first strike force just before 0900. He then altered course due south. The Blenheims reached a position some fifteen miles to the north at 1000 and it was only after circling for fifteen minutes that they sighted the whole panoply of Japanese ships spread out over several square miles of ocean. Two Fleet Air Arm observers flying with them must have been astonished to see such a sight, but sadly they didn't live to tell the tale. Carrying out a formation bombing run at 11,000 feet, their bombs straddled the flagship *Akagi,* and according to Japanese records it was damaged by a near miss. At least it gave Nagumo his first taste of what it was like to be on the receiving end. Five of the Blenheims were shot down by Zeros from the carrier *Hiryu,* and the four that struggled all the way back were damaged. One of the Zeros, piloted by Lt Sumio Nono, was shot down by the rear gunners.

Lt Cdr Egusa's second strike force was having more success. When he reached the coast of Ceylon at 0850 there was no sign of *Hermes* so he turned south. But *Hermes* together with the other ships had reversed course with the forlorn hope of getting fighter cover from China Bay. After twenty minutes Egusa turned north and found *Hollyhock, Athelstone* and *British Sergeant* which were sunk at 0922 by a detached force of Vals. The remainder pressed on north until they came upon poor old *Hermes* and *Vampire.* Their dive-bombing attack commenced at 0954, concentrating on the defenceless carrier. Within ten minutes she was overwhelmed by numerous hits and the attack switched to *Vampire* which, within minutes, broke in half and sank. *Hermes* heeled over and sank at 1020 with a loss of over 300 lives.

Eight Fulmars of 803 and 806 Squadrons had been scrambled from Ratmalana at 0930 to give air cover for *Hermes.* Heading eastward across the island, they arrived to witness the final stages of the enemy attack. Sub Lt Metcalfe recalls that he saw the carrier and destroyer lying stopped, like a couple of beetles being attacked by a swarm of ants. As he dived into the attack, he caught a glimpse of a huge ball of flame shooting up from the carrier. He then became heavily involved with two Vals attacking from either quarter, and realising that whichever way he turned he was done for, he stood the Fulmar on its tail, and since full throttle was not enough to get away, he pulled the boost cut-out and climbed clear. By the time he had levelled out, *Hermes* had gone, and the enemy was disappearing in the distance. As he could do nothing for the survivors, he flew on to China Bay and landed amongst the debris from the enemy bombing.

The Fulmars claimed to have shot down four Vals and damaged two. Two of 803's Fulmars were shot down. The Japanese claim they lost no aircraft and on the way back they were ordered to circle where they were as their fleet was then under attack by 11 Squadron's Blenheims. They finally began landing on at 1150, by which time they had been airborne over four hours. An hour later the fleet turned east to retire from the scene and return to Japan via the Malacca Strait. The twists and turns of the drama were over.

By failing to seek out and destroy the Eastern Fleet the Japanese operation can only be judged a failure. It is surprising that they undertook it in the first place as they clearly had no intention of following it up with

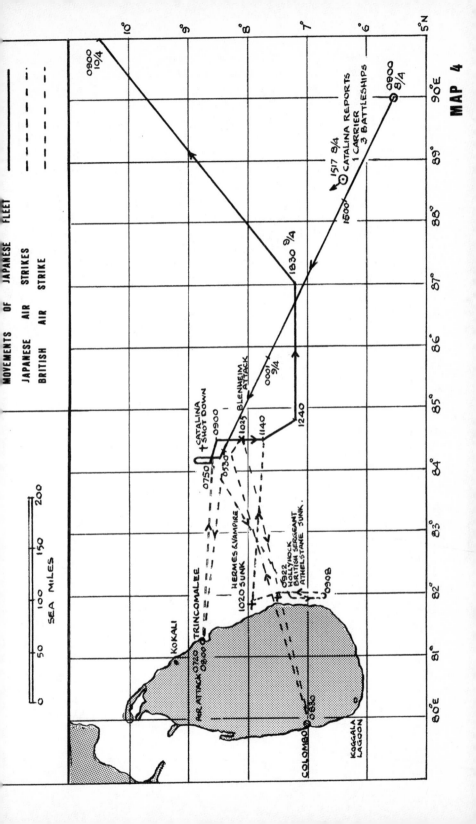

MOVEMENTS OF JAPANESE FLEET

JAPANESE AIR STRIKES —————
BRITISH AIR STRIKE ———————

MAP 4

an invasion of Ceylon or even a continued presence in the Indian Ocean. In the longer term it may even have hastened their eventual naval defeat as I believe they lost more aircraft and highly trained crews than they admit. Certainly they had to keep *Akagi, Soryu* and *Hiryu* in Japan for refitting and working up new squadrons at a time when the American carrier strength was stretched to the limit. In the following May, at the Battle of the Coral Sea the US Navy's two carriers *Lexington* and *Yorktown* might otherwise have had to face all five fleet carriers instead of only the *Shokaku, Zuikaku* and the light fleet carrier *Shoho.*

As for the Eastern Fleet, it was saved by both luck and the somewhat blinkered view of Admiral Nagumo at a time when Admiral Somerville had his neck stuck well out.

For my part, I would dearly have wished to have taken part in the torpedo attack planned for the night of Easter Sunday but never despatched. With the assistance of ASV equipped Albacores from *Formidable* we might have achieved considerable success. Retribution could have been expected from the Japanese the following day. All things considered, it is a good thing that it never took place, for if it had I might not have been here to write of these dramatic events.

Chapter 8
Shangri-La

I awoke on the morning of 9 April with the shakes and drenched in sweat. Willie arranged for one of the docs to come and see me and I was soon in the ship's sick bay. I had had no occasion to go there before so it was a strange experience, row upon row of beds with side rails to stop you falling out and pivoted so that they swung when the ship rolled. Apart from one seaman I was the only occupant so I got more than enough attention. In fact I had the personal attention of no less than Surgeon Commander Patrick who didn't want me to sit to attention this time but proceeded to take a large number of blood samples. He told me that he was sure that I had Malaria and not to worry because on that he was an expert. I didn't worry, I felt too ill — and was hardly aware that we had sailed at dawn and were on our way to Bombay. As always nobody knew why.

Albacores of 831 took off at 0700 on a search to a depth of 200 miles; a trip which lived long in the memory of 'Buster' and observer 'Dusty' Miller. In Buster's words: 'At the end of the dog-leg, 'Dusty' gave me a course back to the carrier, which, according to my back-of-a-cigarette-box navigation, didn't seem to add up. When 'Dusty' went back to his Bigsworth board, he found, to his dismay, that instead of the headwind he had applied on the leg out, we had a tail wind, and were faced with a headwind back to the ship. It was a long haul home. I brought the pitch control back to the stops, on the principle of low revs and high boost giving the most economical fuel consumption. After four hours in the air we managed to pick up the ship's beacon. Great rejoicing. The 64,000 dollar question now was whether we had enough fuel to get there. Fortunately, the skipper turned the ship into wind when they saw the frantic flashing from Dusty's Aldis lamp, and with the fuel gauge beating a tattoo on the EMPTY peg, we staggered onto the deck. My airmech told me, after we had refuelled, that he reckoned that I still had 10 minutes' flying time but 4 hours and 55 minutes in an Albacore is stretching it a bit.'

By the time we arrived at Bombay on the 13th, the medical establishment had decided that I had pneumonia (again), and lost no time in despatching me to a hospital ashore — shades of a dark skinned matron loomed before me and I wasn't at all keen to go, suspecting rightly, that I would be left behind when the ship sailed — but I wasn't in a position to argue so over the side I went the following afternoon, strapped in a stretcher, feet first down the midships gangway with a bevy of grinning squadron goofers to see me off. I think Willie had packed up my kit, because trunk and kitbags followed me down onto the dockside. My clothes must have been a dirty shambles as the ship's laundry had broken down some weeks before and we had been doing the best we could in the bath. The cool peace of the sick bay was replaced by the scorching heat of the dockside and the noise and spicy smell of India. With a swirl of dust an ambulance drew up. I squinted up at the faces looking down and felt as though I was leaving home. It was the last I was to see of them for six strange, exotic weeks.

There was nothing remarkable about the General Services Hospital in Bombay. The officers' ward looked much like Haslar, the nurses were mostly Anglo-Indian, efficient but unapproachable. The doctors I don't remember at all. My days lying on top of instead of in my bed were taken up with a seventeen year old Midshipman who had the bed opposite. His legs, lying along the bed with a pillow under each knee, were emaciated to a state I have only seen in photographs from Belsen. He had cut his feet some weeks before on a coral reef and the doctors had been unable to control the infection. I sat by his bed and talked to him, his grey face seemed like that of a child.

'I think I'll be dead by tomorrow,' he sighed.

'Don't be silly,' I said. But he was. I found it difficult to comprehend.

Jack and Willie came to visit me, also, rather surprisingly, the dreaded Surgeon Commander who put on quite a chummy act. He returned at the end of the week to say that the ship was due to sail and that he was very sorry but he would have to leave me behind. However he had arranged for me to convalesce at Government House. I felt perhaps I had misjudged the portly old boy.

After a couple of days I got a message telling me to be ready to be picked up to go to Government House after lunch. Where was all my kit? I hadn't seen it since I arrived and been issued with hospital pyjamas and dressing gown. I had to search for it in a wire mesh enclosed store and managed to extricate enough to rig myself out in a crumpled set of short whites; my legs felt like rubber. I had no preconception of this Government House so I got a bit of a shock when standing at the hospital door was a black Daimler limousine with an impressive turbaned driver opening the back door for me. Leaning towards me in the back was an elderly gentleman in a dark suit.

'You must be Wallace, I'm Captain Fitzwilliam (Army), an ADC to the Governor. I understand that you'll be staying with us for a while, do get in, it's only about half an hour's drive around the bay.'

I sank back in the luxury and wondered what an ADC was. 'Fitz', as I got to call him, was an old Army man with an abundance of old world charm. Although I was only an insignificant Sub Lieutenant he treated me, as he did everyone, with respect and kindness. On the way he explained that the present Governor of Bombay was Sir Roger Lumley and that he had two ADCs, himself and Lord Wharton, a serving RAF Flight Lieutenant.

You don't motor through Bombay, you weave your way through a brown river of humanity which flows turbulently through wide streets opposite the majestic Taj Mahal hotel all the way down to narrow alleys of dilapidation on the outskirts. A city of brownness and bicycles, dust and heat. Suddenly it was all gone and we glided between wrought iron gates to receive the salute of two Bengal Lancers, immaculate in their striped turbans, white jackets, black jodhpurs, gleaming boots and spurs, flags fluttering from the top of their lances. It seemed ready for Errol Flynn to emerge from amidst the trees surrounding an untropically green lawn.

'You've been put in what we call the Royal Bungalow,' said Fitz.

'Sounds rather good.'

'I think you'll find it very comfortable.'

Typical of Fitz, this was a wonderful understatement. It was more than very comfortable, it had the spacious opulence of a Hollywood film set. One of a number of discreet guest bungalows, it faced the main residence across the lawn. An overhanging tiled portico and veranda led into the entrance hall and then straight on into a bedroom, some twelve metres long and ten metres wide, with a large double bed on the right which had a mosquito net soaring up to a high ceiling. A series of small windows at the very top provided shafts of sunlight into an otherwise dark room. An ornate door led into a bathroom, tiled from floor to ceiling in marble slabs. At the opposite end was a kitchen. Straight ahead a curved arch led into the sitting room, with a bay window across its full twelve metres breadth and looking out over the long curve of the bay; the outline of Bombay was just visible in the distant haze. A veranda dropped down to an immaculate lawn. To the right lay the tennis courts. The room was furnished with more chairs, settees and occasional tables than I could see myself using, but a large desk in the centre, commanding a view over this paradise, became my favourite spot. A pair of turbaned servants appeared from nowhere, like Genii, and carried my old trunk and kitbags into the bedroom. They were dressed as though they were about to appear in a performance of Aladdin in long white aprons with white trousers just showing below. The top of the gown opened to display what we now call a 'T' shirt, brilliant red with a gold crest in the centre. Wide belts and bands around their turbans identified their role in the establishment.

Fitz introduced me to a chubby little Indian with Mongolian eyes, dressed with less ostentation in a white jacket buttoned to the neck, white baggy trousers and a black hat like a shallow fez. Like the other servants his feet were bare.

'This is Santu,' said Fitz, 'he will be your personal servant.'

The little man bowed and put his hands together in the lotus greeting which was unfamiliar to me and I blush to think of the 'howlers' I must have put up during the days that followed.

'The Governor's wife will probably be along to visit you — please remember to address Sir Roger and Lady Lumley as 'Your Ex' when talking to them, warned Fitz with a quizzical grin.

Just out of a hospital bed, I felt particularly weak and was glad to sit down and enjoy tea and cakes brought in by Santu on a large silver tray. I began to think that I was dreaming, but the small, wiry and distinctly formidable lady who entered, unannounced, was no dream. Although I failed to appreciate the fact at the time, I was face to face with the backbone and power of the British Empire — she who must be obeyed. And obey we all did, from the Governor downwards.

'Now young man, whatever your name is, you're here to convalesce so we don't want to see you rushing about for the first few days,' she said, fixing me with eyes of steel set in a deeply tanned face.

'I will arrange for your meals to be brought to you here and you can let one of the ADCs know when you feel ready to dine with us.'

'Thank you very much — Your Ex,' I responded weakly.

No sooner had she left than Santu appeared — his noiseless movements were disconcerting.

'What time your bath, master?' — Did I smell that badly?

'What time is dinner?'

'Dinner at seven, master.'

'OK I'll have a bath at six.'

I opened my trunk and fished amongst the dirty jumble for pyjamas, razor and toothbrush and decided to put off unpacking until the morning. The sound of running water woke me from a doze. Santu was laying out an enormous towel and the bath water was deeper than I had seen for years.

'You like me bring you drink, master?'

'Yes please — whisky and soda.'

Larger than large, in a cut glass tumbler and every night after that for my whole stay, the bath and the whisky were ready at six o'clock. And the cigarette boxes were kept full of both Virginia and Turkish. Wrapped in my Turkish towel I sat back in a chair, lit a Turkish and wondered when the dream would stop. Where was the war? Where was *Indom*? I didn't really care — it was very good whisky.

Dinner arrived with all the hot dishes in tureens which had hot water in their double bottoms to keep them warm, a jumbo sized version of what

Budding Naval airmen of the 45th Observer Course at HMS St Vincent, *November 1940. Author* *right.*

n: Author and parents, summer 1941.

Top: HMS Indomitable *at 30 knots in the Clyde, October 1941.*

Bottom: *Lt Cdr Peter Mortimer RN leads 831 on a dive-bombing exercise over Bermuda, 31 Oc*
1941.

or and Albacore 4C, October 1941.

Top: Albacore over Jamaica, November 1941.

Bottom: Working up problems, December 1941.

HMS Illustrious *after refit in the USA, seen from the quarterdeck of* Indomitable *off Jamaica,* mber 1941.

m: *RAF Hurricane IIBs of 258 Squadron prepare to fly off* Indomitable *to Java, 28 January* (FAA Museum)

Top: *Fulmar Mk IIs of 800 Squadron.*

Bottom: HMS Cornwall *sinking during attack by Japanese dive-bombers, 5 April 1942.*

Left: 'The Royal Suite', Government House, Bombay, April 1942.

Right: 'Santu'.

Top: *Diego Suarez harbour under air attack, 5 May 1942.*

Bottom: *Vichy French sloop* d'Entrecasteaux, *sunk at Diego Suarez.*

Final view of Albacore 4C (T9165) and crew after ditching upside down, 11 July 1942.

om: Sea Hurricane of 880 Squadron flies off Indomitable. (Imperial War Museum)

Top: Indomitable's A1 and A2 4.5 inch gun turrets destroyed by bomb hit from German Stuka du
Operation 'Pedestal'. HMS Charybdis in attendance, 12 August 1942. (FAA Museum)

Bottom: Damage from bomb hit abaft aft lift. (FAA Museum)

'Bisley' (Blenheim V) at Blida airfield, Algeria, November 1942. (Imperial War Museum)

m: 'Bisley' aircrew at Blida, returning from a daylight raid. (Imperial War Museum)

Top: Messerschmitt Bf 109G, Tunisia, December 1942. (Imperial War Museum)

Bottom: Wing Cdr Hugh Gordon Malcolm, VC, CO of 18 Squadron. Killed on 4 December 1942.

(Imperial War Mu

Author's wedding, Gosforth, Newcastle-upon-Tyne, 6 February 1942.

m: Lt Cdr Cedric Coxon RN, CO of 812 Squadron, flies his Barracuda II over RNAS Stretton, 1944.

HMS Vengeance, *Light Fleet Carrier, February 1945.*

Sub Lt(A) Hodgkinson and crew, ditched off Malta, April 1945.

...m: Air-Sea Rescue launch picks up Barracuda crew from their dinghy.

Top: Barracudas of 812 Squadron over RNAS Crail.

Bottom: Author's Barracuda III off Thorney Island after engine fire. Pilot was Lt(A) 'Gus' Hal
RNVR, September 1945.

my mother used for breakfast. Neither that night nor the next did I solve the mystery of how, at the exact moment I had finished each dish, Santu would pad silently around the corner with the next dish. I could find no spyhole and I even tried delaying putting down my cutlery, to no effect.

The next morning I had to face some of the realities. Firstly, I had no money, and secondly, my whites were in pretty bad shape. Santu had already decided to do some unpacking and I could hear him mumbling, 'Tsk, Tsk, Tsk,' as he pulled out each disreputable item. I put the problem to Fitz and he kindly arranged for Paul, one of the ADC staff, to accompany me in a staff car into Bombay where I put my case to a Lieutenant in the navy's local HQ. It was clearly beneath his dignity to speak to so lowly a person but I did manage to get ten pounds in rupees which was duly entered in my pay book — I didn't feel that this would go very far but I wasn't in a position to argue. Paul took me to a rather posh store where I bought some white shirts and shorts — my white shoes hadn't been worn very much and were still adequate. For some odd reason I bought a book of drawings by Augustus John and a sketch pad. On my return it stimulated me enough to try my hand once again at some portrait sketching. The heat in the centre of Bombay had been stifling and, not being used to this amount of physical effort, I felt pretty weak by the time we got back. I met the other ADC, Lord Wharton, about thirty and good looking. Like Fitz, he was always most courteous to me in spite of my lack of rank and style.

Santu, normally impassive, gave the hint of a smile when I showed him my new clothes and more of a smile when he opened the wardrobe to show me all my other clothes laundered to perfection. During the afternoon I noticed that my cap had disappeared off the table. It turned up later in the same place and it was only after careful examination that I was able to see that the Santu had ironed out the wrinkles which aircrew lovingly encouraged.

I thought it about time I put in an appearance at dinner so I informed Fitz on my regular morning visit to the ADC's office where we all met to have coffee and discuss the day's events.

There was an established routine for dinner, ADCs, staff, and guests would assemble at seven o'clock at the entrance porch to the dining room and line up on the right hand side in order of rank. Their Exs would arrive up the red carpeted steps at the quarter hour, greet everyone and be introduced and shake hands with any new guest. The Governor, a small taciturn man of about fifty, mumbled a few words to me, I think they were the only ones during my stay. He never used two words where one would do and always seemed to have his eyes focussed on some distant point. Lady Lumley more than made up for his reticence by keeping up a constant stream of instructions, directions and opinions on any and every subject.

Everyone had his own special 'table boy' standing two paces behind his chair at all meals. Mine had an impressive rotundness and an inscrutable expression; I think he must have indulged in the leftovers as most Indians seemed to be bean poles. He was expert at keeping my large cut glass tumbler topped up with whisky and soda — I had no taste for wine. The food was always sumptuous, the conversation bizarre. I kept my mouth shut — except for eating. I often wondered what the Indians thought of it all.

After dinner we would usually troop off to the Governor's living quarters to gather in the lounge for the ritual of listening to the nine o'clock news on the radio. This was followed by Her Ex regaling us with her views on world events before dismissing us about nine thirty. Almost everybody seemed to go to bed and it was a relief to get out of a high necked uniform jacket.

Breakfast was a gastronomic marathon — you could start with mango, try a little kedgeree, polish off bacon and eggs and finish with a steak.

At the weekends there were special dinner parties to which were invited the higher ranking service officers and top drawer Indians with their ladies. The ladies were a new, exotic experience, some quite beautiful, draped in a wondrous variety of saris and perfect in their English, but somehow remote and unreal. Perhaps they were as shy as I was. All the 'regulars', amongst who I was counted, lined up to shake hands. The Navy top brass alone succeeded in ignoring my existence, even to the extent of refusing my hand. Stuffy lot.

It was after one of these special dinners that I went down with sunstroke — and down was the word for it. I fainted crossing the tennis courts on the way back to my bungalow, falling flat on my face on the sharp gravel. I had been out dinghy sailing that afternoon with Paul and, although wearing my cap, the reflection of the tropical sun from the water must have been responsible. The following morning I couldn't move my head when the doctor was brought in to see me. Later, Her Ex came to check on me and prescribed large quantities of ice cream — a delightful remedy brought with due ceremony by the faithful Santu in a silver tureen. It seemed to do the trick and I was almost sorry to admit my rapid recovery.

There was a private bathing beach ten minutes walk through a tree lined path. I tried a mid morning bathe with Jock, another convalescing Sub Lieutenant just arrived, and found the sand unbearably hot, so we adopted a seven thirty bathing routine. It was somewhat spoilt by being continuously stung by some unseen small sea creature with an effect similar to a midge bite. We also went with Paul to the large swimming pool at the Willington Club where there were English girls. All of them seemed bespoken but at least we could ogle them and, after all these months of monastic seclusion, the display of shapely flesh was disturbing.

With very little money and reliant on official cars to go anywhere we were almost prisoners in our paradise, we couldn't for instance take anyone out for a meal or a drink so there was no way of showing appreciation for all this hospitality and this made me feel increasingly uncomfortable as the weeks sped by.

To fill the day I did some sketching. In the third week the Governor's daughter arrived, wanly pretty but rather an ice maiden. She may have been as shy as I was. I did some sketches of her in my bungalow but there was no touching. How different it all is today — or is it?

Jock constantly played his records of Beethoven symphonies, about which he was volubly enthusiastic. Fitz took me to the silver market in Bombay and pointed out the bargains he could get for me in the filigree work through special contacts. He couldn't have appreciated my almost total lack of cash.

The nine o'clock news seemed to be full of disaster on all fronts and I began to feel guilty about the hedonistic life I was leading — nobody had broached the subject of my leaving. I spoke to Fitz and asked him how I was expected to get back to my ship wherever it was. We had heard about the Madagascar operation but at that time didn't know that *Indom* and *Illustrious* had taken a major part in it on 5 May. Fitz contacted the Naval Office in Bombay and after some days I was told to be ready to sail by merchant ship to Mombasa early the next week. I managed to drag another £10 out of the Navy; I had acquired a total of five servants and Fitz advised on what they might expect. I know it seemed very little.

I said all my goodbyes and thanks the night before and on the morning of 13 May I swept through the gates in the Daimler, lancers saluting, and with Paul to see me off.

The other passengers on the ship must have been expecting someone important as they looked down on our arrival at the dockside. They were not only disappointed, they were antagonistic.

Chapter 9
Kenya

Mombasa meant nothing to me, just some place in East Africa and a long way from Bombay. At ten knots, rolling and pitching continuously, it took ten days but seemed much longer, with so little to do but laze around in a deck chair, eat, and sleep. There were about twenty passengers, the majority Dutch refugees from their East Indies empire. They had escaped from the Japanese onslaught and, for reasons I failed to appreciate, blamed their plight on the British. As I was the only representative of the British services on board I was either given the cold shoulder or harangued about our nation's failure to do I know not what. I swam daily in a pregnant canvas swimming pool rigged in the fo'c'sle, about four metres square, with the sea water sloshing perpetually over its side and only enough for two or three strokes; I was the only one to use it, probably being considered one of Noel Coward's mad dogs. The passage was memorable for the only other British passenger who was returning from tea planting in Assam; a pianist of considerable talent who introduced me to the piano part of Grieg's concerto; its melodies haunted me for many years until I grew to appreciate works with a little more meat and less sugar. I was his only audience and when not playing he retired into his shell. Meals were very good and in the ten days we had ten different curry dishes, all of them excellent. I must have had a good digestion. At the end of the first week one of the younger Dutch girls got to the holding hands and kissing stage out on deck chairs in the cool of the evenings; deck chairs are very unsuitable for that sort of thing and it progressed no further.

Land at last. Past the old fort and the narrow entrance to the anchorage at Kilindini and there were all the 'R's lying squarely at anchor, and there too was *Indom,* easily distinguished by the rust on her bows, adding a touch of colour to the blues and greys of her camouflage. To bring a Royal Navy ship alongside seemed to require a full-scale production using all available hands. The Merchant Navy seemed to manage with a man and boy but I am not knowledgeable on these matters. A signal was flashed to *Indom* to pick me up and I got all my gear up on deck. It was not until I saw the familiar shape of her launch approaching the water side of the ship that I realised that I was going to have to climb down the side on a rope ladder in front of all aboard. If there is a knack to performing on a rope ladder, I have never learnt it. I dared not look down as I swung my legs over the side, trying to look nonchalant and keeping my eyes glued to the side of the ship. The ladder seemed to have a life of its own and a desire to cling to the ship's side instead of maintaining a decent vertical. As far as I know I managed to avoid disgracing the service. My trunk and kitbags followed on the end of a rope.

Coming 'home' was a bit of an anti-climax. Nearly all aircrew had flown ashore to Port Reitz airfield but they trickled back in ones and twos next day and I was able to catch up on operation 'Ironclad' as the Madagascar affair was designated. After the Japanese attack on Ceylon, the Allies became concerned that the strategic port of Diego Suarez, in the north of this Vichy French controlled island, might be their next objective. Not for the first or last time, the Navy was called upon to launch an operation which would have the unhappy result of killing Frenchmen.

Indomitable joined *Illustrious* as part of Force F, under Rear-Admiral E. N. Syfret, to provide air support for the amphibious assault on Diego Suarez. The flagship was the old battleship *Ramillies,* accompanied by the new cruiser *Hermione* and various destroyers.

Illustrious had on board Martlet IIs of 881 and 882 Squadrons, and Swordfish IIs of 810 and 829 Squadrons. She was given the task of attacking any Vichy naval vessels, and giving air support to the assault troops. *Indomitable*'s role was to attack the airfields, drop leaflets, and carry out A/S patrols.

After all these months of flying around the world's oceans I had missed the one and only occasion when 831 was called upon to go into action. It had not been a particularly dashing occasion as there was little opposition from the Vichy French. At the break of dawn on 5 May the first two sub-flights led by the CO and 'Puppy' Kennard dive-bombed the airfield at Antsirane, each aircraft dropping five 250 lb GP bombs and eight incendiaries. Direct hits were scored on the hangar, setting it on fire, the glow from which could still be seen as they circled *Indom* to land on. Jack, flying number 3 in the CO's flight claimed one hit and 'Swee'pea' Morrell claimed to have put four through the hangar door, pulling out so low that he was shaken in the bomb blast. Later in the day and throughout the 6th, A/S patrols were flown as enemy submarines were known to be in the area. That evening word came through that the Marines were going to make a landing on the east coast to attack the town of Diego Suarez in the rear and required air support. The CO and 'Puppy' took off at 1930 loaded with six 250 lb GP bombs, eight incendiaries and about two dozen beer bottles, previously emptied, which they dropped on the target at 2000.

The Swordfish from *Illustrious* saw more action, sinking the sloop *D'Entrecasteaux,* the armed merchant cruiser *Bougainville,* and the submarines *Beveziers* and *Le Heros*. Her Martlets shot down three Potez 63 reconnaissance aircraft and four Morane Saulnier 406C fighters.

On the 7th the third and fourth sub-flights of 831 were briefed for an attack to finally crush the enemy's resistance. The aircraft were ranged, struck down, and ranged again; but at the eleventh hour news of the cease fire came through just as engines were being started.

On 8 May, while entering Diego Suarez harbour a torpedo fired at *Indom* missed ahead by only twenty metres. I also learnt that two larger-than-life characters of 827 Squadron, Jack Pike, his observer 'Colonel' Brown, along with TAG L/A Rough, had failed to return from an A/S patrol on 5 May. Over a month later they returned to the ship to tell a fantastic story. After ditching and taking to their dinghy they had the anguish of watching *Indomitable* pass them by a mile away during the night. Strong currents carried them to a desert island not even marked on the charts. After considerable hardship they survived on raw fish until, almost by accident, a South African Air Force aircraft, searching for Japanese submarines, saw their 'Rescue' message laid out on the sand. They were picked up by the minesweeper *Cromer* on 3 June and put aboard a hospital ship at Diego Suarez. It was a tale that had many tellings. I kept quiet about my halcyon days in the luxury of Shangri-la. After all I had done nothing and achieved nothing.

On 29 May Admiral Somerville sailed for Ceylon in *Warspite* to reform the Eastern Fleet. He took with him the carriers *Illustrious* and *Formidable* and the cruiser *Gambia*. We were rather surprised at being left behind.

In the first week of June squadron aircrew were sent on leave in small groups up to Nairobi. While waiting for our turn we had boating parties with some of our ground crew in the muddy creeks of Kilindini harbour, and played a game of Rugby against the Army on a hard baked field; at the end my lungs felt as though seared by flame. I got talked into crewing in a Fleet dinghy race, this meant walking out along a wooden boom from Indom's boat deck and then down, of all things, a rope ladder. I never learnt. Gybing around the stern of *Resolution* under the supercilious eyes of the Officer of the Watch, telescope under arm, we capsized and ignominiously drifted past. He averted his eyes while we pulled the boat upright and without any baling device and water up to the gunwales, we sailed very slowly until we neared the dockside close by the power station. While tipping the boat up to empty it the Station Manager came up and introduced himself and asked us to come to dinner. It's an ill wind.

At the end of the week Jack and I packed our 'green' cases and flew up to Nairobi in our Albacore to take our week's leave, flying low all the way over herds of zebra and elephants which scattered to the shadow of our monstrous bird. Nairobi is at 6,000 feet and after the sultry heat of the coast the air seemed to have a special sweetness and there was a lush greenness. I don't remember much about the hotel we were booked into because the following morning we received a telegram to report back to the ship immediately.

Indom put to sea on 10 June and landed-on all our squadrons and, much to our surprise, nine Grumman Martlet IIs of 806 Squadron 'A' Flight. I never found out why we were at sea but it was probably due to the Japanese submarine activity in the Mozambique Channel; old *Ramillies* had been hit by a torpedo fired from a midget submarine in Diego Suarez harbour. Two of these midgets were operating from the long range 2000 ton parent submarines *I16* and *I18*. There may well have been fears of a Japanese attack on Mombasa harbour. We flew A/S patrols and the Martlets practised deck landings.

It was something new for the goofers to watch a Martlet taking off, heeling over on its narrow tracked Mickey Mouse undercarriage as its powerful engine built up torque and needing full rudder to keep a straight line down the deck. The only other event was a ditching by one of 800 Squadron's Fulmars flown by Sub Lt Peter Ward. With a failing engine due to a coolant leak he found the carrier giving no sign of turning into wind and was forced to put down in the sea alongside. He was picked up from the aircraft's dinghy by *Indom*'s longboat but his observer, Galloway, was killed. Suffering from a painful back, Peter was taken to the sick bay where some time later the dreaded Surgeon Commander Patrick asked him why he was lying about in bed instead of walking about. On our return to Mombassa at the end of the week a hospital ship came into the harbour and its head MO came over to *Indom* and asked to visit the sick bay. He was somewhat surprised to find Peter walking as he quickly diagnosed a cracked spine for which he should have been strapped in bed. He was returned home and happily recovered.

Back in harbour the ship began a boiler clean and re-paint. We were left to loaf about in Mombassa. The 'in thing' at the time was to have a khaki 'bush' jacket made by an Indian tailor in Mombasa. I went mad and ordered two and rather fancied myself in the final result. It must have been a premonition of things to come because the last week of June saw us all, including ground crew, setting off by train to camp in the bush at a place with the unlikely name of MacKinnon Road some fifty miles up the single rail track towards Nairobi. We just stopped in what seemed the middle of nowhere with nothing in sight apart from a couple of dozen tents pitched on dusty ground amidst low scrub trees. Peter Mortimer was there to greet us sporting a khaki solar bowler. He had flown up with five of our Albacores whose pilots were full of exciting tales of lions roaring at night around the water butts, of deadly snakes, and even more deadly mosquitoes. There were four of us to a tent with camp beds and the essential mosquito nets. The mess consisted of one large tent and meals came from a primitive camp kitchen run by local 'boys' who also waited at table. The food was brought infrequently by train and of doubtful origin. Rumour had it that the meat was Rhinoceros — it was certainly tough and the phrase 'iron rations' is an accurate description. There is a boy scout hiding in most men and the whole affair was regarded as great fun. We even had a camp fire sing song to the great enjoyment of the local boys. I sang one of my old sentimental ballads accompanied by an accordion.

An L-shaped clearing in the bush provided a just adequate airfield. At one end a circular target had been marked out and on this our pilots carried out occasional dive-bombing practice, treating it as something of a sport. I used to go along for the ride and to breathe in the cool air at 6,000 feet.

Tom Troubridge flew up in the back seat of a Fulmar to pay us a visit and was made welcome.

I never saw a snake but it was quite true about the lions at night. There was nothing for all of us to do so Jack and I were well pleased when the CO told us that it was our turn to go up to Nairobi for a week's leave. This time it was by train which stopped just to pick up the two of us and then climbed the 250 miles up country, stopping every so often at isolated halts with usually nothing more than a signal box, a signboard and sometimes a few huts in the bush. We arrived late afternoon and, following our instructions, located the service's hospitality office in the main street. Rather to our surprise we were expected and given a cup of tea while we waited for a lady on whose farm we were to spend our leave and who was doing some shopping before collecting us. The sun hardened lady who arrived was in her mid fifties. She cheerfully hustled us into the broad bench seat of an Oldsmobile estate car and off we set south-east to Konza to start another wartime adventure remote from the imperatives of war.

It was about an hour's drive, fast, bumpy and leaving a cloud of dust swirling behind. But time enough for our hostess to both brief and interrogate us. She was widowed, the farm had become too much for her to cope with, so she had rented it out to one of the bigger estates and lived with her daughter in the bungalow her husband had built in the twenties. Quite a large wooden building based on a large lounge/dining room with bedrooms at each end and situated on the rise of a low hill. You could lean out of a bedroom window and pick an orange. The loo was rather fun, situated some 50 metres at the end of the lawn and a wooden two-seater. I recalled reading of some fellow sitting in just such a loo when a snake chose to cross over his bare knees — I have the customary fear of snakes. Jack and I soon had the equally customary dose of 'trots' one comes to expect from a change of diet and we saw quite a bit of the little wooden house and fortunately no snakes.

The daughter, Gugie, had a friend Lulu staying with her. Both names seem highly unlikely but there they are in my old photo album on which is penned in white ink 'Seven days with the wrong women'. This is grossly unfair, they were jolly good girls and gave us a marvellous seven days leave.

Gugie was tall, well provided in all the right places, tough, and full of fun and Lulu was small, elf like, a bit prissy, but good company. The first thing that was made clear after our arrival was that we were expected to bath before dinner and turn up in our pyjamas and dressing gowns — I suppose I must have had a dressing gown in my gear but it does seem a bit strange. It can be quite cold in the evenings up at 6,000 feet, even in July, and the log fire was always lit. Candles on the dining table set a romantic scene. There was a cook and a house boy who served at table; it wasn't Government House but it was good. Gugie's mother retired to bed after dinner, she suffered from some undisclosed ailment and we saw very little of her throughout the week. Although it will seem difficult for the young of today to believe there was no jumping into bed with the girls in spite of more than enough opportunity; I suppose we had been brought up that way and anyway we were guests in the house. Towards the end of the week there was a bit of mild smooching or whatever the word is these days.

Of our days there in the bright sun and sharp clear air I am left only with impressions of all four of us in the front seat of the Oldsmobile which Gugie drove like a maniac across the surrounding grass plain, swerving from one side to the other, avoiding rocks and clumps of long grass and laughing. Miles with nothing in sight but a few rocky escarpments. It was impressed on us that no British car was any use out in Kenya — I can believe it if that is the normal usage.

Another day a shooting party was arranged as the farm was running short of fresh meat and we all set off in a cart pulled by two oxen with a very old negro as a gun bearer. I don't think Jack took it very seriously as he chose to wear his suit, pullover and solar bowler, the rest of us looked more the part in bush jackets and trousers. It was buck we were after and we climbed a rocky outcrop to scan the vast plain of long grass. Gugie said she could see a herd of Kongoni and gave us instructions on how we were to slowly move around down wind of them, and then creep up very slowly as we would only get one shot before they scattered. I made a spectacle of myself by slipping on the edge of the cart as I climbed off and fell flat on the side of my head nearly knocking myself out. The negro bearer nearly died of laughter, it made his day.

Jack had the rifle and after a long approach through the long grass Gugie whispered:

'Take the fourth one from the left!'

Neither of us could see the slightest sign of buck or anything else. Only after much irritated pointing did we gradually distinguish the perfectly camouflaged beasts.

'Go on, go on!' urged Gugie. Jack fired and with the sharp crack of sound the scene erupted into leaping movement. One beautiful creature lagged behind.

'See you've got it in the hind leg — it's running on three — we'll have to follow it as fast as we can!'

We seemed to run for miles until at last it lay down. As we drew near Gugie passed me the rifle as the poor animal struggled to rise.

'Try and get it in the heart.'

I wasn't at all sure where its heart was. It fell again and turned its head to look at me. I fired and its head dropped, I felt sick. It was indeed dead but I don't know where I hit it. Gugie was elated and drawing a large sheath knife called out:

'Come! I'll show you how to degut it.'

'No thank you, I'll just take a walk.'

'But look, you make a slit and put two fingers in and run the knife between them!'

I went green and strode away.

'You'll have to be blooded,' laughed Gugie and I was then chased by both girls until I finally consented to have a bloody cross on my forehead. I was never cut out for this sort of thing and to cap it all we had to ride all the way back in the cart almost sitting on the carcase. We had some for dinner, it was tough.

When we got to bed that night the girls had made us apple pie beds and there were shrieks of girlish laughter. We decided on some chastisement but they had locked themselves in the room they shared. It may have saved them from a fate worse than death.

We encountered the dreaded 'tick' which gets under the skin around the waist or wherever clothes fit tightly. The standard treatment seemed to be to approach them with the lighted end of a cigarette; as you would expect, the girls thought this great sport. What carefree days, swimming in the large water tank, playing quoits, shooting partridge, visiting neighbouring farms to be shown off.

Suddenly it was time to go and the girls took us in the Oldsmobile to catch the train. A phone message to Nairobi arranged for the train to stop at the Konza signal box. We had a puncture on the way and nearly missed the train. It arrived carrying a number of our shipmates who cheered a rather classic goodbye scene from two tearful girls hanging around our necks.

The next day we packed up at Mackinnon Road and returned to Mombasa to rejoin the ship.

The first thing I learnt was that my cabin arrangements had been changed again — in fact I wasn't to have a cabin at all — I was to sleep on a safari camp bed placed in the aft tiller flat and keep my kit in Trevor Turner's cabin nearby. I had started out so well ten months previously. All this was due to the need to accommodate the extra aircrew of 806 Squadron whose pilots included an above average number of RN Lieutenants, which depressed my seniority to rock bottom. The lights never went out in the aft tiller flat and, while at sea, once every watch, a matelot opened the heavy balanced deck hatch alongside my bed and descended into the steering gear compartment. Returning a few minutes later he closed the hatch with his foot, creating a hollow boom which woke me even out of a drunken sleep.

We put to sea on 8 July with only the destroyer *Lightning* as escort. The Martlet IIs of 806 flew on board followed by 800 Squadron, now re-equipped with twelve Sea Hurricane 1Bs in place of their Fulmars, and with a new CO, Lt Cdr Bruen RN. The rest of us flew on board the next day. Every inch of top hangar space had to be used to accommodate 31 fighters, bearing in mind that the Hurricanes did not have folding wings.

While at Mombasa the ship's engineers had rigged up additional outriggers on the starboard side both fore and aft of the island. This was an American idea which Jack Hillard, our permanent Fairey company engineer, had designed and fabricated so that we could keep fighter aircraft on deck but out of the way of flying operations. It consisted of a U-section steel channel cantilevered out over the side of the deck and supported with stays. The Hurricane's tail wheel was guided into the channel and the aircraft pushed out until the main wheels were close to the edge of the deck.

As usual we were not told why we had suddenly acquired this impressive abundance of fighters, but it was clear that we were heading south fast. Perhaps we were on our way home. It was back to the daily routine of A/S patrols. It was on one of these that the engine of our 4C caught fire. Jack Hillard thought that one of the cylinder heads must have blown so that oil was being pumped out of it as the sleeve valve continued to operate. Leaving a dense trail of black smoke Jack headed straight back to the ship and I fired a red Very light. We expected her to start turning into wind but when there was no sign of this as we turned round her stern Jack bellowed 'Fire another at the stupid bastards!' So I fired directly at the island as we flew past close enough to see all the upturned faces. She began to turn as we crossed her bows.

'I'm going in now!' Jack called.

She was heeled well over as we approached the rounddown. The batsman gave us the 'wave off' and Jack pulled up to port into a slow climbing turn. The smoke was thicker and the vibration had increased as we staggered around for another approach.

'I'm going on this time whether they like it or not so hold on.'

I was fastening my seat belt when the engine finally seized. We were nose high and two hundred metres astern at just over deck height. The old girl stalled, flipped onto her back and, according to the goofers, went into the sea at forty five degrees upside down, then sinking until just her tail and rear fuselage was visible.

I found myself under the water, dazed, and cramped up in some small dark corner I didn't recognize. There was a faint glimmer of greenish light close to my head and I thrust wildly towards it, battering against an obstacle which broke. My head came briefly out of the water before being pulled under. After a frenzied struggle I realised that my parachute harness was caught on something and on the next plunge I banged the release button and with a final struggle broke free to the surface and the glorious brilliance of sunshine.

Jack and Oscar's bobbing heads were close by. The dinghy had inflated but was trapped under the rear fuselage. It floated free as the tail lifted and the old girl sank. When we reached it we found it was upside down and we couldn't turn it over due to the suction, so we just clung on to the ropes around its side. Minutes later a whaler from the *Lightning* was alongside, and we were pulled aboard.

It was not until much later that I realised by what slender chance I had managed to escape from what seemed a death trap. It was entirely due to the many hours my heels had rested on the domed aluminium cover over the bomb sight hatch in the floor and had battered it so out of shape that it was no longer possible to fasten it down with its two wing nuts. Hinged at the front, it had dropped open as we turned upside down and when we hit the water I was thrown against it and the light I had seen through the water was through the perspex roller shutter over the hatch. Although it was a fairly robust affair I managed to get my head through it and eventually escape. The only other way out would have been down through the side door or through the windows of the canopy but it was always my practice to keep a few breaths of air in my Mae West and this was pushing me the wrong way — not that I thought of it at the time — I didn't realise where I was and only instinct made me strike out for the light.

Jack and Oscar had managed to get out without too much of a struggle which is equally surprising. Shivering with shock and dripping bright green fluorescent dye from our Mae Wests we were helped onto *Lightning* and taken below where the ship's MO came and had a look at us. I had a cut on one knee, but otherwise we seemed unscathed. After a most welcome hot bath I remember having to apologize for the revolting mess of green dye and blood I had left all over the floor. Togged out in white shirts and grey flannels we arrived in the small wardroom — never was a large whisky so welcome. Over the next two days we enjoyed such hospitality and friendliness as could only be found on the small ships of the Navy. For much of the day Jack and I enjoyed the sunshine from deck chairs on the after deck where the water foamed past at eye level giving an exciting sensation of speed. From this new point of vantage we could watch the planes taking off and landing on *Indom* as we kept station on her quarter. By a happy chance I picked *Clochemerle* from the ship's library and made the joyful acquaintance with its bawdy characters and their famous 'pissoir'.

We transferred back to *Indom* when she docked for a couple of days at Durban on 13 July. Jack and I had to report to Tom Troubridge in his cabin — he wanted to hear all about our escape from 4C — he was surprised that we had all survived. So were we. He was one of the very few senior officers to take any interest in flying types and was deservedly popular with us.

We only had time for one quick trip ashore at Durban. Like Cape Town it reminded us of home and we could have wished for a longer stay, but there was a sense of urgency as we continued sailing south at high speed.

Our squadron fitters had by now assembled a new Albacore 4C for us, no mean feat at sea, in the cramped space, with the rigging of the folding wings being particularly difficult. Jack was asked to give it a flight test and I decided to go with him for the ride. The ride turned into another drama. After throwing the new kite around the sky in steep turns, stalls and dives Jack decided to try out the front gun and asked me to throw out an aluminium sea marker to act as a target. I tore off the metal sealing strip from the black metal cube and thrust the cardboard inner box over the side. A huge silver disc spread over the sea. 'Cock the gun,' called Jack. This involved scrambling down into the space below the fuel tank — a painful memory — and twisting open the valve on an air bottle. I had hardly got back into my seat before we were diving steeply with the Vickers gun rattling away and splashes breaking up the silver surface. After several dives Jack said 'Shut off the air and let's go back'. It sounded simple but when I looked around there was not a sign of the ship. The sun was high overhead, a copper disc through a thick heat haze, not even a horizon. I had assumed that Jack was keeping an eye on her and had neither tuned the beacon nor brought my chronometer and I had no chartboard. I told Jack to keep circling the sea marker while I tried to control my feeling of panic. I remembered being told about a technique for returning on the beacon with a broken chronometer using the second hand on a wrist watch. But I had never tried it. First of all I needed to tune the beacon receiver and my chances of picking up that once a minute signal were slim, but it was our only chance. I lowered the aerial, plugged in and switched on.

A minute seems a long time when you are close to panic. Silence. I shifted the tuner and waited. Silence. Another minute and then a faint bleep — a tweak on the tuner and it came up stronger the next time round so I noted the position of the second hand on my wrist watch and gave Jack a course due south. When the bleep came up again the second hand was earlier so I asked Jack to alter course twenty degrees to port. Each time the second hand came up early we altered another twenty degrees to port. After ten anxious minutes the bleep came up at almost the same second position and my course corrections became smaller. I told Jack that the ship should now be dead ahead.

'I can see her! I can see her!' he cried shrilly. We had flown around the ship in a decreasing spiral. I felt relieved and chastened — another ducking in succession would have been just too much to bear. We kept this little adventure to ourselves but in later years I used the story when teaching navigation to the young and innocent.

We dropped anchor very briefly at Capetown and then sped on up to Freetown. Our fighters seemed to be flying off more frequently, usually off the booster, and rumours began to circulate about our joining a convoy to Malta. I had little appreciation of the implications and was still romantically lusting for action. We had put in so many tedious hours in the air to so little effect — maybe some odd submarine had been kept submerged and emasculated by our presence but we would never know.

At Freetown we flew our new 4C ashore to swing its compasses; I wasn't too sure if I remembered how to do it — Arbroath seemed a lifetime away — but I managed in spite of the heat and one hundred percent humidity. It even rained when we made a trip into the town and I don't know whether I was wetter with perspiration or rain water. It seemed a ghastly place and it was a relief to be back on board ship, even to my safari bed and the after tiller flat.

On the night of 1 August we weighed anchor and headed out into the Atlantic accompanied by the smart new cruiser *Phoebe* and escorted by the destroyers *Laforey, Lookout* and my old friend *Lightning*. For the next four days, heading north, flying was restricted to A/S and reconnaissance

patrols. On the 5th, a buzz of excitement brought us all up on the flight
deck to find that we had joined up with a force of three carriers, two
cruisers and further destroyers. It was easy to recognize the veteran carrier
Eagle with her large twin funnelled island and scimitar shaped bows.
There too was odd little *Argus,* the very first true aircraft carrier.

It was not until the Captain came on the Tannoy that evening that we
learnt that the third carrier was *Victorious* and that we were to escort a
very special convoy through to Malta. The island was then in a critical
state both for food and fuel.

So after all these months we were to be put to the test, this time there
would be no question of avoiding action. I wondered what part our two
Albacore squadrons would play — perhaps the elusive Italian fleet would
put to sea to provide targets for a torpedo strike. Of one thing we could be
certain, the Italian and German air force would throw everything they had
against us from both Sardinia and Sicily and it would be our fighter
aircraft on which all our lives would depend. On *Eagle*'s deck I could see
Sea Hurricanes. *Victorious* had five Sea Hurricanes kept on outriggers as
her lifts were too small to take them below and she also had a squadron of
Fulmars. *Argus* was a mystery to us, she had Hurricanes on board but all
who knew her from deck landing training days didn't feel she was up to an
operation of this type.

The next two days proved to be a 'goofer's benefit'. With *Indom, Eagle*
and *Victorious* manoeuvring in line abreast, each followed closely by
Phoebe, Sirius and *Charybdis* (for anti-aircraft protection), the various
fighters flew on exercises from dawn until dusk, only interrupted when
one Albacore flew off or landed on from A/S patrols. All this took place
some five hundred miles west of Gibraltar in an unusually calm Atlantic
and under cloudless skies. With the frequent changes in course required by
the zig-zag pattern (to present a difficult problem to any enemy
submarine) the booster was much in use to despatch the fighters and, with
the constant landings the batsman's arms must have felt like lead at the
end of the day. There were moments of extreme excitement but we had no
prangs. *Victorious* seemed to have a lot of trouble with her Fulmars and
one of these ditched. *Argus* wandered around like a lost sheep — it was
reported that she was carrying spare Hurricanes.

During the afternoon of the second day the old hump-backed fleet
carrier *Furious* and the cruiser *Manchester* joined the fleet and kept station
astern. We could see a large number of RAF Spitfires ranged aft on
Furious and it seemed that she was to fly these off to reinforce Malta.

The 8th opened with a scene on the scale of a Hollywood epic — the
rendezvous with the all important freighters of the convoy — fourteen,
including the large tanker *Ohio* — escorted by those wonderfully

impressive 16-inch gun battleships, *Nelson* and *Rodney* and another group of cruisers and destroyers. There seemed to be ships in every direction as far as the eye could see — I counted sixty-seven — a magnificent sight, but what a target. I had gone down to the lower hangar on some errand when an ear shattering series of explosions echoed from all directions. My stomach turned over and thinking the worst had happened I climbed as fast as I could up to the flight deck. There I found the whole fleet was firing all its guns in a practice anti-aircraft barrage — a Brock's Benefit we called it. Up to that time I had never heard the fearsome sound made by our sixteen 4.5 inch guns. It was a foretaste of things to come.

In the afternoon all three carriers flew off fighters from all their squadrons for a 'Balbo' over the fleet. It was a stirring sight to see over fifty aircraft overhead and it was hoped that this display would stiffen the morale of the merchant ship crews who would be just as much at risk as ourselves, if not more so. If it was hoped that the ships' gunners would learn to recognize our own aircraft from those of the enemy it was, as always, to be a vain hope. We Albacore types felt a special sense of pride in our fighter pilots, many of them larger than life characters like Butch Judd and Dicky Cork. And, of course, we envied them.

The convoy passed through the Straits on the night of the 9th while *Indom* was detached to refuel during the night in Gibraltar.

Tom Troubridge's voice came on the Tannoy that evening speaking in his usual forthright and confident fashion. He outlined how the operation would proceed over the next three days and said that we could expect to be a prime target for both submarine and air attack. *Ark Royal,* he said, had been abandoned before it was truly necessary and with a twinkle in his voice he said that should we ever be in that position he would not be giving such an order — but we all had his permission to abandon ship when a list of ninety degrees was reached. There were wry grins all round but an absence of the usual wardroom chatter. The quiet before the storm.

Night and fog cloaked our entry into the Mediterranean. In the early morning the fog cleared, the sun blazed down, the sea was a brilliant blue cut through by the whiteness of the wakes from the serried rows of ships as we caught up with the convoy and took our station in the middle, *Victorious* ahead, *Eagle* astern and *Furious* in a position off in the port quarter.

The curtain was rising on one of the greatest air/sea battles of the war — Operation 'Pedestal'.

Chapter 10
The Most Exciting Moment

The Mediterranean Sea has been the stage for many of the world's great sea battles but never again would it see such as this. Like most great dramas this one had three Acts representing each of the three days out from Gibraltar.

'Day One', 10 August 1942, was a teasing of the nerves, a flexing of muscles, an apprehensive scanning of cloudless skies. Four Hurricanes were ranged on our deck all day at immediate readiness, their engines warmed up at intervals, propellers and yellow painted spinners flashing in the sun like the shields of the Greeks at Troy. The warriors sat, not in their tents like Achilles, but in their cramped, hot cockpits, canopies slung back, helmets off, hair blowing in the wind, waiting.

And what of the enemy? Waiting on the many airfields of Sardinia and Sicily or submerged somewhere close ahead. Our passage through the straits would have been reported by their spies in Spain and there was scant possibility of deceiving them about our route, speed, or objective. Surprise was not an option and was totally lost when, in late afternoon, a Vichy French civil flying boat flew overhead on its way to Morocco. We watched four Hurricanes scrambled from *Victorious* to intercept but, unfortunately, it was allowed to go on its way. It gave a detailed sighting report to the Axis HQ in Italy which gave them ample time to plan their attack.

For all of us with no role to play it was a great innovation to have the officer commanding our Marines, Major Pym, situated in the fighter direction room from whence he made intermittent broadcasts over the Tannoy describing what was happening around us. This was appreciated by all aboard, particularly by those stationed below decks.

That night I took my safari bed up into the passageway just behind the quarter deck and slept fitfully with my clothes on and my Mae West close at hand. I had to be up early as I was to be Duty Officer in the Operations Room. I was pleased to have some small role to play on 'Day Two', 11 August, a day that we knew would bring us within range of enemy aircraft. I had a shower and changed into my white shirt and shorts for the occasion. After a quick breakfast I hurried up to the island to report to a bleary eyed 'Lofty' Logan and got on with my first job of the day — to brew up his very special 'Blue Mountain' coffee which he had purchased when we were in Jamaica. The next job was to chalk up the crews and aircraft details on the blackboard. An 827 Albacore took off for the dawn A/S patrol, followed at 0630 by four Hurricanes of 880 to carry out the first of the days 1½ hour combat air patrols at 20,000 feet. *Eagle* also flew off a section of Hurricanes and I watched them all climb into a cloudless sky until they were out of sight. The convoy was now south of Ibiza and only some 350 miles from Sardinia (see Map 5). It seemed surprising that nothing had happened to disturb the peaceful scene.

When the carriers, with their attendant cruisers, manoeuvred into wind I went out onto the island brow to watch 'Butch' Judd fly off with his section to take over from Brian Fiddes who landed on his section at 0800. As the planes were being taken down the lift for refuelling, Major Pym's voice boomed from the Tannoy to report an enemy aircraft on the radar screen. This proved to be a long range reconnaissance Ju 88 flying at 23,000 feet. This remarkable multi-role aircraft was capable of climbing higher and diving faster than a Hurricane. As was to happen all too often during the battle our fighters failed to catch it and there were many frustrated pilots. 'Dicky' Cork, leading the next patrol, had more success, making an attack on another Ju 88 at 15,000 feet and setting fire to its starboard engine before he had to break off. When he came into the Ops Room he was complaining bitterly about the poor performance of the Sea Hurricane above 20,000 feet. 800 Squadron took over the patrols until lunch time.

At midday I went outside again to watch *Furious*, out on our port quarter, flying off the first of the 41 RAF Spitfires on that long one way trip to Malta. The first group had just formed up and were climbing away to the east when at 1315 the air was suddenly rent with a series of explosions. I looked around quickly to see smoke pouring out of *Eagle*. She had been hit by four torpedoes and was slewing round and heeling over. I rushed into the Ops Room to tell 'Lofty', and by the time we got outside *Eagle* had heeled over so much that we could see one of her Hurricanes sliding off her deck into the water. Then, as we stood speechless, she rolled right over and in as little as seven minutes she had sunk without trace. I felt numbed but there was no time to think about the implications or of what survivors there might have been, she was well behind now as we had increased speed to fly off our next patrol which went off the booster as there was only a light wind and it saved precious time. I tucked away the feeling of relief, it might so easily have been us struggling in the water.

Eagle had four Hurricanes airborne, one landed on our deck and the remainder on *Victorious*. As soon as our own Hurricanes had landed, Commander (F) ordered the flight deck to be cleared to bring on one of the

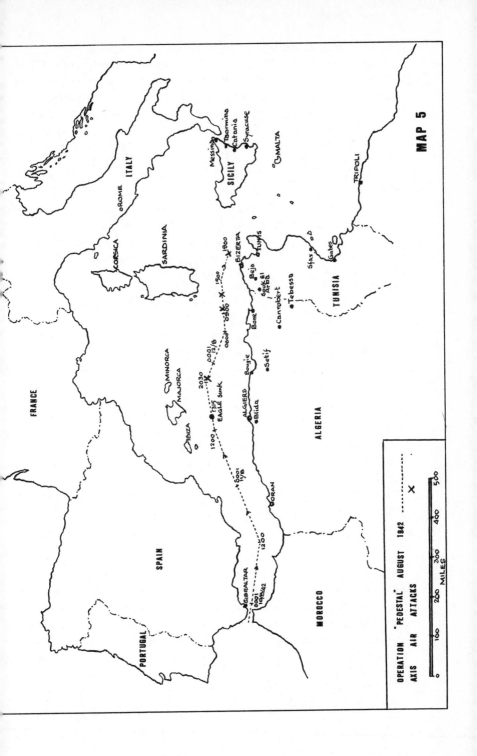

MAP 5

OPERATION "PEDESTAL" AUGUST 1942
AXIS AIR ATTACKS

RAF Spitfires which had developed engine trouble. I don't know why he decided to attempt what seemed to everyone to be an impossible feat; no hook, no deck landing experience and a full load of fuel. I would have baled out and taken the chance of being picked up. Lt Cdr Martin Pares took up his batsman's position, the barrier was raised and the ship moved into wind at maximum speed. Every vantage point was crammed with an audience holding its breath as the pilot made two alarming approaches from well astern (the pilot's view from a Spitfire was far from ideal for deck landing), both of them too fast and too low. On the third he came in fast but well centred and touched down comfortably past the round-down to rush headlong into the barrier below me. Apart from the propeller there was remarkably little damage and the very brave pilot climbed out unhurt. His aircraft was pulled free of the barrier cables, trundled down the deck and pushed over the stern into the sea. In other times 880 Squadron fitters would have lost no time in fitting it with a hook.

We were now south of Majorca and still no sign of an enemy air attack — when it did come we were going to miss the 16 Hurricanes which had gone down with *Eagle*. The Fulmars from *Victorious* were now taking a bigger share of the air patrols and one of them landed on *Indom* in mid afternoon. The pilot came up into the Ops Room. 'Hello,' I said cheerfully. He looked at me, frowned and looked around the room — 'My God!' he said 'Wrong bloody ship!'

At 1535 'Butch' was once more leading his section on patrol and was soon being directed to intercept another snooping Ju 88. Lt 'Johnny' Forrest secured hits on its port engine and Sub Lt 'Steve' Harris completed its destruction. But Forrest's plane had been hit by return fire and he was forced to ditch — we received a signal to say that he had been picked up unhurt by a destroyer.

As the evening approached and all seemed quiet, 'Lofty' sent me down to the wardroom to get some dinner — our sandwich lunch had been disrupted by the *Eagle* disaster — just as I finished the last mouthful the chilling sound of 'Action Stations' came over the Tannoy followed by the order 'All gun crews close up to first degree readiness'. Then Major Pym's voice announced that an enemy force was approaching from fifty miles to the north. The wardroom emptied and I made my way back up to the Ops Room, arriving in time to see the last of 880's standby section climbing away into the warm glow of a setting sun. There was already one section on patrol and two more of 800 Squadron were being ranged on deck so I was kept busy on the blackboard until the last had taken off. The minutes ticked by.

'Our fighters have engaged enemy bombers,' announced the Major. Almost immediately there was the first clap of gunfire over to port and through a porthole I saw puffs of smoke blossom high up where the sky was still lit by the sinking sun. Suddenly the whole scene expanded into a tumult of noise and the sky erupted with shell bursts. With sharp cracks our own 4.5 gun turrets opened up and the darkening sky was lit by arcing lines of tracer. There was a bright flash and loud explosion on our port side aft and I thought we had been hit. A report reached us that one of our 4.5 shells had exploded at the muzzle and severely wounded Lt Cdr Pares who was in position alongside, ready to bat in returning aircraft. His place was taken by his deputy.

The eye and mind were unable to make sense of all that was happening. Ju 88s seemed to be slating down from all directions and the convoy kept making emergency alterations of course as monstrous fountains of black stained water erupted between the lines of ships. Two Ju 88s plunged flaming into the sea, and I experienced a moment of sadistic pleasure, most of the time I felt a numbness and was completely unaware of the passing of time. The attack seemed to have died away when close behind the Ops Room the pom-pom battery began an ominous drumbeat sending arcs of tracer shells flashing skyward. With a shock I realised that they and most of the other ships nearby were firing at our own fighters. Some of the Hurricanes had their wheels down and were waggling their wings — it was agonising to watch, I felt helpless — fortunately most of the gunfire passed behind them but it was not hard to imagine what the pilots were feeling.

Indom increased speed and pulled out of line into wind, the firing had mostly stopped and with the last bit of light we landed on most of our Hurricanes as well as three Fulmars from *Victorious*. One of the Fulmars caught his port wing on the deck and was immediately manhandled for'd and pushed over the bows in order to clear the deck. By this time it was fully dark and both of 880's sections were still airborne having been drawn well away from the fleet while chasing Ju 88s. They were all running short of fuel and Tom Troubridge was faced with the possibility of losing eight fighters and their pilots with the most dangerous of days yet to come. It was typical of the man that he decided to put on the deck landing lights and maintain course into wind although by this time we were well outside the destroyer screen and very vulnerable to submarine attack. Deck landing fighters at night had neither been foreseen, nor practised and was particularly hazardous, however all but Sub Lt Hugh Popham got down safely. Later we learnt that, after circling the fleet and being continuously fired on by all and sundry, he crash landed on *Victorious* with only a cupful of fuel left. Happily he was unhurt.

If there was anything to eat that night I don't remember it. The ante-room was buzzing with tales of the day's events. The general view was that the attack had been only a small probing one made at dusk in the hope that we could not operate our fighters — the range still being too great for the Axis to send a fighter escort. About thirty Ju 88s had been involved together with a few torpedo carrying Heinkel 111s but few had pressed home their attacks and none of the ships in the convoy was damaged.

Before retiring our CO called us to a brief meeting where we were assigned our tasks and action stations for the following day. Some crews were to remain in the ante-room on standby to make a torpedo attack on Italian cruisers which had been reported near Sardinia. Jack Fisher had thought up the idea of removing the Vickers machine guns from our Albacores and mounting them at various positions on the catwalks. I was detailed to man one of these on the port side aft near the crane. It was a good vantage point for the final Act even if the weapon (and the gunner) were unlikely to have any effect on the outcome.

The thought of what had happened so quickly to *Eagle* was much in my mind and once again the corridor behind the quarterdeck seemed the safest place and a Mae West made a very good pillow. I was not alone in my choice.

I was up well before dawn of 'Day Three', 12 August. The wardroom was already full of those taking what might be the last meal of the day — for some the last meal of their lives — I had my prunes as usual and a very large mug of cocoa. We were also given a bar of that hard plain chocolate which the navy issues for emergencies. Dawn was fast breaking when I made my way up to the flight deck equipped with Mae West, binoculars, and tin hat. All around sailed the great assembly of ships — silhouettes on a calm, slate blue sea — it was going to be another hot, cloudless day, but, as I walked down the deck and climbed down into my exposed perch I shivered in the cool early morning breeze. The gun felt unfamiliar and cold, I hadn't touched one since long ago at Arbroath. Long ago? It was only a year. Spare magazines were at my feet, the massive shackle for the seventh arrestor wire at my back and further back the first section of two Hurricanes rocked on their tyres as their engines warmed up. On the starboard side pilots were gingerly climbing into the standby Hurricanes positioned precariously over the side of the ship on their outrigger booms and ready to fly off at a moment's notice should the enemy break through the various patrol levels.

From my seat in the front row of the stalls I could see every movement on the sea and in the air, but I missed having the detailed knowledge of fighter operations which I had had the previous day and had to rely on Major Pym's intermittent commentary from the nearest Tannoy. No sooner had our first patrol of Hurricanes roared past than the Major was reporting enemy reconnaissance planes on our radar screen and that

Fulmars from *Victorious* were being directed towards them. There were few times during this day when we were not being shadowed either by Ju 88s and SM 79s at high altitude or by Cant 1007 flying boats at low level.

Just after 0900 the Major reported a raid coming in from the east. We had expected the first attack to come from Sardinia, which was only a hundred miles away at that time, but it was the Germans heading our way with a force of nineteen Ju 88s flying the three hundred miles from Sicily who were intercepted 25 miles ahead by Hurricanes of 800 and 880. Four Merlins roared into life, starter trolleys were dragged away, and 'Dicky' Cork's section accelerated past me. Hurricanes and Fulmar sections followed from *Victorious* and the first blooms of exploding shells enabled me to focus on the silhouette of a diving Ju 88, then the whole barrage opened up and it became impossible to focus on anything — just brief impressions of fountains of water rising somewhere in the convoy and a Ju 88 cartwheeling into the sea. Even through all the din you could hear the cheers.

Unlike the night before, it was all over quite quickly and around us the air became full of Hurricanes waiting to land. One after another the arrestor wires screamed through their sheaves pulling up each aircraft almost alongside me; most had their red doped fabric patches torn away from over their eight gun ports — I had forgotten to even cock my gun. There was feverish activity from one end of the flight deck to the other to clear it and prepare to launch fighters against another raid which could come at any time; a carrier is at its most vulnerable state when refuelling and rearming. A section of Martlets was hastily launched on the booster to take over the convoy's air cover.

Although at the time it was claimed that the carrier's fighters had shot down eight Ju 88s in the first raid, German records show that six failed to return, two of which were shot down by the convoy's gunfire. Lt Cdr Judd's section also shot down a Cant Z 1007 flying boat and Fulmars from *Victorious*' 884 Squadron sent a Savoia Marchetti SM 79 flaming into the sea. The convoy suffered no damage. *Victorious* lost Sub Lt Hankey shot down in his Hurricane.

There was no doubt that we had won this first round.

There followed an uneasy lull during which our Hurricanes and Martlets maintained standing patrols. The Tannoy was silent except for brief reports that enemy shadowing aircraft were being chased. The sun was now overhead, it was hot and my stomach told me it was lunchtime. I tried some navy chocolate and found it so hard that I needed the knife in my Mae West to scrape off a few slivers.

There was an urgency in the Major's voice as he reported a large number of enemy aircraft forming up in the direction of Sardinia which was by then seventy miles to the north of us. Over the next half hour there were excited reports of our patrol fighters engaging them but it seemed a long time before the raid developed. My eyes were bleary from scanning an empty sky through my binoculars.

'Dicky' Cork's section was scrambled at 1225 and there was gunfire somewhere up ahead, then a massive barrage began low down over to port in the middle of which I caught glimpses of three-engined Italian SM 79 torpedo bombers approaching head on and low down on the water. The battleship *Rodney* was on our port quarter firing her sixteen inch guns to produce an awesome wall of water ahead of the oncoming planes into which they disappeared. It seemed impossible for any to survive this hail of gunfire but I saw only one banking away trailing a plume of fire and smoke. The Italians seemed to press home their attack most bravely, even after being harried by our fighters, but not one of the 43 which took part scored a hit even though they each carried two torpedoes. At least ten of them never reached a dropping position although they were escorted by 26 of Italy's best fighters, the Reggiane Re 2001, one of which was shot down. Before the torpedo attack the Italians attempted to disrupt the convoy by dropping a new type of mine from ten SM 84s escorted by fourteen Macchi Mc 202 fighters. Two SM 84s were shot down and all the rest damaged. Our only loss was Sub Lt Cruickshank who had scrambled with 'Dicky' Cork and had been shot down by two of the Italian fighters. 880 Squadron was now short of three pilots and the day was only half over.

The gunfire faded away as the Tannoy reported a large force approaching from ahead at 11,000 feet. This was a force of 37 German Ju 88s from Sicily escorted by Messerschmit Bf 110 long range fighters. A section of 800's Hurricanes was in the landing circuit and being fired on by some of our own guns. 'Butch' Judd's section was flown off at 1315 and we started landing on the returning section as the barrage opened up again. Cork's Hurricane landed with the rudder fabric in shreds. My ears were blasted by the sharp cracking sound from our own 4.5 inch gun turrets as a stream of Ju 88s dived across the convoy ahead of us. This time I was close enough to see their bombs slanting down and many of the ships were obscured by the huge black and white fountains. But only the freighter *Deucalion* was hit and forced to fall behind the convoy. Due to the efforts of our fighters and the density of the convoy's gunfire only twelve Ju 88s completed their attacks.

I think it is fair to say that we won the second round.

The price we paid was the loss of the COs of both 806 and 880 Squadrons. As the last sounds were dying away, and from a sky smeared with the dispersing gunfire smoke, a lone Martlet came in low and too fast;

its hook caught a wire but was torn out of the fuselage and the plane slewed out over the port catwalk a few feet in front of me. As though in slow motion I watched the pilot, Lt Johnston, try to climb out of the cockpit but the plane turned on its back and fell into the sea. He had been wounded in one of the many air battles. I felt numb. Later I heard that fiery 'old Butch' had been shot down and killed by return fire from what was reported as a Heinkel 111 but was more likely to have been a Ju 88; we had thought of him as indestructible.

With all our planes back on board there was frenzied activity on the flight deck to move them onto the lifts and reposition their replacements: aircrew, dentists and pay branch officers and portly Commanders lent a hand at pushing them, and soon order came out of chaos. I turned my attention back to watching the serene progress of the convoy. In an eye's blink a black painted fighter flew down past our port side at eye level and high speed, and no more than 200 yards away. Since my schooldays aircraft recognition had been part of my life and I saw it to be a Reggione Re 2001, one of the best looking fighters of its day. I was too surprised to open fire and most others thought it was a Hurricane until it dropped two small bombs on *Victorious* which was then on our port quarter. The bombs bounced off her armoured deck and exploded in the sea. I failed to see a second Reggione whose bombs missed the carrier. It was a brave attempt — with a larger force and better bombs it would have wreaked havoc on a flight deck full of aircraft.

The rest of the hot afternoon passed without incident. I had had nothing to eat or drink since before dawn and my legs ached from crouching in the catwalk so I decided to make a quick visit to the Wardroom, hoping to be inconspicuous amongst those milling around the flight deck. When I arrived there were a few fighter pilots in Mae Wests in excited discourse, surrounded by some dozen Albacore aircrew. No sign of Jack, but Willy was there smoking his pipe — it was the last time I saw my cabin-mate. I grabbed a large mug of tea and some bread and jam, wolfed it down and hurried back to the flight deck, feeling guilty.

Depth charges were throwing up mountains of snowy white water a mile away on our port quarter. After focusing my binoculars I was astonished to see a submarine surfacing and one of our destroyers moving towards it at high speed firing its for'd gun before ramming it amidships. [Italian submarine *Cobalto*: destroyer HMS *Ithuriel*.] I watched the tiny figures of the submarine's crew scrambling out of the conning tower and jumping into the sea before it sank. It all seemed unreal and I felt nothing for the poor men. Only minutes afterwards a periscope and the topmost part of a submarine's conning tower emerged from the sea opposite me and no more than one hundred feet away. I fired a quick burst but it quickly submerged and disappeared astern. Depth charging was going on all around us at this time and continued at intervals for the next hour. We had crossed the path of four Italian submarines only one of which got in position to launch torpedoes which missed their target.

It was now late afternoon and we were drawing ever closer to Sicily, so it came as no surprise when the Major's steady voice reported large enemy groups forming up ahead of us. By now we knew what to expect; the uneasy period when our fighters fought their aerial battles far beyond our vision, the dozens of upturned faces scanning the sky, the splutter of Merlin engines being started up. This time the Axis bombers were escorted by as many as forty fighters, Macchi Mc 202s, Bf 110s and Bf 109s. The German dive-bomber force consisted of twelve Ju 87 (Stukas) and 18 Ju 88s and the Italians had 14 SM79 torpedo bombers and 8 Ju 87 dive-bombers, the latter flying from the island of Pantelleria. All these were split into eleven groups which at 1800 showed up on the radar screen at a range of 50 to 60 miles over a wide arc. *Indom* had three Martlets and eight Hurricanes on patrol and we soon had Tannoy reports of them engaging the enemy, but the Hurricanes were nearing the end of their patrol time and were forced to return and land on around 1830 just as all hell was let loose as the first group of bombers arrived.

Everywhere I looked, SM 79s were coming in low through the smoke of the barrage. We boosted off four Hurricanes and continued to land on planes — there was intense activity to get them down the for'd lift — as the first of the Italian Stukas was already diving steeply before releasing its bomb and streaking out at sea level amidst a hail of tracer. Another flew past so close that I could see it's pilot and air gunner, and right behind it, one of our Hurricanes. Both pom-pom batteries on my side fired at it but their tracer seemed to pass closer to our Hurricane than the Stuka. It was the only occasion on which I saw one of our fighters in action and I remember the savage delight I felt when the Stuka started to burn and finally splashed into the sea near *Victorious*. It was the most exciting moment.

The two carriers were then operating as separate units, each with its cruiser and about a mile apart. Our 4.5 inch guns began to fire and I saw the all too familiar shape of Ju 88s diving across a sky pock marked in every direction by the smoke of exploding shells. In spite of the many tons of explosive being hurled at us no ship seemed to have been hit; it seemed that we had the protection of the Gods . If so, they chose not to look our way when just before 1900 the destroyer *Foresight* was hit by a torpedo and then, after the gunfire had begun to fade, I caught sight of a closely bunched formation of twelve Stukas at about 10,000 feet almost directly above us with not a shot being fired at them. I got up and ran onto the flight deck shouting and waving my arms wildly but to no avail. The first Stuka peeled off and I had my first head-on view of its sinister cranked wing heading straight towards us with others following behind. I felt disembodied and without fear, unable to move — not that there was anywhere to move to.

Looking like beer barrels, the 1100 lb bombs seemed to float down towards us as though in some dimly remembered dream. The ship shuddered and the dream expanded into a huge sheet of flame which rose up ahead of the island and engulfed it. There was an enormous explosion just ahead of me and then several behind me which seemed to lift the ship several feet. A wall of water rose alongside to some hundred feet then cascaded down on top of me, washing me into the catwalk. For a moment there was a strange silence such as occurs at the end of a great orchestral performance, it could have been the final moments of *Gotterdammerung*, as flames and smoke billowed near the for'd lift and behind the aft lift.

The ship began listing to port and was moving in a slow circle to starboard. I am told that the list never exceeded ten degrees but it seemed more at the time and I felt the first knot of fear in my stomach, thinking we were doomed and expecting at any minute another enemy attack as we were now a sitting target, unable to operate aircraft, or even land-on all those we still had in the air. The flight deck was a confusion of people and a snakepit of hoses. Tom Troubridge appeared up on the flying bridge, like Zeus, bellowing at the human ants below. I helped to haul hoses along the slanting deck towards the fire at the stern, passing groups of wounded being helped along the deck. I avoided a direct look at them but a glance told me that most had been burnt, their bare skin stained ludicrously with gentian violet.

A destroyer arrived alongside and began hosing water into the stern. The flames died out, the smoke began to clear, and I realised that we were no longer listing; better still the ship was under way again. Half an hour had passed, I looked around, there was no sign of the convoy, we were alone with the cruiser *Charybdis* (of ill omen in these parts) and three destroyers, and heading west into the evening sun. The wind down the deck was still warm, my clothes were nearly dry, but I was shivering and all too aware that I was not doing anything useful. I returned to my position in the catwalk, it began to get dark and there was still no sign of another attack. From the familiar vibrations I was aware that we were cutting through the sea at close to full speed and, as the curtain of night came down on the final scene, a 'stand down' was piped and I made my way over to the island.

At this point my memory fails me. The bomb hit abaft the after lift and had made it impossible to use the cabins in that area and another bomb had exploded near to the port side of the ship, completely destroying the wardroom. There was an all pervading smell of smoke and burnt flesh and, of course, nothing to eat — not that I felt like it. Somehow I was allocated a cabin amidships on the starboard side and did not enquire whose it was but slept soundly in a comfortable bunk without taking my clothes off.

I awoke as usual to 'Action Stations' with a feeling that it had all been a dream. I was in a strange cabin and there was still that sickening smell. The sight of the wardroom dispelled any dream, where the side wall had once been was strung a long green tarpaulin and the splintered remains of a door. Breakfast was available, although everyone seemed to be speaking in hushed tones and it was difficult to stop one's eye wandering to the spots of blood on the remaining walls although a remarkable cleaning up had somehow been achieved through the night. All six aircrew in the wardroom had been killed including my cabin-mate 'Willy' Protheroe and 'Boy' Cunliffe-Owen. There were many other missing faces. Of those of our fighters still airborne when we were put out of action we learnt that Brian Fiddes had been shot down by our own flak, one of the Martlets had ditched short of fuel (both pilots being picked up by destroyers), whilst the remainder had landed safely on *Victorious*.

Jack and I went up onto the flight deck to get away from the smell. It was another beautiful summer's day and from a quick glance all seemed to be just as usual apart from a lack of aircraft. It was only the strange appearance of the for'd lift which claimed the eye: the huge structure had been blown up two feet above deck level, and bent in the middle so that it had a pitched roof appearance. Ahead of it on the starboard side we bent down to examine the round hole the bomb had clearly punched through three inches of armoured deck, its edge turned down with a smooth radius. The adjacent A1 and A2 4.5 inch gun turrets were blackened and the tilting of one told of the destruction below. It was here that most of the ship's casualties had occurred when the bomb exploded at the base of the turret manned by the Marines. It was here too that our Sub Lt Brooks won his D.S.C. trying to rescue the gun crews. Walking back to the stern we found the aft lift jammed in the up position with a large jagged hole behind it penetrating down to the officer's flats. My Vickers gun was drooping pathetically on its makeshift mounting. I carried it down to the lower hanger where our Albacores rested unblooded and undamaged.

We suffered 44 men killed and 59 wounded.

Later that morning all the ship's company, apart from those on duty, attended the burial at sea which took place on the port side for'd of the island. By the end of the service and with the playing of the 'Last Post' I could hardly swallow for the lump in my throat. The words 'Burial at Sea' were just words until this moment, the reality was harrowing. I was only a few feet away from the incongruous wooden chute canted down over the side. The first few white canvas covered parcels, Willy's no bigger than a small case, slid down the bleached wood to disappear with a distant splash. On and on until I could no longer see for tears. All that was left of shy, gentle Willy was a pipe and a few photographs in my album.

Our passage westward was uneventful and on 14 August the unmistakeable profile of the Rock lay ahead. Rounding the headland we entered the bay with the Marine band playing and the ships' company fallen in around the for'd lift to fool the prying eyes on the Spanish mainland. Attached to the inboard side of the island was a smartly painted white board displaying the number of enemy aircraft we had destroyed. As in most aerial battles the figure of 38 was undoubtedly an exaggeration but I believe not wildly so. 880 Squadron lost four and 800 Squadron two Hurricanes in combat while 806 lost only the one Martlet.

Indom went into dock for repairs. The underwater damage from the near miss just aft of where I had been crouching was much worse than I had imagined, a hole forty feet long had been opened up below the waterline, so the damage control parties must have done a very good job to correct our list in only twenty minutes. The destroyer *Ithuriel* was in dock close by, displaying the considerable damage inflicted on her once shapely bows when she rammed that Italian submarine.

Life on board returned to a subdued normality, the smell of battle had thankfully gone and all my clothes were safe in Trevor's cabin. We disported ourselves ashore in the narrow, crowded streets of Gibraltar, with all its many bars, so used to entertaining the world's seafarers. There was Flamenco dancing in a small, grotty upstairs room or the more appealing cellar bar of the Bristol Hotel where we drank a prodigious amount of Tio Pepe. I discovered that the destroyer *Lightning* was lying alongside not far from *Indom* and I arranged for her officers to come on board for drinks during which I let slip that it was my twenty second birthday the following Saturday and as a result Jack and I were asked to join them for dinner. Fortunately Gib's laundry had done wonders with my kit and I was piped on board *Lightning* in well pressed whites. Dinner was excellent and was followed by a long session of 'liars dice' involving the consumption of an enormous quantity of beer and some difficulty in navigating back to *Indom* after midnight. Climbing into my safari bed it began to complete slow rolls when I put my head down so I had to stagger to the nearest bathroom and put my head under the cold tap.

At the time most of us appreciated little of the scale and significance of Operation 'Pedestal'; it was enough to be alive and going home. We were not to know that we had witnessed the greatest battle fought by FAA fighter aircraft throughout the war and the birth of the concept of a carrier force being primarily used for air defence. As a carrier operation there is no doubt of its success: up until the time the main naval force turned back westward on 12 August, no merchant ship had been sunk, in spite of attacks by over 200 Axis bombers escorted by some 100 high performance land-based fighters.

We knew little at the time of the fate of the convoy after we left them bereft of air cover. As is well known, only five of the fourteen merchant ships, including the vital oil tanker *Ohio,* reached Malta after enduring continuous attack from aircraft, torpedo boats and submarines. These started late in the evening of the 12th and continued throughout the following day, during which air cover was attempted by Spitfires and Beaufighters from Malta. These aircraft had great difficulty in locating the convoy and in operating effectively without the radar control and fighter direction which had been planned to be carried out by the specially equipped heavy cruiser *Nigeria,* so badly damaged in a submarine attack late in the evening of the 12th that she was forced to return to Gibraltar. The anti-aircraft cruiser *Cairo* was sunk by the same submarine and proved a great loss to the protection of the convoy on the last lap. The heavy cruiser *Manchester* was sunk by Italian torpedo boats.

Was it worth all the loss of ships and men? The answer surely must be that Malta did not fall to the Axis and continued to play a vital role in throttling the supply line to their forces in North Africa and contributed to their defeat the following spring.

Chapter 11
Entr'acte

We set sail for home on 24 August, patched up and able to maintain over 20 knots.

Back again in an unfamiliar crumpled blue uniform and back again in the after tiller flat. Plenty of newspapers taken on at Gib enabled us to catch up on Jane's stripping escapades in the *Daily Mirror* — what could be more important? No flying. We had to rely on our speed and destroyer escort to avoid any lurking submarine. The ship's carpenters had been busy erecting a wooden ramp leading up to the for'd lift which was still sticking up above deck level. The aft lift was now working and as we sailed up the Irish Channel through almost forgotten showers of rain, blustery winds brought a smell of salty sea quite different to that of tropical oceans. We prepared to fly our Albacores ashore which meant packing in various crates of sherry and enough of our clothes to survive until the ship docked at Liverpool.

We flew off on the morning of 27 August, 1942. If there were any qualms expressed about the wooden ramp they were mostly for dramatic effect; with a strong wind over the deck I remember that 4C passed the island level with Cdr (F)s position. I looked back and down for the last time on the great ship which had been my home and life for eleven months during which we had sailed over 90,000 miles and traversed all but the Pacific ocean.

The lush green patchwork land slid below as we crossed Scotland on our way to the Naval Air Station at Crail, lying on the coast at the east tip of Fife, and famous for its golf course and good food. We had come so far and seen so much that, as our wheels thumped down on the runway and we rumbled round the perimeter track, it was difficult to believe that this really was home. Twelve Albacores lined up in a neat line and grinning faces emerged, bronzed, older, but still innocent.

To those stationed at HMS *Jackdaw* we were just another squadron of Albacores and the best we could do after imbibing vast quantities of ale was to swing any hanging lamp and shout 'Get some sea time in!' As though anybody cared.

The Mess 'phone booth worked overtime as we all announced our arrival to those at home. While away my parents had moved from Heddon-on-the-Wall to Gosforth, a suburb of Newcastle-upon-Tyne, after finding wartime commuting somewhat difficult. It was after midnight when I arrived at Newcastle Central station accompanied by George Marley, another 'Geordie' 831 observer. It was too late for him to get to his home so he stayed the night with my family.

I had no sooner poured forth my travellers' tales to a family that had had enough of the previous war, and too much of the current one, than my mother took concern for my future — a future I was quite happy to put aside for the moment and from what I had seen so far it seemed somewhat precarious, even for immortals such as me. But matchmaking was more on mother's mind.

'There's a nice girl two doors away at Number 36,' she announced, 'Go and ask her to go out to the ballet with you.' In spite of being starved of female company all these many months, I was in no mood to plunge into the unknown and said so, but there was no stopping my mum on this or any other matter and she proceeded to make the assignation on her own. So I was faced with a *fait accompli.*

As far as I was concerned it was 'love at first sight', it took my future wife a few more days to cotton on to the idea as she was already bespoken to a captain in the Tank Corps and her first love, a naval officer, had been killed at Narvik back in 1940.

The programme for the Ballet at the Theatre Royal on this 3 September was: *The Gods Go A-Begging* (Handel), *Hamlet* (Tchaikowsky), *Facade* (Walton),with as an exciting list of dancers as you could imagine — Beryl Gray, Robert Helpmann, Margot Fonteyn and Moira Shearer — early days for all of them and I doubt that I had the sophistication to appreciate them, my mind being more on the gorgeous girl sitting next to me. She was bored stiff. In my usual insensitive way I had omitted to enquire whether she liked ballet. (She only likes those in which the girls wear a tutu.) Ten days passed during which I suffered the quickened pulse and the fever which seems to attend the birth of love. And nights with the ache of unrelieved passion mixed with a nagging doubt about whether my intense feelings were reciprocated. I was due to set off back to Crail the following evening and we were back again at the Theatre Royal to see Patrick Hamilton's *The Duke in Darkness,* a particularly grim affair with an all male cast including Leslie Banks and Michael Redgrave whose fate was to be blinded by a red hot poker. My choice of ballet and Grand Guignol seems in retrospect, more than a little eccentric, and no one could have been more surprised when, later that evening, I popped the question and she said yes. I had not planned to do so, but war breeds its own sense of urgency and in the autumn of 1942 there was no end in sight. Life might well be very short and for me it very nearly was in the coming months.

There was no question of asking her parents for the hand of their daughter as they were spending some days in London; my parents expressed mild surprise and no doubt my father wondered how I intended to support a wife — the thought naturally had never crossed my mind — but they seemed cheerful about it. The following day, my last, saw the buying of the ring and the fixing of the wedding date for 12 December, there was to be no hanging about — or so we thought — but Their Lordships had other ideas.

The overnight train back to Crail via Edinburgh had no heating and it was too cold to sleep, so a dawn arrival at a bleak Crail station found me in a miserable state, cheered up somewhat by being met by a Wren driver. Jack Fisher was about to depart for his leave and I was bursting with my news. 'You must be mad!' was all I got out of him before he left. Mine was not the only tale of romance to be told over many a jar of Scottish ale. 'Cappy' Green had made three attempts to elope with his intended bride. She was over 21 but he hadn't been able to breach the defences her father was putting up; there was much enjoyment in drawing up elaborate schemes to aid and abet his plans but I can't remember whether he was successful. We flew the odd Navex but, as ever, we were told nothing about our future. There were rumours of re-equipping with a new plane called the Barracuda, but more exciting as far as I was concerned was the news that observers were going to be permitted to wear 'wings' on their sleeve, and rather elegant they turned out to be. The local customs officer turned up and relieved me of nineteen shillings in respect of the case of La Ina sherry I had brought back from Gibraltar — I wasn't too pleased about it as having given it to my parents I didn't get the chance to appreciate it.

Much against the wishes of both our parents, my gorgeous girl came up to Edinburgh for the last weekend in September and we stayed at the Carlton Hotel — in separate rooms. Although the young of today will find it difficult to believe, sleeping together was not even discussed. It seemed enough just to be together.

Crail is a cold place, perched right on the sea's edge where Fife thrusts out into the North Sea. It seemed particularly cold that October. Jack came back from leave and took me up in a dual-control Swordfish. His efforts to teach me to make a landing approach into a remote Fife farmer's field were not crowned with much success. I don't think I am a very co-ordinated person and, if they did little else right, Their Lordships were wise to put me in the back seat. It cured me of any romantic dreams I might have had and left me with an even greater respect for the skills of the guy up front. Even more so when I think how young we all were.

Out of the blue the CO called me to his office and handed me a signal which blandly stated that I was to proceed to the RAF Station, West

Raynham on 26 October and report to the Commanding Officer of 18 Squadron. A quick search around the map established that it was in Norfolk some fifteen miles east of King's Lynn. It seemed a bit odd, but no explanations were forthcoming.

'You'd better pack your things and get yourself off on some more leave while you have the chance,' said my CO.

With a hangover from the night's farewell binge it was with very mixed feelings that I set off the following morning, exactly one year since I had scrambled up the gangway into *Indom* for the first time. An operational squadron was a close knit family and we trusted our lives to each other, so I wasn't looking forward to having to fly with another pilot, and I had even grown an affection for the Albacore. There seemed no way of finding out what I would be flying in this new squadron. But on the other hand I was on my way to spend a whole week with the gorgeous girl so I thought to Hell with the war, and planes, and everything.

High on the list of priorities was the purchase of a set of 'O' Wings which were expertly sewn on by the beloved. I also got a loose pair with a pin on the back, although I did not expect to have much use for them, but it was not the way it turned out, and it became a much cherished survivor, being the only item of uniform I still possess.

My future-in-laws seemed surprisingly acquiescent to the prospect of handing their daughter over to me. With no prospects financial or otherwise I must have appeared far from ideal. I had a brief formal 'round the table' with her father and it was a toss up as to who was the most embarrassed. During this happy spell of leave I managed to avoid all high brow entertainments and our sole excursion was to the film *Dangerous Moonlight,* memorable for Richard Adinsell's *Moonlight Sonata* which was to haunt me through the dangerous months to come.

After I left, 831 reformed with Lt Cdr Andrew Leatham as CO. A lot of the original squadron got draft chits, and they worked up the new boys at Crail before going to Lee-on-Solent in December to give their Albacores away and become the first Barracuda squadron. A flap developed and 831 got its Albacores out of mothballs and flew to Hatston — leaving some other poor suckers to kill themselves on the underpowered Barracuda I.

Chapter 12
Neither Fish nor Fowl

Partings amidst the steam and acrid smells of a railway station had become part of wartime life. There was always the vast accumulation of kit requiring an extravagant amount of tipping to get it stowed in the guard's van, the search for a seat, and then the final anguish of the last kiss.

The long journey to West Raynham is a complete blank in my memory. I presume I travelled via Peterborough and King's Lynn to finally arrive late afternoon at one of those classic pre-war RAF stations with lofty hangars and comfortable quarters. But what on earth was I doing here amongst all these light blue uniforms? Arriving at the Mess it soon became clear that I was not expected and the CO of 18 Squadron was off station. Those members of the squadron to whom I was introduced viewed me with curiosity and some alarm, assuming that I might herald much dreaded anti-shipping operations. The squadron had only the previous month been re-equipped with Blenheim Mk V bombers — alternatively designated the Bisley — after having operated Blenheim Mk IVs since May, 1939. An old established squadron with a long tradition and considerable recent success in night intruder raids on enemy airfields.

It was quite late in the day when at last I shook the hand of Wing Cdr Hugh Malcolm who was not at all my preconceived idea of an RAF CO. A tall, quietly spoken man of somewhat donnish appearance, a slender figure with artistic hands and the face of an ascetic. One's eye was inevitably drawn to his forehead which had a broad depression all the way above his eyebrows, the result of a prang in a Westland Lysander in May 1939, in which the plane had stalled at low level and dived straight into the ground. He was lucky to survive with a fractured skull and I found it hard to believe that he had been flying on operations since the earliest days of the war and had reached the venerable age of 25 years.

Although he had been advised of my joining his squadron he seemed to be as surprised as myself at the posting. Looking back, I suspect that it was the stringent security imposed on the forthcoming major operation which forced him to keep me, and all the other aircrew, in the dark. They dubbed me 'The Nautic' and hinted at death and glory daylight attacks on enemy shipping. I knew exactly what they meant; I had so recently been on the receiving end of just such attacks.

During the next few days I began to get to know many of the squadron's aircrew and was surprised to find how much older they were than their equivalents in the FAA, with a high percentage of regular officers. It was a large squadron too, with eighteen aircraft and two Flight Commanders, Squadron Leaders Eyton-Williams and Tucker. A Flight Lieutenant Hugo Dent was tasked with keeping a fatherly eye on me. It was soon clear that I was not to form part of any aircraft crew or take part in any of the current flying exercises, which mainly involved fuel consumption checks on their new aircraft. It even took some persuading before I was taken up for my first flight in a Bisley.

One always feels ill at ease climbing into an unfamiliar aircraft, where to put one's feet, what to hold on to, what to avoid, where to stow one's parachute, where to plug in the intercom — too many ways to put up a 'black' in front of my pilot who was no less than Squadron Leader Eyton-Williams, always referred to as Eyton-Bill. Compared with an Albacore, this twin-engined monoplane looked impressive but was in fact equally underpowered and already obsolescent. I followed Eyton-Bill up the port wing root and lowered myself down through the sliding hatch beside him before squeezing forward into the nose compartment past the periscope pillar arrangement which controlled the movement of the twin rear firing Browning guns mounted below the fuselage in a chin blister. You sat with your feet in an extension of this blister facing to starboard in front of a chart table. To use the bomb sight you had to twist around to the left and view the target through a single, sharply raked window. I was not at all sure that I remembered how to use a bomb sight.

Eyton-Bill called to me to come up and sit beside him for the take-off on a little round seat rather like a bar stool. It was a new and exciting experience to watch an experienced pilot's hands playing a well learnt tune on a console of switches and levers. Both Mercury 25 engines came to noisy life with a cloud of exhaust smoke, cooling gills opened wide into a flared skirt. The rev counters flickered as the magnetos were checked and then it was 'chocks away' as we swung out of the dispersal and made our way to the end of the runway where the engines were run up to full speed, the plane shuddering and straining against the brakes. With flaps selected at fifteen degrees and plus nine engine boost we accelerated down the runway. I remember the acrid oily smell which percolated from the engines at full power, a smell that was to trigger a sense of unease in the weeks to come.

With no bomb load we were airborne in half the length of the runway, then wheels up, flaps up, cooling gills closed, propellers at coarse pitch, we climbed over the flat, featureless Norfolk countryside. I climbed back clumsily into my front 'office'. The autumn sun shone through the expanse of perspex overhead and a green panorama swept below the bomb aiming window — for the first time I was the man 'up front' and it was invigorating. Norfolk was then a chequer-board of airfields and I hoped that Eyton-Bill was not expecting anything in the way of navigation from me. I elected to stay 'up front' for the landing. Unlike the Albacore on the approach, with its mildly skittish response to wind gusts, the Bisley seemed to wallow through the air as though mounted on a ball located somewhere behind me and the close approach to the runway seemed more alarming than my first landing on *Indom*. Taxiing back we passed one or two of the first North American B25 Mitchell bombers to be delivered to the RAF: how different my story might have been had it been our good fortune to be equipped with these fine planes.

A few days later it was announced that all squadron personnel were to draw khaki battle dress and pack up all non essential kit to be sent home. Out came my khaki cap cover, epaulettes, brown shoes and my spanking new pin-on wings. The Delphic oracle spoke of India or Egypt so I 'phoned the gorgeous girl to tell her that a December wedding looked a bit dodgy as we were standing by to leave for 'places unknown' at short notice. Late afternoon on 29 October, Hugo Dent and I, together with all the squadron's ground crew, clambered into a fleet of trucks to be taken to Kings Lynn station where we were packed into a special train which departed into the night for an unknown destination. It wandered painfully slowly in a generally northerly direction, stopping briefly for us to grab a bun and cup of tea on some almost deserted platform, and arriving the next day on the dockside at Glasgow where we embarked on the *Arundel Castle,* one of those very graceful Union Castle liners which graced the Solent, plying between Southampton and South Africa before the advent of the airliner. Hundreds of soldiers streamed up the gangways, a regimental group of the 6th Armoured Division and men of a Parachute Brigade. I was allocated a midships cabin shared with Hugo, a thoughtful, meticulous fellow, who seemed older than his thirty three years but proved a good companion. I dashed off a letter to the gorgeous girl before we left, but she never received it or any of the others I wrote while at sea. Security was particularly tight and events proved it to have been effective.

We sailed on 1 November 1942, and found ourselves part of a large convoy of equally famous liners with a destroyer escort. Apart from simple observation that we were sailing around the northern tip of Ireland and heading out into the Atlantic there was still only rumour about our destination. Although the sea was unusually calm, sea sickness took it's toll of most aboard, and it became impossible to avoid its unpleasantness with all the ship's decks and spaces crammed with humanity. Hugo was laid low. For the first few days I sat almost alone in the glory of the first class dining room enjoying delightful meals in the company of Frank Capra, the American film director; a taciturn man with no sense of humour and quite unlike any American I have ever met. It seemed that he had been assigned to make a film record of whatever it was we were engaged upon. The ship was 'dry' and it was an unpleasant surprise to find how little there was to occupy the day without a session around a bar. My only assigned duty was to take a watch on the bridge as a lookout for enemy aircraft. Occasionally the shadowy grey and white bulk of a Sunderland flying boat appeared out of the clouds but there was fortunately no sign of the long range Focke-Wulf Condor. From recent experience I was expecting a U-boat attack — all these liners packed full of troops and their equipment must have represented many times the value of our Malta convoy — but steadily and peacefully we moved on south. Recently I discovered that we had been lucky, a northbound convoy had drawn off the submarines. When it got warmer we sat out on the deck and watched the waves, the clouds, the ships and each other. In the evenings there was nothing else to do but read a book from the ship's library, although most played cards. I hate cards. Rather out of character I became friendly with the RC padre of the Parachute Brigade and then discovered that another of their officers, 'Tim' Beavers, had been at prep school with me. Both were larger than life characters and we were destined to meet again in the most unlikely circumstances.

It was not until Sunday, 8 November that the Senior Army Commander on board announced on the Tannoy that British and American forces had landed in North Africa at Casablanca, Oran and Algiers under the command of the American General Eisenhower. We were part of the follow up supporting force for 'Operation Torch' and scheduled to disembark at Algiers as soon as it was captured. At that time we were just east of the Azores and about to alter course eastwards to pass through the Straits of Gibraltar. My God, I thought, not all that again. At least we knew now where we were going, and there was much relief that it was not to the Far East. I still could not guess what my part was likely to be in this Hollywood spectacular, directed, no doubt, by Frank Capra, who was to be seen on occasion on the upper decks with a cine camera but remained inscrutable at the dining table.

We sailed through the Straits on the night of 10/11th and, although it was autumn, it was still warm and the sky was that special blue, just as it had been exactly three months ago. But where were the aircraft carriers? It was announced that Algiers had been captured and everyone was in high spirits in spite of the lack of the liquid type. Hugo and I wondered what plans there were to fly out our Bisleys. It would be a very long flight for them without navigation aids, and there seemed no way to avoid crossing the Pyrenees.

I was not so cheerful as the rest and kept a wary eye open for Ju 88s knowing that our entry into the Mediterranean would have been reported, but all I saw was the regular appearance of an RAF Hudson on A/S patrol.

Like Cassandra I warned all my circle of new found chums of the doom and destruction which would descend upon us on the morrow, remembering *Eagle* rolling over so quickly and the onslaught of Ju 88s, so I looked a bit of a fool when we sailed peacefully into the blue bay of Algiers with its cream coloured buildings rising terrace by terrace in the autumn sunshine.

What we did not know was that several squadrons of RAF Hurricanes and Spitfires were already operating from Maison Blanche airfield having flown in with long range tanks from Gibraltar soon after Algiers was captured. The Germans had sent waves of Ju 88s to attack the mass of shipping in Algiers bay during the first two days never expecting to be met by fighters. So few of them survived the 300 mile trip back to Sardinia that, by the time we arrived, they had retired to lick their wounds, having failed to damage a single allied ship.

We came alongside the docks in the afternoon and in surprisingly quick time all the troops were mustered in groups on the quayside with a mass of kit piled up beside them and the air buzzing with banter. 18 Squadron was split into two squads, Hugo with one and myself with the other and off we marched east along the sea front following the preceding columns and without the slightest idea where we were going. The local inhabitants of this very French city watched our passing impassively. After two miles we turned into the gates of a rather bleak park, the Jardin d'Essai, and joined the khaki clad throng sitting in groups on the grass beneath tall palm trees. It soon got dark, there was no food or shelter, and we slept fully dressed in the open — I used my gas mask for a pillow and my greatcoat for a blanket. It rained during the night and there were sporadic bursts of rifle fire in the distance — there was no doubt that our Mediterranean cruise was over.

In the morning we shivered until the sun rose. Some boxes of 'Compo' rations had arrived. This new solution to the difficult problem of feeding a mobile army in the field was used for the first time in this operation. It comprised a series of wooden boxes holding enough to give fourteen men three meals for one day. All the food was tinned, even the tea, sugar and milk mixture (it was hard luck if you preferred it without sugar). Five cigarettes each were included, together with sweets, salt, matches, chocolate and toilet paper. The boxes frequently got muddled up resulting in a diet of nothing but spam, or nothing but sausages, with a particular abundance of toilet paper (and nowhere to use it).

The whole day was spent in a boy scout atmosphere with no one allowed out of the park. We spent another chilly night out in the open and it rained again. It was a dishevelled bunch that clambered into open trucks the next morning and after clearing the outskirts of Algiers, headed south west over a flat green plain with the Atlas mountains rising up some ten miles away on our left. I had thought that North Africa was a sandy desert on which the sun shone all the time, in fact it is much more like the south coast of France. The sun was certainly shining and the swirling dust had the gritty feel of sand.

Blida aerodrome proved to be our destination, famous in the annals of the Fleet Air Arm for being captured single handed by Lt Barry Nation RN on 8 November when flying a Martlet of 882 Squadron from *Victorious*; he spotted a number of gentlemen waving white flags and landed, leaving the rest of his section in the air to cover him, in case of misunderstandings. He accepted the surrender of the aerodrome from the French Commandant and later handed it over to a section of Commandos before flying back to the carrier.

It was a reasonably well provided French colonial air force base with a single runway, hangars and living accommodation.

By the time we arrived on 14 November, the French personnel had evacuated it and our aircrew and Bisleys were already in occupation. I have vivid memories of my first lunch in the Mess with all the aircrew at one long table served by French stewards. The unfamiliar smell turned out to be that of garlic, but after Compo rations the food seemed cordon bleu. There were carafes of red wine in abundance but no water. Unaccustomed to wine I drank far too much while listening to tales told by those who had flown the Bisleys out from England.

All eighteen aircraft had been fitted with long range tanks in their bomb bays and flown from West Raynham down to Portreath in Cornwall. At 0130, on 11 November, they began taking off for a direct flight to Blida, flying singly on a route which took them over the Brest peninsula, across the Bay of Biscay, over the Pyrenees and finally across the Mediterranean; 1100 miles with no navigation aids and nowhere friendly to put down if in trouble. It is hardly surprising that all did not reach their destination in Algeria. P/O Knickerbocker crashed on take-off, but reached Blida on 27 November after his aircraft was repaired. One aircraft returned with a fuel leak and two were delayed with aircraft problems. Of the fourteen which set off on the $8^{1}/_{2}$ hour flight only eleven reached Blida after having a rough time overflying the snow capped Pyrenees which reach up as high as 11,000 feet.

P/O Holloway and his crew were first to arrive. Sq/Ldr Eyton-Williams ran short of fuel and crash landed ten miles from Blida. Sq/Ldr Tucker got off course and landed safely at Oran and had only just arrived at Blida. Sgt Rounding's aircraft was missing but much later it was learnt that he had force landed in Spain and he and his crew returned to England. After his fuel leak was cured Flt/Lt Breakey took off some hours after the other and arrived safely. The remaining two aircraft arrived on the 13th via Gibraltar so by the time Hugo and I arrived at Blida, the squadron had fifteen aircraft available — a remarkable achievement.

Even more impressive was the fact that on the very day they arrived at Blida the aircrew, after a brief rest and assisted by the RAF Servicing Commando which had landed with the invasion force, removed the two 50-gallon long range fuel tanks from the bomb bays and loaded up six aircraft with bombs for an attack on El Aouina airfield at Tunis that same night. Four managed to get airborne around 0220 but two were forced to turn back. The other two, piloted by P/Os Holloway and Hill reached the target 400 miles distant. Hill's bombs failed to release leaving 'Ted' Holloway to have the honour of dropping the squadron's first bombs in the Tunisian campaign. Our fate was soon to be linked.

I found that we were all sleeping in tents on the airfield. The French had left the barrack accommodation in such a disgusting state that it was not possible to use until it had been thoroughly cleaned up. I shall never forget visiting their loos, a tiled room with holes in the floor with positions for the feet either side, but the whole place deep in excreta and the stench unbelievable. The Army kindly built some Elsan type latrines with somewhat crude wooden seats but, by comparison, these were paradise.

Preparations were in hand for a night raid on Sidi Ahmed aerodrome at Bizerta and after a lot of running around I eventually located Wing Cdr Malcolm in the Ops Room tent where I diffidently approached him and asked when I would be required to fly. 'Only when we are called up to attack enemy shipping — and, as far as I can see, we aren't likely to be doing that the way things are,' was his brief reply. All this way for nothing — I was sick at heart as well as from the lunch-time wine. (Wine still does not agree with me.)

During the evening I found out that we were part of 326 Wing comprising 18, 13, 114, and 614 Squadrons all equipped with Bisleys and commanded by Group Captain L. F. Sinclair. The other squadrons had not yet arrived but 114 was due to fly in from Gibraltar the next day. It all sounded mighty impressive and it would have been had we been equipped with Bostons or Mitchells.

I wrote a brief letter to the gorgeous girl whose photo was propped up on my wash stand — she never received it.

I was in the depths of sleep when five of the squadron's aircraft took off just after midnight for the long haul to Bizerta. The weather was not very good and two failed to locate the target and had to bring their bombs back. The other three reported dropping theirs on the airfield. I was still asleep when they returned about 0630. The general feeling expressed around the breakfast table was that it was a helluva a long way to go to drop four 250 lb bombs on an airfield on which no worthwhile target was likely to be identifiable on a dark night. For some unknown reason the RAF did not seem to use flares as we would have done in an Albacore (carrying the same bomb load).

The following day, 15 November, Hugo was preparing to set off with Eyton-Bill on the first daylight raid; a low level attack on Bizerta airfield where it was rumoured the Luftwaffe were flying in scores of aircraft and troops to reinforce Tunisia. I gave him a hand with the maps (he was the squadron's navigation officer) and ran messages. The operation seemed a very risky affair with no fighter cover but they set off at mid-day with Hugh Malcolm leading six aircraft; one was late in taking off and being unable to catch up with the formation he turned back. Later, Eyton-Bill returned with an engine oil leak. Using cloud cover the remaining four achieved complete surprise with little flak and no fighters and dropped their bombs on the hangars at Sidi Ahmed while their rear gunners raked the Ju 88s lined up on the airfield. They arrived back at sunset.

Apart from myself there was no relaxing, especially for the ground crews who were working around the clock with very limited facilities. That same night another six of the squadron's aircraft took off around 0130 for a further attack on Sidi Ahmed airfield.

Once more I retired to my tent, a depressed and frustrated Achilles, with even a gnawing fear about my capability to take my place amongst such experienced aircrew should it ever be required. I was awakened by the noise of the returning aircraft, their propellers sawing the air in fine pitch. I only counted five before going for breakfast — always the best meal of the day. Weary crews came in later. Two had failed to find the target in deteriorating weather and only two managed to drop their bombs but were not very happy with the result due to poor visibility. It was Sgt Eccleston who was missing and he and his crew arrived back safely by train later in the day having bombed the target but, getting lost on their way back, they had overshot Blida and crash landed when they ran out of fuel.

Tramping around the airfield's rough and sometimes muddy roads had worn out the thin soled brown shoes I had bought from Mr Bata in Aden. The RAF supplied me with a pair of black boots and gaiters and they felt like lead weights. Together with all the aircrew I was issued with a tin hat and a .38 calibre revolver, the latter seemed rather dashing at the time but was soon to prove far from a blessing. I never found out why we were given them.

With the arrival of twelve Bisleys of 614 Squadron there were no operations scheduled for our squadron on the 16th so I took the opportunity to badger the CO about my taking part in some flying. He said he was sorry but all the aircraft were fully crewed but I could attend briefings and de-briefings if I wanted to.

Having no contact with the outer world we knew nothing of the progress of the ground fighting. General Kenneth Anderson was in command of what was called the 1st Army. It was not really an army, not even an army corps, nor even a division in these early days; consisting of just two infantry brigades, a parachute brigade and one tank regiment. In fact on this very day they had made their first contact with German ground troops in the north of Tunisia. Our paratroops had captured the important airfield at Bone, close to the border between Algeria and Tunisia, and two squadrons of Spitfire Vs had been flown in. But the German build-up across the short sea route from Sicily had been far more rapid than could be matched by the Allies with 350 miles of supply lines over narrow mountainous roads back to Algiers. The German air force soon achieved air superiority over the battlefield from a large number of well established airfields around Tunis and Bizerta. This was the reason for all the frantic effort being made by our Bisleys and in particular the operation which took place on the following day, 17 November, in which Malcolm led twelve aircraft on the second daylight raid on the airfield at Bizerta.

I attended the briefing in the large tent on the airfield. There was to be no fighter cover, the squadron was to proceed in two boxes of six aircraft to the southern end of Bizerta lake using as much cloud cover as possible, then drop down to 800 feet before sweeping around the adjacent hill, hoping to avoid detection before forming up into line abreast to cross the seven mile width of the lake at 150 feet. Bombs were fitted with 15-second delay fuses and, after dropping, the formation was to break up, enter cloud if possible, and return to base individually. The operation would be called off if there was insufficient cloud cover.

It seemed a very dodgy enterprise to me but Malcolm seemed full of enthusiasm. Lacking both experience and imagination I yearned to be going with them as I watched them climb up into the hazy sky, the Tail End Charlies struggling to catch up with the formation. It was time for lunch and the place seemed empty — spam again. I roamed around the airfield all afternoon feeling uneasy until around 1630 I saw six Bisleys in the circuit. Malcolm was the first to land. Eyton-Bill arrived later with his hydraulics shot away and made a good belly landing on the grass. I went out in one of the Jeeps and helped his navigator, Hugo Dent, extract his gear and got the first hairy account of the affair. They had run out of cloud cover twenty miles from the target but the CO had decided to press on regardless. Rounding the hill there had been a lot of turbulence and he saw two of the Bisleys collide before they made their line abreast approach across the lake. As they crossed the airfield boundary a Junkers Ju 52 transport and two Bf 109 fighters were making their approach to land. The rear gunners shot down the Ju 52 and also fired at the large number of aircraft parked on the airfield. The two Bf 109s had retracted their wheels and swung round to attack them after they had dropped their bombs. It was while trying to get away northwards that his aircraft had been hit.

Five Bisleys failed to return and at the de-briefing it wasn't clear what had happened to four of them. The CO described in graphic detail how his two 500lb bombs had rolled into one of the hangars and the rear gunners had all seen a number of bombs burst amongst the hangars and sheds, the situation being very confused as they split up in all directions after leaving the target. At least one of the Bf 109s was shot down.

After dropping his bombs 'Ted' Holloway gave his engines plus nine boost pressure for twenty minutes instead of the authorised maximum of three minutes and after taking evasive action low down on the deck he emerged unscathed close to Sq/Ldr Tucker who was being chased by Bf 109s and a Bf 110. He had already had his rudder shot away by light flak on the run-in to the target but had managed to drop his bombs. When they both reached the coast the enemy fighters broke off, short of ammunition or fuel. Holloway then escorted Tucker as he struggled back along the coast with one engine losing power and the aircraft difficult to control. He was eventually forced to attempt a landing at the small airfield at Djidjelli during which he over-ran and the aircraft turned up on its nose. All escaped unhurt and returned the next day.

It was never clear how many enemy fighters were involved, but later reports confirmed that two of the missing Bisleys had been shot down by Bf 109s, the crew of one being taken prisoner after crashing near the target. The crews of both the aircraft which collided were all killed. This considerable loss of men and machines seemed to have little effect on the morale of the squadron and it is only when reviewing the history of Blenheim squadron operations over the first three years of the war that I realise how used they had become to this scale of slaughter when flying unescorted daylight operations. With their small bomb load one can only wonder whether it was really worth it.

During the 17th four Bisleys of 13 Squadron and five more of 614 flew in from Gibraltar and the remainder flew in the next day. Our squadron had only four aircraft serviceable and there were no operations on the 18th. Seven aircraft of 614 Squadron made a night attack on Bizerta harbour and airfield to keep up the pressure.

With the influx of aircrew we moved out of our tents into brick built huts with three to a room, still on camp beds but with the luxury of a shower. On the 19th we were given a formal day off and a party of us walked into Blida town for lunch. On the way we passed a number of Arabs riding on mules with their veiled wives walking behind. Their penetrating eyes were glued to our revolvers which it was said they would willingly swop for their wives. We were not inclined to test the theory. We found an excellent small restaurant in the town where we were served enthusiastically with hors-d'oeuvres, enormous omelettes, chicken and steak followed by oranges for dessert. This was a rare treat after Compo rations, and replete with wine and brandy we wove an unsteady course back to the airfield rather pleased with ourselves.

It was back to business again that night. Group Captain Sinclair had decided to lead a combined attack on both the docks and airfield at Bizerta using aircraft from all four squadrons. Nineteen aircraft were detailed to take part. With only four aircraft available our squadron borrowed aircraft from the other three and put up nine crews including the CO. They took off around 0130, one arriving back shortly afterwards with engine vibration. The rest reached the target but three abandoned the attempt to bomb the docks when they ran into cloud and rain. The others arrived over Bizerta to find all the town lights on and the ships in the harbour illuminated. At the de-briefing there were enthusiastic reports of direct hits on both ships and docks. Three aircraft, including Malcolm's, bombed the airfield. This seemed to be the most successful operation so far with no losses.

Group Captain Sinclair never seemed to sleep, attending all briefings and de-briefings. The following morning I was instructed to report to him at his headquarters tent. I was surprised that he knew of my existence and wondered what I had done wrong. He wanted to know if I was prepared to fly in a Beaufighter to make a reconnaissance over the Tunisian ports of Sfax and Gabes where there was a report of the Germans landing troops. I told him that it would be a relief to be doing something at last. The Beaufighters had only just arrived and I got all prepared to make the trip only for it to be cancelled. Was there to be no end to my frustration?

The Germans were now making every effort to reinforce Tunisia by both sea and air, as their North African army was being squeezed between the Eighth Army from the East and the embryo First Army from the West.

A further combined squadron attack on Bizerta's docks was mounted on the night of 23/24 November with eighteen aircraft taking part. Our squadron supplied five crews, borrowing one aircraft from 13 Squadron, but three had to return with engine trouble. Some big explosions were seen in the docks and the operation was judged a success.

Two weeks had passed by and for the first time there were signs of fatigue amongst the aircrew. A number of navigators had fallen by the wayside; Sgt Parker had been injured in a crash landing when an engine cut out on take off; P/O Docherty had gone sick; and P/O John, who crewed with P/O Holloway, had asked to be taken off operations.

And so it came about that Malcolm asked me if I would fly with 'Ted' Holloway. How pleased I was to be given the chance to put my head in the lion's jaw. I celebrated with a good lunch in town and then went out onto the airfield, climbed into one of our Bisleys and sat up front in contemplation.

The following morning Ted and I were briefed to make a special flight along the coast to Bougie to deliver a large bundle of maps to General Anderson. Apparently his troops had advanced into Tunisia beyond those he had available. It is a mystery why we were sent to Bougie as I have since discovered that by then the General had his headquarters near Souk Ahras, fifty miles south on Bone. In any case when we arrived over Bougie we could see no sign of an airfield. There was a rather small field close to the shore but beyond it the ground sloped up steeply. We attempted an approach from the sea but at the last minute Ted decided that it was impossible and put on full power. I watched the ground pass ominously close beneath me until we cleared the top. Unsure what to do next, we decided to fly south to Setif which lies on the Algerian plateau at a height of 4000 feet. The single runway was clear and we made our approach during which I realised that we were being fired on from a gun at the end of the runway. Fortunately their aim was bad and we landed safely to be met by a Jeep containing a quartet of excited Americans who had mistaken us for a Ju 88, a common enough error. With some difficulty Ted got through on the phone to 1st Army HQ and, after being ticked off for breaching security, was told to deliver the maps to the airfield at Bone, 150 miles East along the coast. After a cup of coffee we took off again, dropping steadily down from the barren plateau towards the green, fertile coast. Approaching Bone down a valley between rock-crested ridges, Henry Parsloe, our air gunner, shouted out a warning on the intercom that three Spitfires were making what looked like an attacking run on us. Henry fired the recognition signal and I was relieved to see the Spits formating alongside us. They peeled off as we came into land on the single runway which ran close by the sea. It was a very short runway and we had to brake hard to avoid running into a hardcore of rocks at the end which was to be the base for extending it. We had hardly stopped when an Army truck drove up beside us, from which erupted a very irate Group Captain. We popped our heads out of the top hatch.

'What the bloody hell are you doing here? Get that bloody thing off my runway — there's a German air raid due any minute and I can't have you in the way!'

We explained about our maps for the General, and were told to get them into the truck PDQ. With the help of the truck driver and the Group

Captain we turned the Bisley around and pushed it back as far as we could up to the edge of the rocks — there was little wind and Ted was concerned about getting off on the short runway. He ran the engines up to full power with the brakes on before accelerating and lifting off just before we reached the rocks at the other end and banked away over the sea. I was to meet Group Captain Ambrose Appleton once more in a very different place. I don't know whether the General ever got his maps.

It was an uneventful flight back along the coast until we arrived at Blida. When Ted selected 'wheels down', only one went down. He rocked the aircraft as we flew around the circuit but nothing happened so he decided to make a belly landing and selected 'wheels up', whereupon the wheel that was down went up and the one that was up went down. After repeating this once or twice we came in and made an excellent one wheel landing, only slewing round at the last minute when the starboard wing dropped. We ended up flat on our belly with smoke curling up from one of the engines and I lost no time in scrambling out of the hatch. Within seconds the CO arrived in a Jeep to collect us.

I was glad to have this trip under my belt as it gave me the opportunity to become familiar with the navigator's 'office' and to brush up on map reading. I confirmed the effectiveness of marking my ground track plot every six minutes which had got me out of so much trouble over the sea when the pilot suddenly decided to rush off in an unexpected direction.

I was down to take part in my first operation the following day and Hugo gave me a refresher course on bomb-aiming and the use of the bomb release distributor. I finally finished a long day with a few lines to the gorgeous girl, written in bed with the aid of a torch.

It rained during the night and there was mud everywhere the following morning, with the sky clouded right over. I was not alone in being apprehensive when the briefing detailed another daylight raid on the airfield at Bizerta and this was to be a major affair with a total of twenty-seven aircraft taking part drawn from all four squadrons. We were fielding seven crews, two of them having to fly in borrowed aircraft. We were instructed to proceed separately to the target area and only to attack if there was plenty of cloud cover for the run in. Taxying out in Bisley 'N' we got stuck in the mud and were late taking off. We kept just below the clouds along the coast until, approaching Cape Serrat, the cloud around us vanished and we were naked in the sunlight with a stream of Bisleys flying past us in the opposite direction. We pressed on as far as the Cape but with fifty miles still to go and not a cloud in sight we turned back. Much of the way back we were flying blind in cloud and perched up front I had my only experience of total sensory disorientation and was glad I was not driving. We arrived back safely but Sgt Woodfield got lost and had to force land when he ran out of fuel. Not a very spectacular beginning to my operational career but at least we had not got lost.

The next day we moved out of our huts into one of the French barrack blocks with about ten iron beds ranged on either side of a high ceilinged room on the top floor. It looked comfortable until we found that the mattresses were infested with bugs. Group Captain Sinclair moved in with us and, late that evening, a number of us, including the Groupie, were sitting on our beds when P/O Bill Booth lurched through the door at the end of the room in a well sozzled state and proceeded to play the fool with his revolver. It suddenly went off with an ear splitting bang, the door opened and a very white faced officer entered, looked around, looked at the splintered hole in the door, and said 'Bloody Hell! you nearly shot me you stupid bastard !' Not surprisingly Sinclair was not amused and had Bill grounded and confined to quarters. Perhaps the cracks were beginning to show — it was not to be the end of our problems with hand guns and I am surprised we were allowed to keep them — at least mine ended up in better hands the following week. It was some time before we all settled down to get some sleep and there were the bugs to contend with. Did we really need an enemy?

The night of 27/28th was my first and only night operation which was planned to be a wing attack on the airfield at Tunis by nineteen aircraft with six crews from 18 Squadron. We were on our way out to the aircraft at about midnight when a German aircraft dived overhead and dropped a stick of bombs, one of which landed fifty yards ahead of us as we dived for shelter behind one of the huts. One of 18's Bisleys was damaged and was unable to take part but our 'N for Nuts' loomed up out of the night unharmed. Climbing into a darkened aircraft for the first time is a bruising business, the struggle past the gun periscope with the Bigsworth board catching on every protuberance and then fumbling for unfamiliar light switches and a final struggle back to the perch beside the pilot.

It was 0200 when we started rumbling across the rough ground to find the control point at the end of the runway and it was only when we swung round onto it that I saw the faint glimmer from the two lines of lanterns stretching out into the distance. The green light flooded the cockpit for a second, a pause as the engines powered up, and then the dim lights seemed to be shooting towards us finally disappearing below as we climbed up into the darkness. Back again in my front office I could see the faint glow of surf as we passed over the coast east of Algiers. I had decided to proceed well out to sea before turning eastwards and then to cross the coast again at Cape Serrat. I checked our track by dropping a flame float and taking a back bearing on it through the periscope. There was nothing for me to do for the next two hours as we cruised steadily at 150 mph. The noise and vibration of the engines inhibited chat on the intercom. I was happy with my landfall and we turned south-east. Unbeknown to us, far below in the hills and valleys of Tunisia, the First Army was engaged in a bitter struggle with a superior German army. I now badly needed to have a pee and managed to locate the rubber bag and chrome-plated funnel device but had less success in locating my own equipment which, what with the cold and the constriction of a parachute harness, had shrunk somewhat and produced more of a spray than a jet, with very unsatisfactory results.

'Target six minutes — master switch on.'

I reset the bombsight for the umpteenth time. The coastline of the Gulf of Tunis curved away on our left and then with excited relief, almost disbelief, I could see the airfield, 2,000 feet below with the outline of hangars along one side. No need to make a second approach, with a few course corrections I had them in the sights and pulled the rotary bomb switch around. There was a loud thump, more felt than heard, as four 250lb bombs hit the spring loaded doors. I reported 'bombs gone' and gave a course home. I had expected flak and searchlights but there was nothing to disturb the darkness. Henry reported seeing the bombs bursting but not whether they achieved anything. It was 0500 so at least we must have spoilt their sleep. We saw no sign of any other aircraft and the flight back was uneventful but tedious. It was just getting light when we landed at 0750. What a way to spend a night. Two of the squadron's aircraft had been unable to find the target which boosted my ego, only to be deflated when it was pointed out that I had failed to release the four 40 lb bombs we carried.

During the morning P/O Sims and his navigator F/Sgt Litchfield were injured, when he crash landed after an engine had cut out on take off. This was an old problem going back to the early days of Blenheims — a Boston or a Mitchell could climb away on one engine.

Bizerta airfield took another hammering on the night 28/29 November from nineteen aircraft of the Wing with four crews from our squadron taking part. P/O Knickerbocker was forced to return with a locked up aileron but managed to land safely. The other three were quite successful. This was the last operation from Blida but a greater challenge lay ahead.

Chapter 13
Death and Glory

To follow the events that ensued it is necessary to look at what was happening in Tunisia to the mis-named First Army. General Anderson had split his meagre force into two mobile columns, an infantry force in the north and an armoured force thirty miles to the south. By 28 November 1942, his tanks, with parts of the 11th Infantry Brigade, had pushed forward with such energy that they were within fifteen miles of Tunis. But the German build-up across the short sea route from Sicily had been far more rapid than the Allies could match over the hundreds of miles of rudimentary roads and a primitive single line railway all the way from Algiers and they came under heavy attack both on the ground and from the air. Tunisia was well provided with airfields but most of them were in the Tunis and Bizerta area. Our nearest fighters were based at Souk el Arba and Souk el Khemis, seventy miles to the west of Tunis, and too far away to provide continuous fighter cover over the forward troops even if they had had sufficient aircraft. Enjoying air superiority with the Bf 109Gs , the Germans were able to use their Stukas with impunity over the battlefield (although they achieved very little).

The famous German General Rommel, by now squeezed on two fronts, found General Anderson on his rear, as the latter pressed eastwards towards a link up with the 8th Army. The gamble to reach Tunis might have come off had the Germans not been able to land just enough tanks in time. As it was the First Army began to withdraw at this time to form a defensive line along the hills running from Medjez el Bab north to Cape Serrat (see Map 6).

Their call for increased air support led to the decision to move 18 Squadron to an airfield at Canrobert (now known as Oum el Bouaghi) 250 miles to the east, high up on the plateau south of Constantine and well off the beaten track. This gave it some immunity from air attack, being difficult to find and 160 miles behind the front line (see Map 6).

Out of the sixteen of our Bisleys which had arrived at Blida we were now left with only seven, for which we had twelve crews. It was decided to bring the squadron once more up to sixteen aircraft and crews by drawing on the other squadrons in the Wing who provided nine aircraft and four crews.

We packed our kit on Monday, 30 November and loaded it into our aircraft. Several aircraft took a member of the ground crew as passenger as there would be no maintenance crews at Canrobert when we arrived. We were one of the first to get airborne in 'Nuts' and climbed steadily up over the 4,500 feet sandy brown peaks of the Atlas mountains. There was a flash of light and an explosion below and to the left of us which looked ominous and in fact was Sgt Proud's aircraft out of which none survived the impact. When we arrived at Canrobert situated close to a prominent hill which rises from an arid plain 3,000 feet above sea level, there seemed to be no sign of an airfield and, joined by one or two others, we began to circle and finally watched one brave character making a landing approach to a hedge-lined field which looked a very dodgy proposition. But he made it, so down we went and with some heavy braking we made it too and taxied over towards a narrow road alongside a small barn. This was found to be the hangar for a small French light aeroplane of unfamiliar type. Thirteen Bisleys got down safely before darkness fell as it does quite suddenly in Algeria at this time of year. Some cars had just arrived from the village when we heard the unmistakeable sound of a Bisley overhead. It was Hugh Malcolm, who had been held up at Blida completing all the arrangements to move up the ground crews and equipment. And now here he was circling this small dirt landing ground with not a single light to guide him down. With magnificent improvisation cars were driven with their headlights switched on to mark the boundaries and all who could find a torch were sent out to form a line across the field, pointing them skywards. Hugh came thundering in like a black shadow with his landing lights blazing from the port wing. There was a sickening crumpling and tearing noise as the aircraft's undercarriage was torn off crossing a ditch before sliding to a stop on its belly. Hugh and his crew emerged unscathed.

Sgt Eccleston had returned to Blida with a dud engine and flew in the following day.

We were quartered in a French villa, sleeping on mattresses, cheek by jowl, on the mosaic tiled floor of an unfurnished room. There was hardly enough room to undress and I don't recall getting anything to eat or drink, so drink can't be blamed for Knickerbocker shooting himself in the thigh when standing no more than a couple of yards from me. God knows how he came to do it but when my ears had recovered I remember the surprise in his voice when he said 'My God! Look! It's gone in here and come out here!' Fortunately there was not a lot of blood as I am prone to faint at the sight of it. I have no idea what happened to him afterwards but I don't suppose that he was very popular with the Group Captain.

It was freezing cold at dawn on 1 December and when we arrived at the airfield we had to sweep the white frost off the aircraft's wings. With only the one or two ground crew we laboriously refuelled the aircraft ourselves from five gallon cans, piercing them with an aircraft axe. Further ground crew arrived in a US Air Force C47 Dakota and, with everyone's help, bombs were winched up and all thirteen aircraft took off, circled until all were in formation, and set course for Bone. We crossed over the Medjerda mountain range before dropping down into the lush green coastal plain. This was my first experience of being in a formation of Bisleys and there was nothing for me to do but enjoy the view, watch the gentle rise and fall of each aircraft and the flashing of the sun on the gun turrets as the rear gunners swung them. I squeezed myself down into the half kneeling, half sitting position which one had to adopt to fire the pair of rear firing Brownings and swung them about to see whether I could take aim through the periscope on our 'Tail End Charlies'. It left me with a distinct lack of confidence in my being able to use this unwieldy arrangement and I rather hoped that there would be no occasion to use it. I was wrong again. As we had already discovered, the single runway at Bone was a short one, running close to and almost parallel with the sea shore. As we banked steeply over the sea it reminded me of an approach to *Indom*. Safely down and pulling back the top hatch, the balmy, pine scented air filled the cockpit. Spitfire Vs were dispersed around the field, otherwise this lovely part of the world seemed as Aeneas must have once found it. The Germans had found daylight bombing raids on fighter airfields to be a costly business and now only came at night. We could only heartily agree with them.

The bar of the aerodrome cafe was the 'Ops' room and it was here that the CO briefed five crews to attack an enemy column reported to be on the road leading north west from Mateur and approaching the front line near Jefna. Eyton-Bill was to lead with our 'Nuts' as his number two, Wray Eller was to lead on his left with Georges and Armstrong tucked in behind. For the one and only time we were to have twelve Spitfires flying top cover; I never saw them, keeping my eyes well glued to what was going on below, but it felt comforting. We crossed the coast over Tabarca and I could see the fishing boats drawn up on the sand near the causeway which leads out to the old Genoese castle. Ted reminded me to cock my Brownings as we entered the infamous Sedjenane Valley which had all the wildness of the Scottish Highlands and was the scene for the next four months of the most bitter fighting of the whole campaign. Flying at 2,000 feet the rocky tops of the hills reached up to 300 feet below us with the narrow road and single line railway snaking between them. It was impossible to locate the front line and the road seemed deserted (both sides kept off it during daylight). We circled once and then returned to Bone at lunchtime with our bombs. Armstrong in 'R' came in late and reported that he had bombed a truck and troops — it made me wonder whether the policy of wireless silence was worth it.

Operating from 100 miles behind the front line involved a delay of at least an hour before we could respond to an army request for support and it is hardly surprising that our target had moved off the road long before we reached it. This probably accounts for the decision to operate from the fighter airfield at Souk el Arba ('Market at the Crossroads' now known as Jendouba) to which the CO took the other eight Bisleys in the afternoon (see Map 6).

I was sitting on a grass knoll eating a Compo tin of Spam in my fingers — quite revolting — when I saw a Fulmar coming in to land. I dashed off to speak to the RNVR pilot and found that he was on his way from Malta to Gibraltar. I dashed off a brief pencilled note to the gorgeous girl which she received on 10 December, being the first time she had heard from me.

We returned to Canrobert in the afternoon and the boys from Souk el Arba in the evening after a wasted afternoon with no target being given to them. Sgt Eccleston arrived from Blida, bringing our aircraft up to fourteen; but by the morning only ten were serviceable — our few ground crew had worked miracles with no facilities and most of the time in icy darkness. We took off early on 2 December for Souk el Arba. It lies in the green and fertile Mejerda valley and was the base for two squadrons of Spitfires, Nos 72 and 111, whose crews lived in tents pitched amongst olive groves close to the Arab village. The grass field was of comfortable size and we dispersed ourselves on the eastern side. Nearby was an enormous bomb crater, at least fifty yards wide, which we used as our loo, hoping that lightning would not strike the same place twice while we had our trousers down. The CO set up his 'office' out under the sun with a folding table and chair and a mobile radio set nearby with which to contact the Army. The rest of us just sat around on the grass with Sweet Fanny Adams to do.

At 1030 the Army called for an attack on enemy artillery in a cemetery three miles north of Tebourba. The CO detailed Sq/Ldr Tucker to lead six aircraft but one had trouble starting and only five took off. For some reason or other the Spitfire squadrons were unable to provide an escort and it was obviously a high risk operation with the enemy airfield at Djedeida only five miles from the target. However they all bombed successfully without interception and returned to Canrobert, leaving us uneasy about their fate.

It was our turn next and, with Hugh Malcolm leading, four of us took off at 1230 to attack a concentration of tanks reported to be near the road four miles north of Chouigui. With no fighter escort we flew at 1,000 feet down the Mejerda valley with the peaks and ridges of the Teboursouk mountains rising up on our right and the cluster of white buildings of Beja on our left. I found map reading difficult with such irregular features and the narrow winding roads often obscured. I gave the 'Six minutes to target' warning as we passed over the densely wooded hills to the west of Chouigui and then we dived down towards the plain of Tunis. Malcolm banked left so steeply that flying number two we swung wide and lost formation. Levelling out at 100 feet, the ground was so close that I had to bend my head back to see ahead. And there they were — tanks spread out in an olive grove — there was no time to think or speak, just a quick rotation of the bomb switch. 'Bombs gone', and we were catching up with the others to climb back over the hills to return to Bone. I can't remember why to Bone and not to Canrobert. In my excitement I had forgotten to release the four 40 lb bombs. Henry saw our bomb bursts but with eleven second delay fuses they were then some half mile behind and there were no medals for going back to see what effect they had — if any. It was only now that I realized that we hadn't run into any 109s. Luck was all in this game and it wasn't to last much longer.

We flew back up to Canrobert in the late afternoon to the monotony of our Compo rations and a bottle of local red wine. I can't imagine what we did with our evenings, there was nowhere to go and the nights were cold. With Knickerbocker gone and Bill Booth now on his best behaviour we had no more emulations of the OK Corral.

Back again in Bisley 'N' to Souk el Arba early on 3 December. Sgt Stott in 'G' (one of the few 18 Squadron aircraft still flying) lost an engine on take off and crash landed without injuring the crew. We were all becoming very nervous every time plus nine boost was selected; there were probably some only too glad to see the demise of another unloved Bisley. Ten of us arrived to while away the time lying on the grass or visiting the 'crater'. We were lucky to have fine weather, soon it would break and the airfield become a sea of mud.

With five others and led by Eyton-Bill we took off just before noon for the first of the day's operations. Once again the target was tanks in the Chouigui area. For some reason we got separated from the rest and proceeded on our own, putting my very low level navigation to the test for the first time. Wind speed and direction didn't come into the equation but I used my familiar six minute system, correcting my track whenever a clearly identified feature passed below. We swept over the last ridge of hills and down their slopes until we were rushing over the flat, featureless plain at 500 feet. Ted saw the tanks first in a line on the road running north from Tebourba and dived down to 100 feet. This time I got all our bombs away. There was a bang and a sudden rush of air which blew all my maps off the chart table. I thought we had been hit, but it was only the cap covering the camera hatch in the nose which had blown in and was soon forced back into place. As we banked around to the west Ted called out that there was a column of troops on the road and to man our guns. By the time I had got into position Ted was already firing his wing gun. I got a confused, blurred impression of road and running men and squeezed the triggers. If I hit anyone it could only have been luck. Henry was able to get in a better directed burst from his turret guns. I felt unreasonably elated and it was some time before I was able to settle down to the business of setting the right course back to Canrobert where we arrived safely an hour later.

P/O Sims had arrived from Blida in 'J' of 614 Squadron. The CO returned later in the afternoon with the other four aircraft having also bombed tanks near Chouigui. They had seen 109s in the target area but fortunately these were engaged in combat with US Air Force P38 Lightning fighters from Tebessa. We had been lucky so far; unbeknown to us we had been operating for the last three days within five miles of two German airfields, but the fortunes of war only allow so much luck. Ours was about to run out.

Friday 4 December 1942 dawned crisp and clear. The sun was only just lighting up the face of Canrobert's singular hill as our wheels skimmed over the edge of the small field and over the forlorn wrecks of two of our Bisleys. I was beginning to feel queasy with each take-off and it was a relief to be climbing on a steady engine note; if Ted felt the same he never looked other than imperturbable.

Eleven of us arrived at Souk el Arba to await the army's call for support. It was not long in coming and the CO took off at 0945 with six aircraft with instructions to attack whatever targets he could find in the now familiar Chouigui area from whence the Germans were massing for their major thrust against the over exposed British forces. There was some grumbling about no fighter escort being available once again from either of the two Spitfire squadrons. To be fair to them I doubt that we appreciated the problems facing a fighter squadron attempting to escort very slow bombers at low level with insufficient aircraft to give both high and low level cover. They would have been sitting ducks. This time Malcolm stumbled on the lion's den, an enemy satellite fighter airfield six miles east of Mateur. Fortunately the lions were caught unawares and all six Bisleys dropped their bombs in a formation pass and returned unscathed to Canrobert where they were immediately refuelled and re-armed before flying back to join us shortly after 1400. They must have been fairly tired by now having been in the air for three and a half hours. It demonstrates Hugh Malcolm's 'press on' nature; many COs would by then have called it a day. Even more so when he received an army request to make a further attack on the same satellite airfield. He decided to take all eleven aircraft and to approach the target low from the east, taking advantage of the last of the Teboursouk range of hills to give some element of surprise. He must have known the risk (see Map 6).

On the way out to our aircraft Wing Commander Pieter Hugo, the South African commander of 322 Spitfire Wing, approached and for the first and only time Malcolm lost his composure, complaining bitterly about the lack of fighter escort. Hugo replied that all three of his squadrons would be carrying out a sweep over the target area around the time we were due over the target. Malcolm shrugged in disbelief and stomped off. I naively remained convinced that our luck would hold and was more concerned about engine failure at take-off.

We took off at 1515. F/O Armstrong, a 13 Squadron pilot, burst a tail wheel when taxiing and got left behind. Sims, our most accident prone pilot turned back after fifteen minutes with engine trouble and crash landed on the way back to Souk el Arba. That left nine of us flying in three boxes. As usual we flew number two on Eyton-Bill in the second box with Wray Eller number three. I cocked both my guns and took a quick look through the periscope at the tail enders gently rising and falling in the bumpy mountain air. Looking up through my curved expanse of perspex there was not a cloud in the sky. Reaching the Sidi N'sir junction we turned east, following the road through the valley to Chouigui. We must have crossed the front line about 1545 with no sign of the violent struggle going on in the hills below. Just past the village of Chouigui we turned north east with the Teboursouk hills on our left and the wide plain stretching out to Tunis on our right. I flicked the bomb master switch and buttoned up my face mask. It was just then that Henry's excited voice reported a large number of fighters high up above us. I looked up and it was like a swarm of bees, more than I had ever seen before, even in the Malta convoy. I assumed that they were the Spitfires promised by Hugo.

We were now some ten miles east of the target and after turning to a westerly heading towards Hill 394 we began a shallow dive. I was concentrating on the lead aircraft, ready to release bombs but when we reached the hill we began a wide left hand circle. It seems likely that Malcolm was unable to locate the target. I never saw it, believing it to be some three miles further west. Catching a quick glimpse of a Bf 109 flashing low across us from ahead I yelled on the intercom and almost immediately Henry called out that we were under attack from a swarm of 109s from all directions. I saw Malcolm's section dropping their bombs and hurriedly released ours although I could still see no target and we were in a shallow dive over hills. Eyton-Bill's aircraft started dropping down and passed close below my aiming panel with it's starboard engine on fire and streaming a plume of dense black smoke. There was an almost

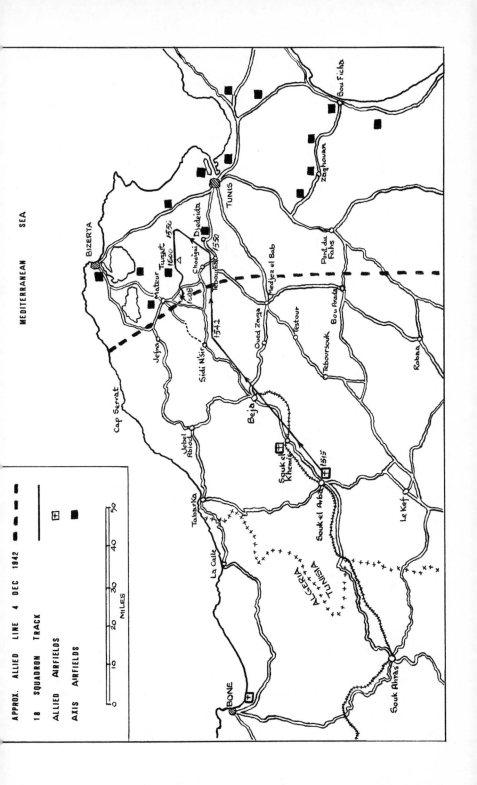

MEDITERRANEAN SEA

APPROX. ALLIED LINE 4 DEC 1942

18 SQUADRON TRACK

ALLIED AIRFIELDS

AXIS AIRFIELDS

MILES
0   10   20   30   40   50

BIZERTA

TUNIS

Bou Ficha

Zaghouan

Pont du Fahs

Bou Arada

Medjez el Bab

Testour

Teboursouk

Robaa

Mateur

Tunget 1550

1600

Chouigui Djedeida

Tebourba 1550

El Bathan 1208

1542

Sidi N'Sir

Oued Zarga

Jefna

Beja

Souk el Khemis

Souk el Arba 1815

Le Kef

Cap Serrat

Jebel Abiod

Tabarka

La Calle

BONE

ALGERIA

TUNISIA

Souk Ahras

continuous rattle from the rear turret guns overlaid by a terse command from Henry to break to the right.

We banked away from the formation and were now so low that I could see a line of cannon shells stitching the ground in front of us. Mesmerized by the sights and sounds, I was slow to react and only then began to struggle into position to fire my own guns. As we banked left under full boost in an attempt to rejoin the formation I felt the shocks as we received the first hits on the starboard wing. All I could see through my periscope was a blurred view of the ground as we continued violent evasive action. We were hit again in the starboard engine which went on fire. The intercom went off and Henry was no longer able to give Ted any help in evading the continuing attacks. I could feel the aircraft shudder as we continued to be hit. That distinctive orange glow of flaming petrol lit up the cockpit as the fire spread along the wing to the starboard inner fuel tank and began to come into the cabin alongside me. I began struggling back aft.

Although having the utmost difficulty in controlling the aircraft Ted managed to belly land it on the side of a rock strewn hill some six miles south of Mateur. The rumbling and tearing of metal was followed by a surge of flame with the heat penetrating my throat but I was free of the narrow passage and rapidly pulled open the top hatch and dropped down onto the ground. Ted followed almost immediately and helped Henry to climb out from his rear hatch, his left leg covered in blood where a cannon shell splinter had entered his calf. Our aircraft was now an inferno of flames from which oily black smoke boiled up. A single Bf 109 roared low overhead and Ted shouted to us to hit the deck but it didn't open fire. Ammunition in the aircraft began to explode and we stumbled as fast as we could up the hill and sat down. There was a large explosion — it was four 40 lb bombs which once again I had forgotten to release — it was only a miracle that they didn't go off when we hit the ground.

My concern of the moment was the loss of my binoculars and my father's old camera. I was vaguely aware that both my hands were burnt but avoided looking at them closely and felt no pain. All three of us were blackened with soot. The only sign of life was an Arab sitting motionless some distance away. I passed out around this time and must rely on Ted Holloway's account, remembered clearly over forty five years later: 'A Bren gun carrier emerged manned by two soldiers (ours fortunately). I noticed that it appeared to be following a line of white tape to our hillock. It was just as well we had not moved around much as it transpired that the whole area was mined. We had come down between the two armies. We were taken in the carrier to the forward HQ of the First Parachute Regiment.'

I came round lying in the corner of a small stone-built farm outhouse and was surprised to recognize the RC Padre with whom I had become friendly on the voyage to Algiers. He failed to recognize me at first, and then recalled my once white, now singed, polo-necked sweater, and my unusual rig. It was my good fortune that their medical orderly dressed my hands in Vaseline gauze, a new treatment at the time and still favoured today.

We had to stay put until nightfall as Bf 109s regularly strafed any vehicular movement during daylight. With a morphine injection time passed in a haze, and I was unaware that Ted had been taken to the site of another crashed Bisley half a mile away and had the unpleasant task of identifying the pilot, P/O Georges of 614 Squadron, who had either attempted to bale out or been flung out before his aircraft hit the ground, all the crew being killed.

All nine aircraft were lost that afternoon in as little as five minutes and only three crews survived. I knew none of this at the time and have only recently been able to piece together what happened in those few minutes.

The records show that between fifty and sixty German fighters were airborne, mostly Bf 109Gs and some Fw 190s. Henry Parsloe estimated that as many as twenty-six 109s made the initial attack and a pilot of the German Gruppe JG53 [which also took part in the attacks on the 'Pedestal' convoy] reported that they were almost queueing to make their attacks on what they thought were USAF Bostons (operating at that time from Tebessa). Closing to within one hundred yards, Eyton-Bill's aircraft was hit almost immediately. Sgt Stott was probably next to go down and both crashed behind enemy lines near Chouigui with no survivors. F/O Irving, flying number three on Malcolm, broke formation and found himself separated from the rest of the formation by three 109s; he flew down a valley at ground level taking evasive action against repeated attacks during which his starboard aileron and port engine were hit. His air gunner put in a good burst at a 109 which turned on its back and another broke off with smoke pouring from it after which his guns jammed. Irving continued flying on one engine before belly landing some fifteen minutes later four miles east of Souk el Khemis, all the crew being unhurt.

Henry Parsloe got in a long burst from his twin gun turret at a 109 which closed to within 25 yards and it turned away, going down. He obtained hits on three more before we too went down.

Wray Eller's experience was remarkably similar to our own. Having joined up with Malcolm after Eyton-Bill fell back, he too had to break formation when attacked. His gunner, P/O Eckersley, hit a 109 in the belly at 100 yards and he saw another 109 crossing the formation at ground level with smoke pouring from it. His starboard engine was hit and with both hydraulic and electrical power put out of action he made a successful belly landing half a mile south of us. The aircraft caught fire and Eckersley was trapped in his turret, but Eller and his observer Tony Harding broke the perspex and got him out to find that he too had injuries from cannon shell splinters. Tony was wounded by a bullet which passed through his forearm.

F/O Georges' aircraft was seen by Army officers being attacked by six 109s. The cockpit was on fire and he too crashed close to us.

The remaining three aircraft were seen by the army with at least ten 109s attacking them. All three were shot down and crashed near Sidi N'sir with no survivors. When two soldiers and an infantry officer arrived at Malcolm's aircraft only minutes later they were able to recover the body of P/O Robb, his observer, but the flames and exploding ammunition made it impossible to recover either Malcolm or Grant, his air gunner.

Hugh Malcolm, aged 26, was awarded a posthumous Victoria Cross, the thirteenth won in the air during World War II and the only air VC to be awarded in the entire African campaign. I like to think that the award was given to all Blenheim crews, including those of 11 Squadron who flew out to attack the Japanese fleet off Ceylon.

Chapter 14
Wounded

I remember little of the forty-mile journey by Army ambulance to the Casualty Clearing Centre at Beja other than the very bumpy ride which caused audible distress to the injured army officer opposite me. We were all put down on stretchers on the floor of a large room which I believe was part of the old castle built on a hill in the days of the Byzantine empire. There were about fifty wounded with no more than six inches between each stretcher. Next to me was a German. In the dim light I found that I no longer had my white sweater, my battledress blouse or my revolver. I had a little white bag tied around my neck, but, unable to use my hands, it was a long time before I found out that it contained my pay book, my wings, my epaulettes and my father's scarab ring which had been cut off my finger. Ted had accompanied us to Beja and then decided to make his own way back to Canrobert — 150 miles to the west. He set off after dark and was fortunate enough to be picked up by a Tank Corps Brigadier in a scout car, who gave him a lift to his HQ where he got a meal and a bed for the night. He was sent on his way to Canrobert in a jeep the next morning, where he was horrified to learn that none of the eleven aircraft had returned, and he was the first survivor to turn up.

I never saw Henry Parsloe again, and believe he was killed on operations later in the war. I was not to meet Ted Holloway for another 46 years.

I woke with the sun up and a very pressing need to pee; not surprising since the last time must have been before take-off sixteen hours earlier. Trying not to step on all the stretchers I struggled out into a high walled courtyard and was directed to primitive facilities against a wall. I discovered that the male sex has a problem if he is unable to use either of his hands. It required a painful surrender of one's dignity to ask a stranger to unbutton one's flies, with an added reminder that there was still the need to extract the essential organ. On the way back I felt dizzy and fainted — it may be said from 'over exposure' — and woke up back on my stretcher where I spent the rest of the day being fed countless cups of tea and chocolate. Stretchers came and went like a grim game of musical chairs and there was a sickly stench of blood and sweat. I tried to speak to the German next to me in French but got nowhere.

Sometime in the evening I was carried across the cold, dark courtyard and into the blinding light of a makeshift operating theatre; like a scene from the

TV series M*A*S*H but without the nurses. A Scottish 'Hawkeye' bent over. 'What's your trouble laddie?' he enquired, untying the little white bag around my neck. I mumbled something about my hands being burnt in a plane crash and without another word a mask came over my face and a voice said 'Start counting'. I woke up retching with a very irate 'Hawkeye'. 'Another one with too much tea and chocolate!', he growled. 'Look laddie, you've been sick, so we'll have to start all over again — start counting!'

I woke up lying in a tent in the dark with each arm tied to a bar above and behind my head. For a while I thought I must be having a nightmare. I could hear the drone of aircraft overhead and the unmistakable whistle and crump of bombs falling fairly close by. I must have made some sound. 'Are you OK?' a voice asked from out of the darkness. 'Jerry's bombing Beja down in the valley,' said another disembodied voice in a thick accent. At least I was not alone but felt more than usually vulnerable tied up and stretched out on my back like a sacrifice; it was a relief when the sounds died away and fitful sleep took over.

With daylight I found that there were three other bandaged bodies in the tent; soldiers from an infantry brigade. Compo rations arrived, they untied my hands and I sat up and was fed like a baby. My hands throbbed if I lowered them but, looking at the others I had little to complain about. They carried out a ceaseless banter all day woven with the customary obscenities. One of them wrote a brief letter for me to the gorgeous girl on a small scrap of paper which purported to be an Air Mail Letter card and was sealed with adhesive tape. Surprisingly it reached her on 31 December.

I sat outside in the sun in the afternoon and a lone Bisley flew past to the south going east leaving me wondering when I would see them all again and whether Hugo Dent had survived. He had gone down with Eyton-Bill and the memory of their flaming Bisley was still vivid.

In the evening, after dark, we were taken by ambulances down to Beja station to be packed into the oddest of trains. Those on stretchers were fitted one above the other in racks which were spring mounted on hangers from the carriage roof. I and other walking wounded were perched to one side on small metal seats. It was a journey into Hell.

I doubt if there is half a mile of straight track in all the ninety miles from Beja to Souk Ahras. We lurched violently at every corner and bumped over each ill matched joint. The stretchers bounced and banged on their springs resulting in a purgatory of moans, cries and screams from their tortured occupants. Sleep was impossible, there was no escape and no relief until we pulled into Souk Ahras station just before dawn. We transferred into a conventional train with compartments and corridors but with their inter-connections open to the elements and protected by side railings.

It is the story about my difficulty in making arrangements to have a pee in the train which opens this book.

The single track line to Algiers winds in a demented fashion up over the plateau through Setif. Up there it was cold with only a single grey blanket and we dozed much of the time to be awakened by a belated visit from an army orderly with Compo rations and bedpans. I imagine that the seriously wounded required most of their attention and I was relieved that they were out of sight and earshot. The captain's wounds seemed serious to me but no doubt there were others much worse and, although moaning in his sleep, he never complained.

It took two days to reach Algiers, arriving late in the afternoon of 8 December to be whisked off in a fleet of ambulances to a hospital high up on the hill behind the town. Beds, lovely beds, and pyjamas, but no nurses; the ship bringing them out had been torpedoed off Oran.

It was the last I saw of my boots and battledress trousers; from now on I only possessed my vest and underpants. I never saw the wounded Army Captain again — wounded are like flotsam and have no identity. I don't remember seeing a doctor but I did have my bandages removed by an orderly who took such care that the process seemed never ending. Squeamishly I avoided looking and maintained a senseless chatter together with a pretence that it didn't really hurt.

The ward I was in was much like any hospital apart from the tiled floor and the flies. With no nurses on the scene, vulgarity reigned supreme; having no talent for this I felt out of place and was relieved when on 12 December I was taken — in pyjamas, dressing gown and slippers — down the hill to the harbour and onto a Royal Naval hospital ship, spotlessly white and boldly emblazoned with a red cross. I was soon bedded down in a small officers' sick bay with some six beds which had little side rails to stop you falling out, just like those we had on *Indomitable*. And nurses. In immaculate blue and white, efficient and distinctly no nonsense.

'Let's have your hands young man. Burns is it? Well shall we have a look?'

What had previously taken half an hour took less than a minute. If the pain level was high, at least it was over quickly. The doctor who arrived took a quick look at them.

'Well boy, do you want that left hand to be bent like that for the rest of your life?'

'No Sir,' I replied weakly.

'Well you'd better do something about it hadn't you. Keep pressing it back, otherwise you're fingers will end up touching your arm and we don't want that do we?'

I had only subconsciously noticed the behaviour of my left hand which had taken the worst of the burning on the inner wrist. With my hands once more encased in vaseline gauze and bandages I gave a gentle push. The pain made me feel sick so I didn't keep it up for long. I am not brave.

Suddenly it came to me that this was the day, Saturday, 12 December, that the gorgeous girl and I had set for our marriage. It could have been worse — I might have been dead.

The crisp white sheets, the excellent food, the nurses and the cheerful company of the other four patients — it seemed to be too good to be true. It was. The scene shifted swiftly back to the macabre when just before we sailed that evening the door into the passageway opened and two sick bay attendants struggled to bring in a stretcher. It bumped the door and there was a high pitched scream unlike anything I had ever heard coming from a man. He cried out at every slight movement and again when he was moved onto his bed at the end of the row. He was almost entirely encased in plaster and his ashen grey face seemed old, but in fact he was a young army Commando who had been blown up by a shell. He received a lot of attention but everything done for him seemed as though it was torture. He whimpered or cried out throughout the night and none of us slept. We tried talking to him but he didn't seem to hear or understand. I even tried to shut out the sound by putting my head under the pillow, but it was useless. In the dim light the nurses fluttered around him from time to time but apparently there was nothing they could do for him, he had had all the drugs he could be given.

When morning came at last I felt emotionally drained and escaped at the first opportunity onto the deck. Cleaving through a calm, blue sea, without any escort, it was hard to believe that four months ago *Eagle* had been sunk not many miles to the north amidst that great assembly of ships. Was it all a dream? As I pressed my hand back, the physical pain was almost a relief from the mental anguish of those long night hours. The sun was chasing us eastwards but it had lost that fierce strength of earlier days and the chill drove me back inside. Daylight seemed to make the agony more bearable.

At first I thought we were on our way home but the Algerian port of Oran was our destination. Oran. A name which evokes painful memories. Here in 1940, and much against his will and judgement, Admiral Somerville carried out his orders to destroy the Vichy French Fleet in harbour to prevent it falling into Axis hands. Many French sailors lost their lives and I doubted that we British would be welcome. I am happy to say that I was proved wrong.

Being a major naval base it lacked the elegance of Algiers, more like a Mediterranean Portsmouth. We arrived late afternoon and our sorry cargo of casualties was slowly disgorged into an oddly assorted fleet of ambulances. We were dispersed to several of the city's hospitals and I never learnt the fate of the Commando officer. A nurse told me that he was not expected to live.

I was taken to the American 7th Station Hospital which, prior to its being taken over by them, had been a French maternity hospital and in consequence it had an unusual layout. There were no wards, only single rooms which were allocated to the most severely wounded. The rest of us filled every corridor and open space. Equipped with smart new pyjamas and dressing gown I was put to bed by an attractive young nurse outside the lift on the fourth floor amidst a mixed group of American officers.

After the perfection and efficiency of an RN Hospital Ship I was in for a culture shock. I had then and still have the expectation that the Americans are really British with an elusive speech and idiom, bearing no relationship to their Hollywood image. The nurses were straight out of a not too well rehearsed *Dr Kildare* programme. Whether out of shyness or prudery, they showed a disinclination to handling my private parts, so I chose the lesser indignity of asking help from able bodied patients. The first time my hands were dressed, a young lady with a deep southern accent took half an hour to remove the bandages and vaseline gauze, piece by piece with a pair of tweezers, and was concerned that she might have been hurting me. When she unsealed the new bandages from their immaculate containers she carefully lifted them out with her tweezers and placed them down on my side table amongst the flies and orange peel. The doctors wore pyjama bottoms, blood stained vests and continuously smoked cigars; they might have been the inspiration for scenes in M*A*S*H.

I found Tony Harding, Ray Eller's navigator, on another floor. He was rather gloomy as the the doctors had told him that he could expect to lose the use of his hand; this proved not to be the case when he returned to the UK. He was in fact discharged before me.

I also discovered that Group Captain Appleton was in a room on the floor below. Shortly after our untimely arrive at Bone with the maps for General Anderson he had been blown up by a bomb and badly injured, losing one of his legs. I visited him and found him a grey-faced ghost of a man, clearly in such pain that conversation was difficult. We played draughts.

On another floor were some British nurses who had been wounded when their troopship was torpedoed on the way to Algiers. They had seen many of their friends drown.

On my floor was the oddest bunch of American characters to which the word casualty could apply. In the next bed was a Roman Catholic padre with gonorrhoea. He had a high twittering voice and complained non-stop about everyone and everything; he was the only person to receive magazines and when a batch of *Esquire* magazines arrived he would lie on his back clutching them and giggling, never letting anyone else touch them. He was loathed by everyone.

A very smart, good looking Captain in the US Army Signal Corps came in one day to visit a friend. On the way out he tripped on the kerb, broke his ankle and ended up a patient close by me. One of the world's charmers, he chatted up every nurse in sight and kept us all entertained. After a week the doctors told him that he would have to be circumcised (don't ask me why), and when the day arrived, all who could walk lined up outside the entrance to the lift, and saluted, as he was wheeled through to go to the operating theatre. Afterwards we were regaled with what he had said to the doctor while under local anaesthetic about being careful with his manhood. The story did not end there, the circumcision went septic and because of his reputation as a leg puller he couldn't persuade any of the nurses to come and look at it and was only saved from further disaster by the eventual arrival of a doctor. He was still there when I left a month later, chasing the nurses on a crutch.

One of the nurses developed a crush for one of the young officers who had lost his right arm and was morbidly sorry for himself. She would come and hold his only hand throughout much of the night. I thought it very soppy, but was probably jealous.

The treatment for my burns was now to immerse them for fifteen minutes in jars of warm salt water. The first few seconds of exquisite pain were followed by a blissful numbness and the scented nearness of a blonde head as small fingers replaced the bandages. My right hand improved enough for me to write to the gorgeous girl; the letters which survived are mawkish.

It was never boring. I had to suffer the continual insults about the evils of the British Empire which I was ill equipped to defend, having been brought up to be proud of it. There were the visits from the ladies of the American Red Cross with cigarettes, toothpaste, Hershey bars and stationery, wheeled around with the heartiness so common to those who wish to do you good. And there were mealtimes with such strange flavours as sweet potato, sweet corn and peanut butter, all served up on those uniquely American metal trays which in their multitude of dimpled pockets brought to close proximity everything from sausage to ice cream. I think maybe because of the general sweetness it never seemed to satisfy and by late evening I was always hungry. I had developed a particular taste for peanut butter and managed to persuade the night orderly, a Red Indian no less, to raid the kitchen and bring me rye biscuits spread with it.

By leaning out of the window at the end of our passage we could look down into the street below and watch the customers going into the brothel whose entrance was adjacent to that of the hospital. It was an officially approved establishment with an American Military Police guard and specified times for officers and other ranks. A veritable 'Irma la Douce' affair and as popular. Perhaps that is where the abominable padre had become a war casualty.

Christmas was approaching. My right hand was now reasonably operational and I was at last able to shave myself and wipe my own bottom. But I still had a problem, no money and no clothes. The signals Captain suggested I borrow his uniform so, much to everyone's enjoyment, I tried it on and found that everything fitted, including shoes. With two silver bars on each shoulder and crossed flags, it felt strange but looked smart and without a word to anyone I nipped down the stairs and out onto the busy streets of Oran, waving to the gang leaning out of the window up above. The American forces in the city were going through a period of strict attention to saluting and it was fortunate that I had the use of my right hand as I made my way towards the docks looking for some Royal Navy presence. Fortunately I got directions from an RNVR Lieutenant, and I wasn't exactly surprised that my arrival at the naval office became something out of a pantomime. I produced my tattered brown paybook and was shuffled from one to another explaining my plight and eventually extracted from them francs to the value of £5. The story went down well back on the ward, particularly when I reported that I had received a salute from the MP on brothel guard duty. The unaccustomed exercise left me weak at the knees (I don't mean the brothel).

'Dreaming of a White Christmas,' sung by a chorus of nurses remains in my memory like a scene from so many movies of those days. There was plenty of turkey but no alcohol and it seemed difficult to get in the mood. I was smoking too many 'Camels' (and they were well named).

After Tony Harding left I palled up with an Army Commando. A wild buccaneer of a fellow who, had our acquaintance been longer, might well have led me astray.

'It's time you and I got ourselves out and about and away from all these poncey Yankee abstainers!'

'What about clothes?'

'Leave it to me — they're bound to be able to come up with something.'

So we both got issued with a GI (Government Issue) soldier's uniform, the khaki shirt, the stringy tie, the bosomy waterproof blouse, the tight trousers and the strangely shaped, rubber soled boots. I added my epaulettes and wings. There was no cap.

'Well Captain, what do you think of an American uniform?' asked one of the nurses.

'Well my dear', he said. 'Do you see that building over the road there?'

Algiers Jan '43.

E.N.S.A. SHOW!

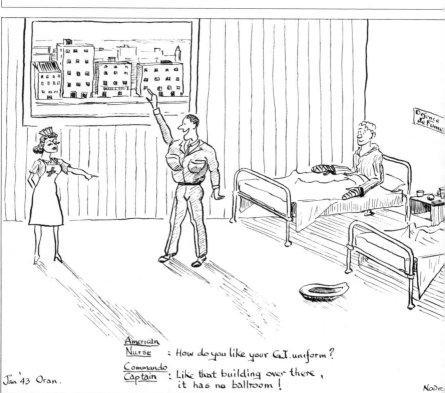

Jan '43 Oran.

American Nurse : How do you like your G.I. uniform?

Commando Captain : Like that building over there, it has no ballroom!

Contemporary cartoons by the author.

'Yes!'

'Well it's got no ballroom has it dear?'

'No!'

'Well neither have these trousers!'

Young American nurses appeared to have little sense of humour and this exchange passed way over her head.

'I hope you boys have permission to go out,' she said.

'Certainly we have, my dear, straight from General Eisenhower!'

We toured the bars, then we took a box at the theatre for a variety show. The box overhung the stage and there was continual badinage between the Captain and anyone on the stage who took his fancy. Another night we met a bunch of RNVR characters who took us to an 'Exhibition', pronounced in the French manner and best left to the reader's imagination. My father would have said 'Just like a lot of fish on a wet slab!' I was rather too sober to get much enjoyment from it but no doubt it was one more facet of joining the Navy and seeing the world.

But suddenly he was gone, back to war, and my world seemed less bright. The Americans were pale shadows by comparison, except for the Signals Captain, and he was still flat on his back.

But the New Year, 1943, brought forth unexpected compensation in the rather attractive form of Odette Teboul; a French girl of eighteen or so who came to the hospital to assist the American Red Cross. She was dark, olive skinned, and spoke English with a delightful accent. Pretty and shy, it was brave of her to come into our world of oddballs. I told her so in my limited schoolboy French and got myself invited to lunch with her family, which put me up a peg or two with the Yanks.

Lunch had its fair share of minor embarrassments. Monsieur et Madame Teboul and younger daughter spoke no English and the Aunt only a little. A strange green plant with thick leaves, sitting in melted butter, was on my plate. Everyone looked at me, clearly expecting me to start and I hadn't the slightest idea what to do with the thing. Even had I known that it was an artichoke, it wasn't the easiest thing to eat with only one hand. And, of course, the vegetables all came separately and with only one knife and fork for the whole meal I was soon left with none at all until my original set was rescued from the kitchen. If nothing else I gave them some amusement but I doubt that I showed the appreciation they deserved for taking me into their home after the tragic events in 1940. I saw Odette as often as I could over my last few days in Oran, she played the piano rather well and was usually chaperoned by either Aunt or younger sister, not that I was much of a threat to her honour.

Around the end of the first week in January, I was beginning to feel restless and that I ought to be getting back to the squadron. The doctor wasn't very keen on me going so I got to see the boss, a Colonel (never seen by anyone before) who said he hadn't any authority to keep me, so if I wanted to go I could go. And where did I want to go? Blida seemed to be the only place to aim for and he thought I ought to be able to hitch a lift with the USAF.

So, after saying my goodbyes and kissing all the nurses, I left in the morning in a Jeep for Tafaraoui airfield. No baggage, no overcoat, no cap, but several rolls of bandages in the bosom pockets of my blouse. I think it was only because I was in an army vehicle that I was allowed into the airfield in my unorthodox rig. But once inside it was just a question of hanging around and drinking coffee for an hour before I was climbing into a dark green Dakota with a mixed company of gum-chewing Yanks. The trip was noisy and bumpy and I had time to wonder what I was going to do when I got to Blida, having very little money, no kit and spurred on only by a romantic notion of getting back into action. And anyway, what else could I have done?

Two hours later we thumped down onto the familiar runway. There were Hudsons and Wellingtons but no sign of any Bisleys; I was pleased to see a small group of Swordfish parked quite near and made my way over to them and bumped into Lt Cdr C. Hutchinson RN, who had been one of my course officers at Arbroath, and was now CO of 813 Squadron. I told my story and explained my predicament. He was most helpful, taking me over to their 'office', where he made enquiries about 18 Squadron. It was then I heard for the first time that none of our aircraft had returned on that fateful 4 December. He was told that the squadron had been disbanded (this was not so, in fact on this very day 7 January, Ted Holloway was flying on his first operation from Canrobert after a rest period at No 326 Wing base at Setif). He then phoned the FAA Staff Officer at the Allied Forces Headquarters at the St. Georges Hotel in Algiers. This officer turned out to be Lt Cdr A. J. T. Roe RN, who had been in charge of our course at Arbroath. I travelled there by car and it took some hard talking before I got past all the American guards. I didn't realise that it was Eisenhower's HQ.

Lt/Cdr Roe received me most kindly in his office in what must have once been the cellars of the hotel. He listened to the story of my adventures and then told me that he was making arrangements for me to be sent back home on the first returning transport ship; meanwhile I could stay in an RAF transit centre. This was a strange place through which officers passed both going up to the front as well as returning to the UK. Here I met Peter Coulthard who was a student with me at de Havillands before the war and now a fighter pilot in the RAF, waiting to go to one of the front line squadrons. If he survived, he was not one of the few who returned to de Havillands after the war, but at the time he appeared to be enjoying an affair with a French young lady. I never possessed the talent for this sort of thing, which has probably saved me a lot of trouble. However I was to get a surprising sensual stirring. With some misgiving I turned up for a local French version of an ENSA show in the small mess hall. There must have been no more than thirty of us and somehow I ended up on the front bench. I have forgotten all the acts but one, a fabulous belly dance by a strikingly well shaped Arab girl. I have seen many since, but nothing to compare with this dark pagan creature, with eyes made up in the classic eastern fashion and gyrating so close I could have touched her. It was much more erotic than any strip tease and I spent a restless night on my camp bed.

Visiting the many bars and reading the French newspapers I was able to get some impression of the progress of a war that had begun to seem quite remote in the winter sunshine of a surprisingly peaceful and attractive city. Rommel had been driven back as far as Tripoli by the Eighth Army and after their defeat at Stalingrad the Germans had been forced to retreat from the Caucasus. It seemed impossible to find out how the battle was going in Tunisia. I felt slightly ashamed of the relief I felt knowing that I was out of it all.

I don't remember the name of the troopship in which I embarked on 14 January. Typical of this period I found myself appointed in charge of some fifteen RAF other ranks with instructions to see that they arrived safely at a transit centre in London. I saw nothing of them during the voyage as within a day of sailing I went down with a severe bout of 'Gyppy Tummy' and spent ten of the twelve days as the sole patient in the ship's sick bay. With a very high temperature and an over-long period on Sulfa drugs I wasn't in the best of shape when we docked at Liverpool on a bleak, cold 26 January. I collected my RAF bods and mustered them on the dockside with their kit. For the first time I felt conscious of my American GI rig and was thankful it wasn't raining.

Once again I was in a fix about money; I hadn't got any! While we waited for transport to the station I located the RN port office where I was received with the total apathy I had come to expect. An improperly dressed Fleet Air Arm Sub Lieutenant asking for money and backing it with an unlikely story of being shot down with the RAF I waved my bandaged hands at everyone and eventually received a very grudging £10, duly entered in my pay book. The returning hero cut no ice, but £10 would go a long way in 1943.

On arrival at Euston we were all waiting in the station yard for transport when I noticed a couple of American Army MPs eyeing me with obvious suspicion. They hurried off and we all reckoned that they had gone to find an officer before checking up on me. As we climbed onto our truck they reappeared with an officer in tow just as we pulled out; we gave them a wave. The RAF officers' transit centre turned out to be a requisitioned hotel close by the station, and here I left the others.

As soon as I had booked in (where was my kit?) I phoned the gorgeous girl and my parents to announce my return, but was unable to say when I could travel up north. The first thing I did the following morning was to visit Gieves in Piccadilly where I asked a po-faced assistant to let me have a Royal Navy cap with a khaki cap cover. 'Will we be wearing it or shall I wrap it up for you?' he enquired. 'Wearing it, thank you,' I replied, sticking it straight on my head. At last I felt dressed and walked out into the winter sunshine. How different London seemed. The last time I had been there the Blitz was still raging with the shadow of unease in everyone's eyes. Now the streets were bustling with life, uniforms of every description, Americans, Poles, Free French, Canadians, Indians, Australians and New Zealanders. I blended into it all and hurried back to the hotel, feeling cold without a coat; the idea of wearing a naval greatcoat on top of my 'Doughboy' rig was just too grotesque.

There was a message for me back at the hotel to report to Adastral House the following morning. So someone somewhere knew of my existence, but I hadn't the slightest idea what they wanted of me. Meanwhile I poked my head into the lounge, crowded with the blue uniforms of RAF aircrew, too many of them showing obvious signs of injury. Here I came face to face with the full horror of what might so easily have been my own fate. Here were young men so severely burnt that one had a face resembling an egg with just slits for eyes, nose, mouth and ears, and a few tufts of hair. Another, a Flight Lieutenant Navigator, introduced himself and held out a hand which was webbed between the fingers, the right hand side of his face was more or less normal, the left had no eye or ear and had the nightmarish lack of any feature to display its humanity. 'I'm meeting some girls in a local dive — do you feel like coming along for a jar or two?'

The three of us piled into a taxi and were soon ensconced in one of those basement bars so typical of London. I can't remember how many girls arrived or what they were like; the party was dominated by the exuberant spirit and charm of 'webbed hands'. 'Feel them dear, feel them!' he exclaimed. 'You'll soon get used to them and they don't hurt! And keep this side of me, which is the good looking side!' And so he held court as we downed our pints of beer — like nectar after the rough Algerian wine. And never did cheese and pickles taste so good. I found out later that he had baled out of a flaming Wellington and had grasped the red hot door frame as he pushed himself out. At that time I knew nothing of the wonders which were to be achieved by surgeons in re-building burnt faces and I hope this great character received their very best efforts. I was more than a little relieved that the gorgeous girl would not have to face the disfigurement which would have resulted from just a few more seconds in our Bisley.

Friday morning found me entering the impressive portals of Adastral House where I was given a full medical and given a grading which only allowed me to fly below 5,000 feet and not in any cold climate; this apparently was to avoid frost damage to the newly formed skin on my hands. I then had a brief interview with a very charming Air Commodore who wanted to know how I had received my burns and finally told me to proceed on leave for three weeks after which I could expect to receive instructions from the Admiralty.

Could all this have really happened in just three months?

Chapter 15
Clipped Wings

'We're getting married next Saturday!' announced the gorgeous girl, meeting me in Newcastle-upon-Tyne's dim, dour Central Station, with its pervading acrid smell of steam-borne soot; now only a memory. Only my generation could contemplate the arranging of a full blown church wedding in seven days but that is what was achieved without much help from me, being more or less in a state of shock, and my intended who was much of the time in bed with flu.

The sun shone brilliantly upon us through the stained glass church window on that morning of 6 February 1943. My brother, now a RN Commando officer, was my best man and Jack Fisher and his wife came down from Crail. The gorgeous girl looked truly gorgeous in powder blue and for going away had a feather in her hat, perhaps to signal her capture of a male of the species. Not that I was much of a catch with only a Sub Lieutenant's pay, a poor prognosis for survival, and naught to show that I would be able to keep her in suitable style should the war ever end.

We began well with a no expenses spared honeymoon commencing with three nights at the Dorchester in Park Lane where we arrived early in the evening, weary and bedraggled after sitting on our cases in the corridor of the train most of the way down to London, and then lugging our cases through the underground as there were no taxis.

Confetti erupted from our cases when we opened them and spread all over the room. After a brief attempt to pick it up we gave up and went down for dinner to find ourselves at a table surrounded by sleeves inches deep in gold braid; a scene straight out of one of Bateman's cartoons. At least I had a pair of wings on my sleeve and a bandaged hand. A dance band was playing somewhere around the corner.

'Come on, let's dance,' said my new wife. 'After all we are paying for it!'

Ballroom dancing has never been my forte, and the pocket sized dance floor just had to be empty when we reached it. I would have been happier facing a diving Stuka, but there was no escape, and now I was under new command. I had a lot to learn. And so to bed — and much to learn there too.

Oh the supreme luxury of ordering our breakfast in bed. And when it came it lay under a large tureen which, when opened, disclosed the dreaded scrambled dried egg from which there seemed no escape, not even at the famous Dorchester.

The sun shone in Hyde Park and there were red squirrels; out of sight of uniformed humanity there might have been no war on. But there were plenty of uniforms at the Grosvenor House tea dance and at Sunday Night at the Palladium (with Tommy Trinder).

Allowing for a ten per cent reduction for being in the services, our bill amounted to fifteen pounds, nine shillings and three pence for our three nights. Wildly extravagant. And then off by the Great Western Railway to the delights of the Imperial Hotel at Torquay, delights hardly touched by the war and blessed through all nine days by spring-like weather, the sun flooding our large, luxurious bedroom, and warm enough to sit outside for a coffee. I don't think we realised how lucky we were. Far away in Tunisia, Ted Holloway was still battling away in a Bisley of a re-formed 18 Squadron and was about to make his first solo flight in a Boston with which they were soon to be re-equipped. The front line ran in much the same place as it had in December but Rommel had retreated into Tunisia and was now using his experienced Panzers to good effect against Allied tanks. Bisleys no longer made suicide daylight raids and confined their operations to night operations. RAF Wellingtons had taken over the nightly bombing of Tunis and Bizerta, with USAF Fortresses continuing by day. Hurricane fighter-bombers gave army support and by the end of February the Desert Air Force joined in the air war over Tunisia. The combined forces from East and West at last won air superiority and by May had virtually destroyed the German air force in Tunisia, leading to the defeat and surrender of all Axis forces in North Africa on 12 May 1943. This was the turning point in the war. On the Russian front the Germans were retreating after their defeat at Stalingrad and in the Pacific the aircraft carrier battles of the Coral Sea and Midway had torn the heart out of the Japanese navy.

In the first week of March I was instructed to report to NA2SL [Naval Assistant to the Second Sea Lord — responsible for Fleet Air Arm Appointments] and duly presented myself one morning at Queen Anne's Mansions after crossing a spring-like St James' Park and Birdcage Walk. It was a long way to go just to be told by an expressionless Lieutenant RN that I was being sent to Observer School at Arbroath as an instructor. It was just two years since I arrived there in my bell bottoms. One wonders how they arrived at this decision but it all turned out rather well in many different and unexpected ways. It allowed my Joan and I to live together for a whole year, getting to know each other and laying the foundations for a marriage extending happily over nearly half a century, few were so lucky at this time.

I was also lucky to get some very good lodgings in Carnoustie with a dour but unobtrusive Mrs Brown. Rationing hardly seemed to affect Scotland and there was an abundance of good food and my Joan proved to be an excellent cook. To occupy her time she took a job as a clerk in a local company building cranes. I think she had a rather boring social life, there were no social occasions at HMS *Condor* and not many of the instructing fraternity were married.

It was a pleasant surprise to find that 'O' School was under the command of 'Lofty' Logan, ex Commander (O) on *Indomitable*. The course officer was Lieutenant the Hon Walter A.C. Keppel DSC RN, always referred to, but kindly, as 'Wacky' Keppel. From an old aristocratic naval family, he was far from a typical navy man, never raised his voice and treated everyone with respect, never interfering with his team of instructors if all seemed to be under control. A true gentleman.

I was apprehensive about the new role of instructor thrust upon me. With no experience of teaching, and no advice from anyone as to how to set about the task, it proved, as in most affairs of war, a matter of jumping in at the deep end. I had survived long enough to have learnt most of the tricks in navigation and I had the lung power to reach to the end of any classroom full of drowsy Acting Leading Airmen. Promotion to Temporary Acting Lieutenant did much to boost my confidence and my pay.

The 61st Observer Course proved to contain more than its fair share of ex-policemen who were on average two or three years older than me. An unruly lot and very prone to heavy drinking. There were also the young innocents straight from school. Their keenness to become aviators was never in doubt, which meant that we were all on the same side. A novice teacher is not always so fortunate.

The start of their flying programme was marred by tragedy. Two of my Dutch Navy pupils were killed quite unnecessarily on their very first flight which was to familiarise them with being airborne and to look for familiar landmarks. At the briefing I had fortunately warned the pilots not to indulge in anything other than straight and level flying at one thousand feet. Apart from the middle-aged pilots, those posted to 'O' School squadrons were often pilots who had failed their operational training course and regarded their role as a reflection on their manhood, seeking any excuse to demonstrate their unappreciated flying prowess. And this was just such an occasion. When I went outside onto the control tower balcony with my binoculars all I could see in all directions were my aircraft cavorting around the sky in steep turns and dives.

The Swordfish bearing my two innocents spun into the sea off the Bell Rock lighthouse and none survived. Both young Dutchmen, on my strict instructions, would have been tethered to the floor of their cockpit by their 'G' straps and probably unable to manipulate the quick release coupling with gloved hands. Their bodies were never recovered and I had a miserable time at the subsequent enquiry where the adequacy of my briefing was put into question. It was not the best of starts in my role as instructor. Happily they proved to be the only casualties in over one hundred pupils. I doubt if, at the time, I appreciated the work of the pilots, flying boring exercises in all kinds of weather, out over a sea of minefields with a pupil who might not be sure of the difference between east and west. It also says much for the reliability of the Swordfish, Albacore, Lysander and Proctor aircraft in which they flew, and of the quality of their maintenance, that I recall no other losses.

In the classroom I tried to make the navigation exercises as realistic as possible giving unexpected interruptions and making as much noise as possible. I always felt that it was the continuous noise of the engine, interspersed with chatty interruptions from one's pilot, which induced the observer to make mistakes in his navigation.

Vivid memories were awakened when I read on 23 April that Hugh Malcolm had been awarded the VC and Ted Holloway, Wray Eller and Eckersley the DFC. Some weeks later a reporter somehow managed to locate me up at Arbroath and came to interview me. A garbled melodramatic story was published in the national and local press which bore minimal relation to the facts. It was embarrassing, but our families enjoyed it all. The BBC asked me to go down to Edinburgh to record a broadcast. The script they had prepared was even more embarrassing and I found it difficult to get the words out, sitting alone in a little glass-enclosed room in front of a microphone reading from a script which no persuasion could make them alter, and with a man outside waving hand signals when he wanted me to start, slow down, or speed up. I was given £4 and lunch in a pub in Princes Street which was the best part of the affair.

The episode closed with our being invited to dinner by Hugh Malcolm's parents who lived in a fine old house in Broughty Ferry just down the coast from Carnoustie and where our old Walruses still struggled reluctantly into the air from the river Tay. The wives of both Hugh Malcolm and Eyton-Bill were there and it was an occasion of well concealed anguish. Eyton-Bill was still on the 'missing' list and his wife asked to see me alone, hoping that I might give her some hope of his survival. I could only tell her that we went down in much the same way and survived.

The summer months rolled by and I settled comfortably into the daily routine of an instructor. On the sunny days I cycled to the air station.

When John Jameson arrived (ex 45th course and 821 Squadron in North Africa and Malta) to take a course in astro-navigation and eventually to become an instructor in this seemingly irrelevant art, he brought his wife Kitty and family to live close by us in Carnoustie and we shared in the purchase of an old Morris Minor (£30). Its steering could best be described as capricious, making unpremeditated dives to either side of the road, and our survival was only due to the lack of traffic. Rather bravely my dear young wife managed to drive me home in it after the end-of-course party held at the Seaforth Hotel. The wild ex-policemen made it their night's objective to get me incapably drunk. They succeeded.

About this time, and to our surprise, my wife discovered that she was pregnant. All the best rubber must have been used for aircraft tyres. However it seemed the right thing. The war might go on forever and we soon got used to the idea.

Bob Woolston, who had been in 800 Squadron on *Indomitable,* arrived with his glamorous wife to live nearby and to join the Naval Air Signal School. Frank Hemingway also arrived (ex-45th course) to join our own staff as an instructor.

The 63rd Observer Course arrived in October. They were very different to the last one, being on average no more than eighteen and straight from school. Uninitiated into the demon drink and oh so keen to fly. I felt an old man at twenty-three.

Navy blue battle-dress was approved by Their Lordships at this time and proved a much more practical rig for daily life and even better for flying, although the only flying I took part in was a search in an Albacore for a plane lost in the sea from Easthaven and an alarming trip in a Barracuda Mk 1, which 'Lofty' Logan asked me to undertake to report on its good or bad features from an observer's point of view.

Rumours had reached us that this Fairey monoplane replacement for the Albacore was not much loved by the squadrons which had received them, including my old 831 who for a time went back to operating their old Albacores. At first sight it was impressive and just missed being a good looking aircraft by having a strut braced, high mounted tailplane; a modification to the original design necessary to avoid the severe buffeting caused by the unusual Youngman designed flaps which could also be used as dive breaks.

The observer's cockpit under the long perspex canopy was everything one could desire. The floor-mounted seat was surprisingly comfortable with a magnificent view below the wing out of the two perspex 'bow windows'. With a compass mounted in each bay, bearings could be taken through nearly 360 degrees. The view standing up was equally impressive and there was even a small hinged windscreen from which you could look forward over the pilot's head. The only snag was that if either this or the air gunner's canopy was raised the pilot would complain about tail buffeting. To achieve the observer's view the Fairey designers had found it necessary to adopt a shoulder-mounted wing, which was too high above the ground to permit a conventional single strut retractable undercarriage; the result was the ungainly and heavy system hinged to the fuselage. The high wing also required a complex arrangement for wing folding, involving the folding back of the rear centre sections of the wing, and the lowering of hooped hand holds from the wing outer panels so that the ground crew could reach them and pull them back to engage their spigots in the tailplane.

In the landing configuration the Barra could be likened to a flying Christmas tree. I am told that it was easy to land the monster on a carrier, with the pilot having a good view over the nose and the undercarriage capable of taking a lot of punishment.

The Japanese had by now replaced their Kates with the Nakajima B6N2 (Jill) and later with the cranked wing Aichi B7A1 (Grace), both of which looked and performed better than the Barracuda, and were two-seaters.

Our take-off that day used every foot of the runway and we only just cleared the tops of the runway lead-in lights before staggering into the air. After the ungainly undercarriage had lifted up into the wing my pilot came through on the intercom, 'Sorry about that chum, but these Mk 1s are absolute cows to get off the ground'. And this without a torpedo. Only a handful of this mark were built, being seriously underpowered, having the same Rolls-Royce Merlin 30 engine as the Fulmar II with a three bladed propeller, and the Barracuda nearly 50% heavier.

I carried out a very successful shadowing exercise on the little steamship which patrolled the mineswept channel and served both as target and rescue vessel. I felt very much at home and reported favourably to Lofty on my experience. It was the beginning of a love/hate relationship with this oft maligned aircraft.

The winter of 1943/44 was surprisingly mild even this far north and there were not many days when our pupils were unable to be airborne. The death and glory business seemed to be in another world. Intelligence summaries came our way, and there were startling photographs of the Fleet Air Arm's battle with the U-boats; Swordfish, armed with rocket projectiles, and the massive American built Grumman Avenger, were to be seen flying off the tiny decks of the new Escort Carriers. We even seemed to be winning the war. The Axis had been driven out of Sicily and, seeing the way the wind was blowing, the Italians had given up the struggle and signed an armistice when the Allied armies invaded their mainland. After all it had endured, Malta was now free of threat. New American fleet carriers of the Essex class equipped with Hellcats, Dauntless and Avenger aircraft were now more than equal to the Japanese and were beginning to drive them, one by one, out of their island bases by means of carrier supported amphibious assaults. The Russians were pushing the Germans steadily back in the Ukraine.

John and Kitty Jameson with their young daughter joined us for Christmas Day — how lucky we were to be spending our first together. Joan was now visibly pregnant and in February she left for Newcastle. I took quarters at HMS *Condor* where on 21 March 1944 I received the news that I had a son. I made a quick trip down to make the acquaintance of my hefty offspring and a rather drowsy wife. It had not been an easy birth and both were still in hospital. It was fortunate that her family was able to look after them.

With the 63rd course now in its final month I began to feel that it was about time I got myself back into the flying game so I put in a request to return to an operational squadron. My pupils had done well and departed to await their commissions before going on to Greenwich. I was not expecting to see their eager young faces again but, as always, I was in for a surprise.

It was not long before I received a signal to join 812 Squadron at Stretton on 1 June 1944. I cleared up my office, bade farewell to all at HMS *Condor* and went on leave. If my wife was fearful of my going back to flying she never showed it. Kenneth Michael, as he was now christened, was proving more than a handful and so were both grandmothers. Nappies and disturbed nights were the order of the day.

Chapter 16
Barracudas

812 Squadron reformed at RNAS Stretton (HMS *Blackcap*) on 1 June 1944, and was equipped with twelve brand new Barracuda II aircraft. It was a squadron with a long history, being first formed as far back as 1933 when it operated the ungainly Blackburn Ripon, and later the Baffin, on HMS *Glorious,* finally re-equipping with Swordfish in 1936. At the outbreak of war *Glorious* sailed for the Indian Ocean to search for German 'raiders'. In the spring of 1940 the ship returned home and the squadron operated with RAF Coastal Command from shore bases on the Channel coast until it embarked on *Furious* in July, 1941 to take part in the raid on Kirkenes and Petsamo in Norway. The squadron was operating from the *Ark Royal* when it was torpedoed and sunk in November 1941, after which it operated in an anti-submarine role from the airfield at Gibraltar. With its Swordfish now equipped with ASV radar it was the first squadron to sink a U-boat at night. On returning home, night operations were carried out in the Channel with Coastal Command until the squadron was disbanded in December, 1942.

By great good fortune my new CO was Lieutenant Commander Cedric Coxon RN. Just turned twenty-three, he was one of the youngest of that rank in the Fleet Air Arm. A lovely man in every way, tall and good looking with an almost perpetual wide grin and most expressive hands which he would use to great effect when describing some flying manoeuvre or, if he could be persuaded, when giving one of Stanley Holloways monologues — 'Albert and the Lion' or 'Sam and his Musket' — he was surprisingly shy and it took a lot of persuasion (or beer) to get him to perform these party pieces. I missed my last chance of getting him to make a recording when he unexpectedly died recently, and this part of my story will lack the reminiscences I had hoped to draw upon. Although ill qualified to judge I would rate him as one of the Navy's finest pilots. He received his wings at No 1 Flying Training School at Netheravon on 2 May 1940. After a period of operational training on Sharks and Swordfish his flying ability resulted in his being lent to the RAF as an instructor on Fairey Battles and Avro Ansons. After a torpedo course at Crail and a deck landing course at Arbroath he joined 810 Swordfish Squadron on *Ark Royal* in May, 1941. In July he volunteered to fly one of the six replacement Swordfish to 830 Squadron and to join this hard pressed squadron in its nightly attacks on Axis shipping taking vital supplies to Rommel. He made seven night attacks and achieved six torpedo hits. His exploits are dramatically described in Kenneth Poolman's *Night Strike from Malta.* He returned home in March 1942 and was posted as a torpedo instructor to 786 Squadron at Crail where he became familiar with, and mastered, the idiosyncrasies of the Barracuda.

Lieutenant 'Spike' Regan RN, was our senior observer. A dark, dapper Irishman with a square jaw and a sardonic wit, he enjoyed nothing better than a quick trip to the nearest ale house — and there were plenty of them in Cheshire. I was destined to fly with the senior pilot, Lieutenant Peter Poole RNVR, later generally referred to as Peter 'Effing' Poole as a result of his constant, but seemingly unconscious, use of the scatological adjective regardless of his audience. No doubt the dear young Wrens who kept watch on the R/T had heard it all but to make it worse he was the worst offender in leaving his microphone on 'transmit'. A short, wiry little cockney with dark impish features and a mercurial nature, he was the most unlikely of naval officers. But he could certainly fly a Barracuda and throughout my time with the squadron I don't recall a single dodgy moment in the air and rarely a dull one as he kept up a constant stream of cockney comment over the intercom. From afar he could be identified by his battered cap which had a shiny top due to his using it to clean oil off his windscreen. He never wore battle-dress and I think he only had one uniform which he brushed vigorously for several minutes each morning. My TAG was Petty Officer Casey of the strong jaw, sallow face and impassive expression.

Seafires with strange, broad, black and white stripes on their fuselage and wings appeared briefly during the first few days and on 6 June we read that the Allies had begun the Normandy invasion. In the middle of the month a batch of young pilots joined the squadron, newly commissioned and trained either at Kingston in Canada, or at Pensacola in the USA, where fortunately they had put in most of their flying time in monoplanes, and did not suffer conversion to the Barracuda so badly as those used to the forgiving nature of the Swordfish and Albacore. For two weeks they had been on a special conversion course at Stretton with 798 Squadron. The Pensacola boys — and they were really just boys — thought that they would be given Dauntless or Avengers and were not too impressed with their new kites. A cheerful rivalry ensued between the two groups. Mostly a sober lot apart from two wild characters, Sub Lts 'Ace' Throssel and 'Johnny' Cookson. Throssel considered his flying prowess to be superior to the rest of the herd, and Cookson, with a few pints on board, had an urgent need to hit someone and, as far as I remember, always missed. Lt 'Pop' Bristow, an old hand, also joined to stiffen the ranks of the pilots.

Apart from 'Spike' the only other observers at this time were Sub Lts 'Tommy' Dewsnap and 'Toby' Tobias, the one blond and apparently guileless, the other dark and saturnine. They were always clowning. Their particular forte being a send up of two American airmen which always began with 'Well Major, what is your mission today?' and carried on with that strangely formalised manner which is so much at variance with the macabre irreverence of most British airmen.

The main body of our observers was not posted to the squadron until some months later, so we few observers went airborne mostly for the ride and to try out all our new gadgets. Our Mk II Barras, delivered spanking new from Fairey's factory at Stockport, were lavishly equipped with all the latest radio magic. Mk II N radar (ASV) with its display console conveniently mounted to swing down between one's legs, a new American crystal controlled R/T set for short range communication between aircraft, and a new American type homing beacon receiver. The pilot had a low-level radio altimeter designed to assist him in making night torpedo or A/S attacks giving him a yellow, green or red light below 400 feet. The green light was supposed to operate between 100 and 200 feet but did not inspire much confidence when it frequently still showed green with the aircraft's belly nearly touching the water. The TAG had the latest high frequency W/T set for longer range communication and, as a token for defence, a pair of .303 calibre Vickers gas operated guns stowed under a sliding hatch. Raising the hatch to fire the guns caused severe tail buffeting by its projection into the slipstream. The range and hitting power of these guns was totally inadequate against cannon-firing fighters and they might just as well have been dumped in the sea to save weight.

One wonders what operational role Their Lordships expected these aircraft to fulfil at this late stage of the war. The Italian fleet had surrendered and what was left of the German fleet rarely put to sea. In the Pacific theatre the dive-bomber had been shown to be the dominant naval weapon against capital ships and we were only three weeks away from the Battle of the Philippine Sea which virtually wiped out Japanese naval air power. There was still the continual submarine threat but the war against these was mainly being carried out by the Escort Carriers and their support groups. The Barracuda was certainly not the aircraft for all weather operation from a small deck and after all these years it could not match the range and speed of the old Japanese Kates and Vals. It was, like the Bisley, underpowered and obsolescent before it went into service.

But none of these thoughts crossed our innocent minds in June, 1944. We just climbed into our new Barras and flew across the Lancashire and Cheshire countryside enjoying being able to talk to each other and to ground control even if we needed an interpreter to understand my new pilot. Over Liverpool one day he decided to give me a taste of dive-bombing. I stood up to enjoy the view and watched the big flaps move to the unorthodox up position as we rolled over at 19,000 feet and plunged into a steep dive. The whole machine vibrated uncomfortably and the tailplane was shaking with a life of its own. Over the engine noise I heard intermittent words over the intercom and could only make out the one word 'parachute'. I quickly pulled my chute out of its storage, clipped it onto my harness and pulled back the hatch. The noise increased and the ground loomed up ahead. I hesitated, imagining myself slamming straight into the tail and found myself being pressed down into the cockpit as we started to pull out of the dive. When we were at last flying straight and level in comparative quiet I yelled 'What was all that about parachutes?'

'Ow well!' replied Peter, 'I thought as 'ow you oughter get a bit a practice putting the effing thing on!' I was speechless and it was not until we were back on the ground that I told him I had been half way out of the aircraft and might have been in someone's backyard at Liverpool. I have yet to meet an observer who baled out of a Barracuda to ask about that tail.

There are some fine old pubs in Cheshire and most evenings we old naval rakes piled into the CO's Bedford utility, christened 'Tilly' and went out for what Spike always called 'a bit of a thrash'. Cedric's driving, like his flying, was 'sportif'. He enjoyed keeping some two feet behind the bumper of the car in front through bends and twists for mile after mile. For lesser mortals it was an alarming experience but demonstrated his remarkable reflexes.

Spike's birthday party was a very boozy 'do' in the mess during which I climbed up on a couple of tables and scribed 'Fighting Twelfth' in large lettering on the virgin ceiling. The station CO Commander Madden, was not at all pleased, having just had it repainted to remove previous graffiti. I was old enough to know better, he said, and sentenced me to report for one week to the duty officer i/c the early morning parade.

The last two weeks of the month were devoted to familiarisation and formation flying for the new boys. Dummy torpedoes were fitted to give them flying experience with the extra weight. Midshipman John Dickson made a name for himself when he burst a tyre before take-off. After this had been replaced he took off again. 'And how did you find it handled?' asked Cedric on his return.

'No problem,' replied John, 'Just the same as before!'

'I'm not surprised,' exclaimed Cedric. 'You left your torpedo behind on the deck!'

On 28 June the squadron flew all twelve aircraft up to RNAS Crail (HMS *Jackdaw*) passing over my home town on the way up to Scotland which enabled a proud father to pick out his first-born in his pram in the garden and broadcast the fact to a disinterested squadron.

812, 814 and 837 Barracuda squadrons were the first TBR units in which the pilots carried out their full operational training, including deck landings, as a completely formed squadron rather than drawing on pilots trained individually at specialist establishments. This was the reason that a full complement of observers did not join us until later as they were not needed for the torpedo attack phase about to commence at Crail. None of us realised how protracted this training programme was to become.

The next week I was despatched to my old stamping ground at Arbroath for a week's course on the Mk II N ASV equipment. The flying was mostly in 737 Squadron's old Ansons fitted out as flying classrooms. I learnt that the heart of the ASV was the Magnetron valve and it was drummed into us that it needed a lot of cooling and if the fan providing it was to stop the unit would melt. If you heard it stop you were to give the casing a good slap and cross your fingers — standard procedure for most radio gizmos.

There was time for sitting out in the sun in a deck chair and a lot of time for drinking. It was around this time that I got the nickname 'Blood'. I am somewhat vague on the subject but it seems that I got more than a little hooched one night in the mess and decided to address everyone present over the Tannoy about the need for more action, death and glory, etc. etc. As if there wasn't enough of that going on all around the world.

Sadly, the Gods of War must have heard me for I was no sooner back at Crail than Petty Officer pilot Steve Blakey, flying solo, was killed when he crashed into a deceptively sloping cornfield while shooting up his girl friend's house. There was very little left of the aircraft. The long march behind the coffin through country lanes was depressingly sad and the 'last post' produced the usual lump in the throat. Cedric's admonishments probably fell on deaf ears as there were boasts of rolling and looping the Barra from the likes of Throssel. Peter did not go in for these aerial antics.

Day and night the squadron took to the air, formed up into flights behind Cedric, and practised the difficult routine for a co-ordinated torpedo attack. In some respects it was easier than in the days of the Albacore being able to transmit commands over the R/T (if Peter refrained from leaving his transmitter switched on). And no longer was it necessary for the pilot to aim ahead of the target as the latest torpedoes could be set by the pilot's computer to alter course automatically after entering the water. In spite of this there lurked a new hazard as deadly as the enemy.

There had recently been a number of occasions when Barras were seen to dive into the sea after levelling off low over the sea in the final stage of a practice torpedo attack and there had been no survivors. I witnessed one of these incidents and saw a bright flash and a splash in quick succession; it seemed as though the aircraft exploded, but the opinion at the time was that it was due to a high speed wing tip stall caused by skidding the aircraft to correct the aim and what I saw as a flash was the sun reflected in the light blue underside as it flicked over on to its back. Captain 'Winkle' Brown, the famous naval test pilot, reports in his book *Wings on my Sleeve* that he located the source of the problem as the interaction of the dive brakes and the rudder when operated simultaneously. Much was expected of a pilot who had to fully retrim his aircraft after retracting the dive flaps when only some 150 feet above the sea and at the same time avoid other kites coming in to the target from all directions. These dive brakes caused our boys other problems being responsible for some very heavy landings when accidentally put into this position instead of flaps down. 'Buster' May, who became CO of 817 Squadron, told me recently that he forbade the use of dive brakes.

To make matters worse our ebullient 'Ace' Throssel burst into the ready room one day full of excitement. He had discovered an effortless technique for pulling the Barra out of a steep dive. None of that pulling back on the control column, just wind back on the tailplane trim and out she would come on her own. Apart from the obvious dangers of retrimming at high speed and low level, this procedure seriously overstressed the wings and was stamped on by Cedric as soon as he got to hear of it. But I suspect that the likes of Throssel paid no heed, and as the months sped by the effects of overstressed wings became increasingly apparent with gaps opening up in the top skin of the wings and various cracks appearing.

In the first week of August Cedric flew me all the way down to RNAS St Merryn (HMS *Vulture*), near Padstow in Cornwall where I was to take a three week Air Strike course at the new School of Naval Air Warfare. It was a lovely trip, slipping in and out of clouds over the Cambrian mountains and then across the Bristol Channel before following the romantic coast of Devon and Cornwall with Atlantic rollers tracing a white outline around their coves and rocky beaches.

It was soon evident that this was no run of the mill course. The fighter pilots, TBR pilots, and observers taking part were all two ringers and long in the tooth by wartime standards. We flew in Barracuda IIs, the fighter boys in Corsair IIIs and Spitfire Vs of 736 Squadron and there was never a dull moment. We were there to be taught the latest techniques for the attack and defence of strike formations. The instructors were an enthusiastic bunch and approached the subject with a gay abandon somewhat lacking in realism. The philosophy was that if we were set upon by enemy fighters there was no need to lie back and die with nobility, we could be up there doing something about it. As far as TBRs were concerned the 'something' turned out to be a violent 'corkscrew' manoeuvre, first introduced by the RAF and designed to disrupt the aim of a fighter making an attack from any angle. To add to the excitement of the manoeuvre, which in the back seat felt like what I imagine one experiences on a bucking bronco, we were expected to carry it out while flying in formation. This involved a change in the time honoured vics of three aircraft, and adopting a formation of two groups stepped down in line astern, flying parallel some fifty yards apart. It was the observer's job to scan the sky and report enemy sightings on the clock system so dramatically highlighted in the film *Twelve O'clock High*. The observer in the lead aircraft would call out on the R/T 'Corkscrew Left' (or Right) when he judged the enemy to be about to open fire. Lead aircraft were fitted with fighter type VHF sets for communication with a fighter escort and this added further weight to an already overweight aircraft. The sight of sixteen Barras violently gyrating in the sky is unforgettable.

We were introduced to the magic of the gyro gunsight, developed in the USA and used to good effect in the mid upper and central gun turrets on their Fortress bombers. The twin Vickers guns in our 736 Squadron Barras were equipped with a gyro sight linked to a small movie camera. Perched in the unfamiliar TAG's cockpit we took aim at Spitfires and Corsairs approaching from positions which required us to have the skills of a contortionist. Their favourite attack was to peel off some five thousand feet above us and dive vertically through the middle of our formation. They too had gyro gunsights and cameras and the SNAW staff had devised a technique of analysing the films to establish whether attackers or defenders had made any hits.

I fail to see what good this did to observers — it was not possible to get oneself from the observer's to the TAG's cockpit — however it was great fun, especially when carrying out very low level exercises on one's own, weaving between trees, through valleys, around houses and generally scaring the living daylights out of the locals. The Spitfire or Corsair pilot on one's tail, was in considerable danger of flying himself into the ground in his efforts to put us in his sights. My particular pilot 'Nobby' Clarke was a virtuoso on the Barra and could make it do things beyond the call of duty.

During the second week I persuaded my wife to leave our offspring in the hands of grandparents and make the long train journey down to Padstow where I had booked a room in a small boarding house. Scrumpy cider in scruffy little pubs was all that Cornwall could offer, the sea was too rough to bathe, but we enjoyed each other's company, and it was summer.

The next flying trick they had us perform was to climb in two-column formation up through dense cloud, on a compass course, and with only the tail wheel of the aircraft in front to be seen gently rising and falling just above our propeller tips. Anxious moments were followed by the exhilaration of bursting out of a grey nowhere into brilliant sunshine with its light glinting on the wings of Corsairs high above us as we proceeded to a dummy dive-bombing attack on Lundy Island. On another day we attacked Yeovilton and encountered their defending fighters who mixed it with our Corsairs. This was the way wars should be fought — cameras and no bullets. It had all seemed rather different in our Bisleys in some other world.

The final part of our jousting involved the firing of our rear guns at a drogue towed by a Miles Martinet on a range off the coast. Colours painted on the bullets were supposed to show up on the drogue but as far as I recall we achieved very few hits even with a gyro gunsight at close range. There was nothing in this experience to change my view that these guns were not worth their weight, a view expressed some months later which got me into a lot of trouble. We all got a fun type certificate to certify that we had graduated from SNAW and were exhorted to spread the 'gospel' to our various squadrons.

I returned to Crail to find the boys in the final stages of their torpedo training dropping 'runners' (just like the real thing but with a buoyancy chamber instead of explosive). John Dickson was not very popular when his torpedo broke up on entering the water as they cost a lot of money. The squadron was now up to sixteen aircraft and pilots.

Peter was still haranguing all pilots at all times over the R/T, and me as well over the intercom.

'Where are they all Blood? Have you counted them all? Close up Blue Two! Where's the effing target Blood?'

Cedric seemed to have given up on his earlier insistence that we all fell in for PT at 0700 followed by a pint of milk each. Perhaps he was putting on weight.

During these last three months some of the greatest dramas of the war had been unfolding; the fall of Rome and then Paris, the V1 Buzz Bombs landing on London, the Russians pushing the German Army back into Poland, and the Americans regaining the Mariana Islands with their increasingly powerful naval air strength. All this we read in the newspapers, but it seemed to be in another world as once more we packed up our kit ready to move on.

On 7 September we flew in loose formation across Scotland and down the coast to RNAS Burscough (HMS *Ringtail*), seven miles east of Southport in featureless flat countryside. The spare seats were occupied by ground crew; always anxious to get airborne. This was to be the wrong day for one of them flying with Sub Lt 'Les' Terry with Tommy Dewsnap as observer. They had an engine failure, and ditched safely in shallow water off the beach at St Annes. They were rescued by the Blackpool lifeboat after spending two hours in their dinghy. Dewsnap was only concerned about his uniform which he was to wear at his forthcoming wedding.

Waiting for us at Burscough was our full complement of observers. To my surprise, all of them were from my last batch of pupils at Arbroath; apparently they had asked to be sent to the same squadron and it seemed most unlike Their Lordships to have acquiesced. In their crisp new uniforms they looked even younger than I remembered them. Their average age must have been no more than nineteen, the youngest was Midshipman 'Bambi' Brook who was only eighteen. They had been waiting our arrival with some apprehension having heard grim tales of the Barracuda which older hands took macabre pleasure in spreading. I think that with my arrival they felt that at least they had someone to hold their hands.

But first we all went on ten days leave for which my dear girl had rented a bungalow overlooking the sea at Bamburgh and close by the grim walls of its timeless castle. Firstborn was now six months old and already a heavyweight — it was the first time he had consciously seen me and I don't think he was too impressed. His pram could be found daily outside the Crewe Arms. Nights of passion were generally disturbed by his noisy needs.

On Sunday, 17 September the 'black out' was officially deemed to be at an end after four long years; the German Air Force was too busy defending the Fatherland. We were the only people in Bamburgh to celebrate and our bungalow glowed like a beacon during the night as well as emitting clouds of smoke every morning when I battled to light the kitchen range.

We grasped our brief idyll gratefully, it was still warm and sunny and never at any time had the war seemed so remote. And yet we never allowed ourselves to talk of its ending. All too soon prams, cots, cases and baby had to be packed into the train back to Newcastle and then for me it was back to Burscough, to rain clouds and fog sweeping in daily from the west.

Intensive working up with newly formed crews was now the order of the day. Weather permitting, we flew our Barras in all the routine exercises — Navexs over the Irish Sea, dive-bombing targets in the mud flats off Fleetwood and night torpedo attacks on a target ship using ASV to locate and flares to illuminate. Cedric had great expertise in attacking ships at night gained the hard way in Malta and I flew with him on a number of occasions when we led the squadron into the black pit of a moonless night, only the flickering glow from the Merlins' exhaust stubs and the green shimmer from the ASV screen throwing any light on the scene. I had to ask the other observers to keep their ASV sets switched off as I soon found that they caused interference on my own, so they had little to do apart from keeping a check on my navigation (which I doubt they did) in case they had to return to base on their own. Cedric found it a great help to be able to communicate with all aircraft on the R/T but discouraged loose chatter. It was a change after being used to Peter.

With October came the cold and the rain. There seemed to be mud everywhere and short wellies became the rig of the day, I even wore them in the air rather than inflict mud on my flying boots. If a Barra got its wheels off the edge of the taxi track it could be stranded like a fish out of water and even twist its rear fuselage in an effort to escape.

Our living quarters was the ubiquitous Nissen hut equipped with standard model iron beds in opposing rows, four a side and, most important of all, the cast iron stove in the centre around which all would cluster. Here, into the small hours could be found Dewsnap and Tobias playing bridge, a game that seemed capable of producing much bad feeling. Anyone considering themselves good enough to join them was subjected to an inquisition.

To go to the bathroom you had to venture out partly dressed into the elements with the wind blowing up into one's nether regions. Most of us developed severe colds and the evenings often found me in the sick bay inhaling Friars Balsam under a towel.

In this bleak part of the country even the booze was now in short supply. Only one bottle of whisky was brought out in the Mess bar at 1900 hours and a small queue would form for those like myself for whom this had become a favourite beverage. With most of our young observers joining the navy straight from school, they had had no time in their young lives to get into the pub crawling or boozy mess party habits which were so much a way of life for us 'older characters'. It was almost impossible to get them to join in our antics and this worried us — when the going got rough, how would they relax stretched nerves or turn their minds away from grim realities? The pilots seemed to be made of sterner stuff and in spite of an intensive programme of day and night flying, often in atrocious weather, there were no serious accidents. John Dickson selected 'dive brakes' instead of 'flaps' after a night ADDL [Dummy Deck Landing] and ran into a hedge when trying to take off again. Either the Barra was not so much of a handful as some have reported or we had a particularly good batch of pilots.

We had our first glimpse of the Curtiss SB2C Helldivers of 1820 Squadron; as ungainly as the Barra and reported to be even more of a handful in a dive; so much so that they were disbanded shortly afterwards and never went into service. The American squadrons which operated them asked to be given back their Douglas Dauntless. I was very envious of the Fairey Firefly F1s of 1772 Squadron which appeared briefly and gave us some fighter evasion experience. At this stage of the war it seemed to be a more effective aircraft than the Barracuda and could carry two 1000lb bombs.

It is difficult to find anything agreeable to say about the local village of Burscough. There was the odd 'foot on the brass rail' bar where one could chat up the ATS girls or visit the cinema to be surrounded by a swarm of boisterous local children. Southport had more to offer but more often than not we were too 'flaked out' to bother.

By the end of October the squadron had settled down well and, apart from a lack of deck landing experience, was ready to go to sea. I wish we had been able to do so. With news reports of successful actions taking place on all fronts and especially the defeat of the Japanese fleet at Leyte Gulf in the Philippines, there was a strong desire to get on with it — whatever 'it' was to be.

On 16 November the squadron moved to RNAS Fearn (HMS *Owl*), twenty-five miles north east of Inverness on the Moray Firth and just about as far away from civilisation as you can get. If Burscough was cold, Fearn was colder, but a brisk cold with clear skies.

814 and 837 Barracuda squadrons had arrived the week before. What on earth were Their Lordships going to do with this bevy of Barras? It seemed more than likely that we were destined to go out to the Far East and by now we had all heard the horror stories of Barras failing to take off with a full war load on a hot tropical day.

With some hundred commissioned aircrew arriving, accommodation was stretched to the limit. I was lucky to get a large room to myself in a wooden hut half a mile from the mess. It had its own delightfully Victorian cast iron stove and even a telephone. The small mess became like a hive when all were squeezed in, bringing an uninhibited feeling of mateyness in which old and new songs could be sung and terrible tales could be told of the 'Beastly Barracuda'. As always in Scotland, the food was good and there was plenty of grog.

As for flying, it was the same old routine of dive bombing, anti-submarine and torpedo attacks in which Peter and I took little part. We had already seen too much of it and were happy to lounge in the crew room trying to keep warm by the stove.

The only novelty to break the monotony was what was called a 'carrier ranging exercise' in which we joined either 814 or 837 Squadron to line up on the end of the runway in threes as though we were on a carrier deck, and then, after individually taking off, we formed up as an attack group.

These exercises usually resulted in an almighty shambles, mostly due to the Barra's lack of engine power making it difficult for a delayed aircraft to catch up with the rest of the boys and resulted in the squadron's first major calamity on 25 November. It was the usual frosty morning, John Dickson took off late due to a jammed cartridge in the starter breech and was unable to catch up the others, leaving a gap in the formation. Sub Lt Muncer manoeuvred to fill the gap from below and at the same time Petty Officer Hunt attempted to do the same from above. Both aircraft collided and crashed into Lake Eye. Out of the six crew members only Sub Lt Saggs, who was Muncer's observer, survived. Sub Lt Crosthwaite, who was Hunt's observer, was knocked unconscious when his head hit the radar console, being only restrained by his simple lap-type seat belt, and drowned before he could be rescued. I had already come to the conclusion that this is what would happen when ditching in a Barra and decided that if it ever happened to me I would stand up pressed against the for'd bulkhead, putting my head against crossed arms and holding the windscreen bar. Nearly a year later it probably saved my life.

There were some ill winds, and, at times snow blowing over Fearn. At least they blew some good to our much respected boss, Cedric. He met Muncer's widow at the funeral and fell in love, although we didn't learn this until some months later.

One snowy night I was detailed for 'runway control' dressed like a Michelin man in every bit of clothing I could lay my hands on, standing on the end of the runway in a wilderness of white with my red and green Aldis light the only colour apart form the wing tip lights of our Barras which appeared out of the snowflakes like noisy phantoms.

At the end of the month 'Bibby's boys'[Lt Cdr Bibby, 787 Squadron] arrived with their Seafires to give all three squadrons exercises in fighter evasion, all very dashing and exciting but somehow I couldn't see us faring any better against Bf 109s or Zeros than poor old 18 Squadron in Bisleys, with our two .303 calibre pop guns in the back and not even a turret. At least the Grumman Avenger had a .5 gun in a turret, as well as a bomb bay big enough to take a torpedo or four 500lb bombs.

Our work-up seemed to be endless. It was already December and we had been skylarking about for six months. All three squadrons had been brought up to a strength of 18 Barracudas with additional crews, but there was still no gen on our future destiny. There was even talk of the war in Europe being over by Christmas — but that was before the German offensive in the Ardennes. There was also a promise of two weeks leave over Christmas. Apart from the odd flic shown in very cramped conditions, and boozing, there was damn all to do in a winter at Fearn. I never even ventured into Tain, which was the nearest town, and recall no local pubs.

On 12 December 1944, the squadron mounted a dummy dive-bombing attack on RAF Crimond against opposition from Seafires. It all seemed like a game by now but it was good to see that we were beginning to play quite well as a team and there had been no more accidents which says much for both pilots and ground crews, the latter having to work on the aircraft with near frozen hands. One of my greatest regrets is that I failed, throughout my flying time, to express appreciation of the efforts of our ground crews. We saw little of them except when climbing in or out of our aircraft, but there is no excuse for my not visiting them while they were doing their maintenance work, especially as I had started on a career as an aeronautical engineer.

In the middle of December we all departed on leave. For me it was back to home and beauty and the delights of sleeping in a double bed with a loving wife, even if at times interrupted at critical moments by a particularly boisterous nine-month-old son.

Instead of reporting back to Fearn I received a cable instructing me to proceed to RNAS Burscough for a three week ASV course. I saw the New Year in on the train in the company of three army types and a rather attractive ATS young lady. Burscough was no more inviting in January 1945 than it had been in October and just as wintry as Fearn. To make it worse I had arrived ten days too early for the course and had to hang around without any oppos. I was pleased to see 'Toby' Tobias and 'Snappers' Dewsnap arrive on the 10th, having been flown over by Jack Birch from Ballyhalbert, an RAF airfield on the Northern Ireland coast some miles east of Belfast to which the squadron had moved on the 5th. They brought the news that we were to join the new light fleet carrier *Vengeance* after some intensive dummy deck landing practice [ADDLs] at Ballyhalbert.

A nice bunch of very 'clued up' instructors tried their best to make me understand the theoretical aspects of radar. I regret that it went in one ear and out the other. On the other hand with daily flying in 735 Squadron's Anson classrooms, and in Barracudas I got to be able to operate a Mk II N ASV set with some degree of skill.

I put in some good drinking time with Toby and Snappers, bumping into the Captain's car one night while sliding like children on the icy road leading into the station, not exactly the behaviour of officers and gentlemen. My dear wife travelled to Southport to spend the weekend with me in a somewhat seedy hotel. The highlight of the weekend was my falling through the ice in my best blues and greatcoat when we attempted to cross the boating lake on the sea front, followed by an unsuccessful attempt to dry my clothes in front of the small gas fire in our bedroom. This resulted in the Hotel Manager knocking on the door to ask if we were using the fire as he hadn't enough gas pressure to cook the lunch. So Joan took them to a dry cleaners and when we got them back, still somewhat damp, we went to see Bob Hope and Bing Crosby in *The Road to Rio.*

While we pottered about on the last week of our course the boys at Ballyhalbert were making their first landings on the deck of a carrier, not in the forgiving Swordfish or Albacore, but in a Barracuda in rough winter weather on a much smaller flight deck than that of a fleet carrier. It was a lot to ask of them and yet all twelve who left Ballyhalbert on 26 January landed safely on *Vengeance,* which was sailing in the storm-swept waters of the Firth of Clyde. This was a remarkable achievement and they deserved the party in the wardroom that night at which all the grog was free. Those pilots who had been put aboard before the ship sailed made their first carrier take-offs and landings the next day. They even took with them their observers and TAGs which, in hindsight I feel was an unnecessary risk, but all went well. On the third day, after taking part in an ALT on the ship, 'Poppa' Bristow made a bad landing and ended up half way over the side of the ship.

Not knowing about all these capers, Toby, Snappers and I finished our course and were told to join the squadron at RNAS Ayr; another grim place with poor accommodation. When we arrived it was difficult to find out what was going on as the squadron seemed to be split up all over the place, some at Ballyhalbert, some on *Vengeance* and one or two at Ayr. The weather was dreadful but most of the crews arrived back on board by 5 February to get their first experience of being boosted off the 'accelerator' (as it now seemed to be called) and, for most, their first sighting of an Admiral, when the Flag Office Carrier Training (FOCT) flew aboard to see how things were shaping up. The flying display put on for him included an ALT in the morning and dive bombing in the afternoon; it was all a bit of a shambles due to thick cloud, but considering that it was only two weeks since the first deck landing I was surprised it all went off without an accident.

There was work to be done getting the ship ready to sail overseas and the squadron flew ashore to Ayr on 10 February.

Cedric dashed off on leave and it was quite a surprise to hear that he had got himself married at Wetherby; fast work, but who was I to talk. Spike was best man. When Spike got back, he and I were kept busy organising W/T exercises and Navexs over the Firth of Clyde. We did no flying ourselves, being the older generation.

I hadn't even seen *Vengeance.* We were all due to fly on board on 26 February, however rain stopped play and we didn't get off until the following morning with eleven aircraft. How the years rolled away as I looked down again at the glory of a carrier steaming at speed over a white flecked sea. Three and a half years had gone by since my first landing on Indomitable, but this time there was a refreshing, if bizarre, difference to the procedure. Jackie Fisher never spoke a word when landing — Peter Poole never stopped.

"Ook down! Is the 'ook down Blood?'

'Yes the hook's down Peter!' (You could just see it by leaning out into the blister.)

'Right! Wheels down! — Is the 'ook down?'

'Yes it's down!'

'Right! Flaps down! Are you watching Blood?'

'Yes!' (The observer had a grandstand view of the approach through the port blister.)

'Well look at that silly f——— waving his b——- arms about — if he thinks I'm going to pay any attention to him he's f——- wrong!'

(The approaching deck now looks very much smaller than *Indom*'s.)

'Right now! 'Ere we go!'

(Following my decision not to fasten my lap strap, I braced myself as the flight deck panorama flashes by followed by a good old thump and the usual deceleration.)

'There now! What d'y think of that eh? Beautiful! Beautiful!'

I don't think a reply was expected — it seemed OK to me. Any landing from which I climbed out onto the deck was OK by me and, whether or not Peter paid any attention to the batsman, I never had a single prang with him.

The barriers went down and with a burst of engine power we taxied over it and braked to a halt. Not another word from Peter as he initiated the somewhat hilarious procedure for folding a Barracuda's wings by setting the flap jacks to fold the trailing edges of the wings up and over each mainplane alongside the canopy of my cockpit. From there on there was none of the elegance of the powered, birdlike wing folding of the Avenger. For one thing, the wing was so high off the deck that it was not possible to reach it until retractable hoops were lowered from the wing tips. It needed four men of the deck crew to unlock, fold back, and secure spigots on the top of each wing tip to the tailplane. It was these quite tall spigots together with ASV antennae on top of the wings which gave the Barra its Christmas tree appearance. And so to the steep climb down from the top of the wing stub onto the port wheel and finally onto the rain-swept deck to feel the tremor of the ships engines making full speed.

Ahead of us was the awe-inspiring sight of a Vought Corsair IV of 1850 Squadron which had landed just before us. Their CO was Lt Cdr 'Mike' Hordern RN, an elegant and experienced fighter pilot who had survived the tribulations of 803 Squadron in Ceylon in April 1942. They had joined the ship two days before us after carrying out their deck landing training on our sister ship, the *Venerable*. From my spell at St Merryn I was familiar with this cranked wing fighter of such massive proportions, but at the time I was unaware of its fearsome potentiality — it could fly further and carry more bombs than a Barracuda and match any naval fighter of its day in combat. We had heard the tales that the American Navy had found it too difficult to land on a carrier and had dumped them on us, but with a modified undercarriage capable of absorbing the heaviest landings the boys of 1850 seemed to do the job remarkably well even if their approach to the deck in a sweeping curve looked particularly fearsome. It was an alarming sight to see them start their 2000 horsepower Pratt & Witney Twin Wasp engines; an enormous gush of flame would erupt from its exhaust pipe and deck crews frequently sprayed a fire extinguisher into the pipe during the start.

Peter and I shared a cabin on the starboard side aft, with access up a short stairway to the flight deck. It was more comfortable than I was expecting, having a desk with a gimballed lamp, and a small washbasin unit. For the first time I was introduced to the early morning Peter Poole ablutions, a performance which produced cascades of water from a vigorous face wash, followed by a prolonged lathering with shaving soap, and then a meticulous use of the razor. The whole performance, including shaving, was repeated. Then there was the brushing of that poor old uniform and, of course, that shiny cap.

Somehow I ended up having the top bunk bed which was all right except when climbing in after a heavy night. As always, in the colder climes, I wore the woolly bedsocks which my mother considered an essential item of nightware for all civilised people. And of course, pyjamas — none of that vest and underpants between the sheets.

Vengeance was in most respects a scaled down version of an *Illustrious* class fleet carrier, with a single hangar which could accommodate 18 Barracudas and 24 Corsairs, and with large, square-shaped lifts at each end. There were no 4.5 inch gun turrets, only 40 and 20 mm Bofors guns to provide defence. The flight deck was fitted with eight arrestor wires and the usual two barriers.

The most striking aspect in the mess was the preponderance of VR types and how young they looked. Regrettably the higher echelons of command did not reflect the wind of change that had blown through the Air Arm since 1939. You might have expected that we would have had battle-hardened Commanders with recent aircrew experience. It was said, unkindly, that Commander (F) had last flown a Fairey Flycatcher, while Commander (O) had spent most of the war in the British Embassy in the USA.

As always, the mess was alive with 'buzzes' about our imminent sailing for the Mediterranean and on to the Far East. I wasn't surprised and I can't say that I was all that keen on the prospect of taking on the Japanese in what was going to be their own backyard.

On our first morning at sea we were all up before dawn for the boys to make their first take-offs and landings in the dark. Once again it says much for their training and ability that there were no accidents.

Flying continued for the next two days during which I went up to get some experience with the new type of American homing beacon which, instead of rotating, sent out a discreet Morse letter in each of twelve sectors over 360 degrees. Knowing the disposition of the sector letters, it was a simple matter to fly the appropriate course once one had picked up the signal in the beacon receiver, even if more than one letter could be heard as the carrier drew nearer. It was a piece of cake compared with earlier days.

Almost everyone in the squadron now had an 'oppo' and being 'on board' had drawn everyone together. The boys de-bagged Cedric at a party one night and at last I felt that we were a real squadron with an identity and a pride.

After putting into Greenock for a day we were back at sea again on 4 March. What should have been a quiet Sunday was livened up by Lt Charles 'Bum' Wintringham stalling on the approach and ditching. Fortunately everyone got out safely, but, as ever, it showed that there was no room for mistakes in this game; flying proved to be just as much a threat to survival as the Germans or the Japs. I have often wondered how many more died in accidents rather than in action.

Back again in Greenock all aircrew were sent off on three days' leave. I think everybody knew that it would be the last we would see of home for a long time and when I took my parting from the gorgeous girl and lusty son I seemed to have lost a little of that feeling of immortality. I like to think it didn't show.

We returned from leave to find the light fleet carriers *Venerable* and *Colossus* anchored close by with Admiral C. H. J. Harcourt flying his flag on board *Venerable*. The next day we all fell in on deck for Sunday Divisions and the Admiral came over to carry out a Ship's Inspection. There must have been some high level discussion of the problem arising from cracks in the wings of our Barracudas; these had begun to appear in the cutaway in the port wing which housed the landing light and camera, and there were also ominous gaps appearing on the top inboard skins of the wings. In front of numerous squadron onlookers the Admiral climbed up a ladder to inspect the crack and, in the booming voice Admirals tend to affect, announced that he couldn't see how a small crack like that could cause any problem and told everyone that a crack twenty feet long hadn't caused any problem on his last ship. The remark didn't go down very well or inspire much confidence in his knowledge of naval aviation, and here we were, over five years into the war and the top brass still didn't seem to know what it was all about. I am probably being unjust, but that's how it seemed to us at the time.

At 1300 hours on 12 March, *Vengeance, Venerable* and *Colossus* weighed anchor and sailed from Greenock [forming Aircraft Carrier Group 11]. It was soon announced that we were bound for Malta and we didn't need to be told where after that. As we were passing through the North Channel that evening, the ship went to action stations and we were called to the crew room where we were told to standby for an anti-submarine strike.

One of our destroyer escort began dropping depth charges and the old adrenalin began to flow, but moving at high speed we would have been a difficult target and my luck held never to have had to face being torpedoed.

By morning we were ploughing west out into the Atlantic with visibility clamped right down. Anti-submarine patrols were flown from dawn to dusk. It appeared that Commander Fenwick RN, who was Commander Operations, was unsure of the best routine for these patrols and Spike and I were called up to the Ops room to give an opinion. If a bit out of date, he made up for it by his charm and readiness to listen to our views. I was rather pleased that all our young observers found their way back to the carrier in spite of the weather, some of them having to home in on the beacon.

The weather improved when we turned south and Commander (O) set up a night exercise in which the aircraft were to patrol around the carrier at a ten mile radius. I told him that I was a bit concerned about our young observers being able to cope with the navigation problem and after some haggling he agreed that Peter and I could carry out the exercise leading the others in formation. I didn't find it too easy, there was no moon, and we never saw the ship from beginning to end, but it was possible to judge our position from the ship on my ASV. I hoped we wouldn't be asked to do it again.

By 16 March we were down by the Azores and turned eastwards towards the Straits of Gibraltar in glorious sunny weather. In the afternoon we launched eleven Barras and twelve Corsairs, making a combined ALT and strafing attack on the fleet, all of which was rather fun until it came time to land when the rise and fall of the deck at the round-down, due to the heavy swell, caused numerous wave-rounds, dodgy moments and much panic, particularly for the Corsairs with their high approach speeds.

Commander (F) called a meeting of senior aircrew to discuss operational problems. I made the suggestion that, from my experience, TAGs, their

W/T radios, and their guns should be made redundant to save weight and improve performance. This was received like a lead balloon, as also was my idea for keeping spare radio and radar sets near the flight deck (which I did anyway in my cabin).

On 17 March I flew with Cedric ahead of the ship to Gibraltar, to take some official paperwork and mail. The Rock was a magical sight seen from the air for the first time, as though it had been placed there by the Greek Gods to guard the entrance to their world. With the African and Spanish coasts diverging into the haze to the East we banked around the white rain collecting sheets covering the east face and were bounced about by the air turbulence as we came into land at North Front airfield, which eighteen months ago had been the staging post for all the squadrons which took part in the North African operation.

We had both forgotten to take our caps with us and were stopped while walking down the main street by an RN Captain and chastised like a couple of naughty boys for being improperly dressed. After a couple of La Inas in the Bristol Hotel's cellar bar (no longer there on my last visit) we bought as much fresh fruit as we could carry and flew back on board to find that one of the Corsairs had nosed over on the deck and had to be cleared away before we could land.

White cap covers were again the order of the day, and with the sun and calm sea we might have been on a Mediterranean cruise as we steamed along the North African coast for the next two days, passing within sight of Algiers and Cape Bon. How different it all seemed to those drama filled days of 1942 when fighter pilots spent their days in the cockpit, and every daylight minute one could expect a Ju 88 to be on the scene.

The Corsairs flew off to Malta on the 19th and we were boosted off on the accelerator early on the morning of the 20th. Malta was a sort of home coming for Cedric for it was here in 1941 that he had played such a successful part in the night attacks on Axis shipping and we had been told great tales of the rugged life on Hal Far airfield, the shattered mess, and the weaving between bomb holes to take off and land. And here we were on a bright sunny morning with everything seeming shipshape and Bristol fashion. The white painted, balustraded mess was immaculate, and the food was good; I particularly remember poached eggs on toast for tea. The Nissen huts we slept in were as good as Nissen huts can be.

By the time the Barracudas and Corsairs of 814 and 1851 Squadrons had arrived from *Venerable,* it must have seemed to the Hal Far staff like an invasion. We thought that it was to be a brief stopover on our way to the Pacific and everyone would have been happy, if not enthusiastic, about this. But no, it was back to even more concentrated working-up which was all beginning to seem a bit pointless. It would have been worse had we known that we would be in Malta for two whole months, attractive though the place might be for a holiday, if a little bare and dusty and without good beaches. As if to rub in our situation the Fleet Carrier *Implacable* sailed past on its way to action in the Pacific, equipped with two squadrons of Seafire L IIIs and one each of Avenger IIs and Firefly FR1s. With 814 we made a combined dummy strike on her on 24 March, with our squadron dive-bombing and 814 carrying out a torpedo attack against its defending fighters. I wouldn't like to have been doing it for real.

Almost every day we seemed to be dive-bombing little Filfla island with practice bombs. At night there were the attractions of Valetta which, in spite of all the years of relentless bombing, had made a remarkable recovery. As is well known, the Maltese girls are very attractive and, with the Navy still quite popular, the boys seemed to have a good time. For an old married character it was either eating out (if one's nerves could stand the 'sportif' performance of the average Maltese taxi driver) or sitting on a hard bench seat in the mess cinema or getting a thick head in the bar. I didn't know how it started but almost all aircrew began growing beards apart from Cedric, Peter and myself, and there was a lot of muttering into these hairy appendages when ordered to shave them off three weeks later.

With the coming of April there was no let up in the flying both day and night except for the odd Sunday. On 4 April I was photographing the flight dive-bombing of Filfla with a big F15 camera when Sub Lt Hodgkinson radioed that his engine was on fire and that he was going to ditch. Peter followed him down and I photographed the whole of the ditching sequence from the first impact when the flaps broke off to when the crew were clambering out of their cockpits to haul in the dinghy on the end of its lanyard. We stayed around until the RAF Air Sea Rescue launch arrived to pick them up.

After a mine laying exercise to Tripoli on 5 April the squadron carried out a dummy dive-bombing strike on Syracuse harbour on the morning of the 6th, with strafing by escorting Corsairs. On the way back I picked up a call on my VHF that one of the Corsair pilots was having to bale out and I saw him floating down some miles behind. Shortly after landing Peter and I took off as part of a search for the pilot. We didn't expect too much difficulty in locating him as his position was reasonably well established, but after three hours we all returned without finding him. I felt very upset and Peter and I took off again and carried out a progressing search at 500 feet using aluminium markers to ensure an accurate coverage. We kept this up for another three hours without success. A night search was organised from which Sub Lt Jack Birch and his observer Sub Lt Dave Robbins and TAG L/A Ham Hamill failed to return. I had now lost two of my ex-pupils from the 63rd Observer Course and for the first time in the war the loss depressed me. They all seemed so young.

The following day was a significant milestone in the war in the Pacific: US Navy dive- and torpedo-bombers sank the massive new Japanese battleship *Yamamoto,* thus completing the destruction of all major units of the Japanese Navy which, in its own way, was to reflect on the future utilisation of the Barracuda. I might have saved myself a lot of anguish had I known this.

By now we had turned our hand to dive-bombing a target towed by an old Italian destroyer. I was sent aboard this ship one evening in Grand Harbour to co-ordinate the squadron's first and, I think, only attempt at night dive-bombing. It was all delightfully comic opera. I have no Italian and they had little English but by the time I had knocked back a few glasses of Marsala in the Captain's cabin we seemed to be getting on famously. It was a bit chilly up on the open bridge but there was a general air of noisy jollification all around. The target was streamed and its bow wave could just be seen in the darkness, it didn't seem much to aim at. The boys arrived overhead more or less on time, only detectable by their engine noise. I flashed a green Aldis light in their general direction, and the sky was lit up by a descending lopsided curtain of flares followed by a rising engine note and then the unmistakable whistle of a bomb which hit the water with a sharp crack close alongside. When I looked around I found myself quite alone on the bridge and it was some time before I persuaded anyone to return, by which time the boys overhead had departed and I was quite unable to assess the results of their efforts. The only thing left to do was finish off the bottle of Marsala, too sweet and sickly for my taste, but strong enough to induce demonstrative affection between ex enemies.

Friday the 13th lived up to its reputation. Peter and I were up with the boys knocking hell out of Filfla with 250 lb SAP bombs, the first time we had dropped the real thing. On the way down on our last dive a more than usually excited Peter came on the intercom announcing that there was something wrong with the elevator controls. There was nothing for me to do but pray, but somehow, at times like this it never occurred to me — I had the usual feeling that it wasn't really happening. That we levelled out a few hundred feet above the sea was just another of my lucky escapes. The flying control locks [fitted on the ground to prevent the control surfaces from sustaining wind damage] were kept in a special canvas bag in my cockpit. They had worked loose and partially jammed the elevator controls.

With all this dive-bombing the weakness in the Barracuda wing was becoming increasingly apparent, rivets were pulling and top skins could be seen to have gaps where they should have been butted together. Cedric couldn't hide the fact that he was worried and the morale of the squadron was not what it should have been.

It was at this time that I have to report an action which later I came to realise was foolish. I wrote a letter to Captain Neame in which I expressed a lack of confidence in the Barracuda being of any operational use in the Far East and suggested that we be re-equipped with Fireflies. [It is ironic that the squadron was re-equipped with Firefly FR1s in February 1946.] Cedric knew all about the letter and he should have stopped me sending it but he was even younger than I and was undoubtedly feeling the strain of the prolonged working up. He was even more aware than I of the deficiencies of our aircraft. Who the Hell did I think I was? What did I expect the Captain to do about it? He certainly wasn't the first carrier Captain to be saddled with inadequate aircraft. The repercussions were some weeks in making themselves felt and there was no acknowledgement that my letter had been received.

At the end of the week we started packing and all eighteen aircraft flew on board on 23 April. Cedric caused quite a stir when he reported to Commander (F) that the state of most of the aircraft's wings made them unsafe for operational use.

The ship's doctor assigned to the aircrew (a recent innovation) called me to his cabin and asked me my opinion of the squadron's morale. I told him that I was surprised that, with all the concentrated flying during the nearly year-long working up, we had had so few accidents. I was, however, fearful of the future and if there was not some let up — or some real action — I thought that morale might sink dangerously low. Was I, perhaps, fearful for myself but not prepared to admit it?

The upshot of all this was the grounding of our aircraft until the ribs around the wing camera recess had been strengthened, and seven days leave in Sicily for all aircrew. The leave turned out a never-to-be-forgotten experience. How could it be otherwise in Taormina? Probably the most beautiful place in the whole of Sicily, and staying at the magnificent San Domenico hotel, not so long ago the headquarters of General Kesselring when in command of all Axis forces in the Mediterranean.

Peter and I left with the first batch on 30 April, sailing to Catania at the extraordinary speed of forty knots in a brand new Italian destroyer. It had a narrow beam and rolled mightily, so that we had to sit with our feet braced against a mess table; it was rather like being on a fairground ride. Our arrival at Catania was a bit of a pantomime. We came in too fast and rammed the jetty at an acute angle. Officers on the bridge lent over and shouted at ratings on the deck and ratings shouted back, arms were waved about or hands clasped to heads in anguish, as the ship drifted aimlessly, engines stopped. Great stuff.

The road winds for thirty miles along the coast to Taormina, with the sea on the right and Mount Etna dominating the scene all the way on the left with a wisp of smoke rising from its top, nearly 11,000 feet up. Taormina lies at its foot, perched well up on a hillside with narrow roads winding up and down between the low, flat-roofed, white painted dwellings and shops which are to be found everywhere in the Mediterranean. The sun cast sharp shadows, and everywhere there was a unique and pleasing odour of dried orange peel.

For such a small place there was an abundance of luxurious hotels discreetly situated at all the best vantage points. We were all split up between them, Peter and I sharing a lovely room in the San Domenico, tiled throughout and with an enormous marble bath. The gardens were ablaze with spring flowers and in all directions from balconies and verandas, the view was enchanting. Transport took us down to bathe in the crystal clear, deep water off a shingly beach surrounded by rocks. The water in May was cold, but what joy to come out into the warm sunshine.

Meals were served in the dining room as though we were the grandest of tourists. There were bars to visit at night which stayed open until all hours and there were dark Sicilian girls who I was told, were accommodating all night, as they must also have been for the Germans. It was now nine months since they had been driven out of Sicily and the only evidence of their having been in Taormina was the graffiti on the walls of an observation post cut into the hillside, some 1,500 feet up and a stiff climb up a narrow path on a hot day.

The Sicilian folk seemed friendly enough and claimed no love for the Germans but we must have seemed like just another set of invaders from whom they were keen to extract what money they could. They were clearly very poor.

Although the Eighth Army had passed through en route to Messina, the ravages of war seemed happily to have missed this paradise, loved equally I imagine by the Romans who had built there a small theatre in a hollow surrounded by Cypress trees and looking as though it was awaiting their return.

Before my week was over I developed a raging fever and was carted off by ambulance to a British services hospital in Messina where I was kept in bed in a large, airy, private room for a week with no one to talk to and nothing to do but read. And nobody seemed to know what was the matter with me. My only visitor was a swarthy Sicilian who came in to shave me with a cut-throat razor, which made me uneasy as he looked like a cut-throat himself.

I was there on 8 May when the war in Europe ended. An anti-climax as far as I was concerned, but later I was to hear of the sometimes more than lively goings-on back on *Vengeance* which, with the rest of the fleet, was all lit up at night and it is said that some of the wilder characters tried to push a Barracuda over the side (an unconfirmed story).

Messina is not much of a place. While recuperating I sat almost alone on a long stretch of sand looking over the straits to Italy and recalled the trials and tribulations of Virgil's *Aeneas* which meant so much to me at the age of fifteen. I was feeling washed out and lonely with no letters from the gorgeous girl.

After nearly two weeks I was declared fit and put aboard the Africano Scipiano, a brand new Italian light cruiser. Light was the right word for it, the top structure was built almost entirely of aluminium, including the 20mm gun mountings. We sailed down the dramatic Sicilian coastline at forty knots, the stern settled down in the water like that of a destroyer. The captain was a grim fellow, unlike any Italian I had met so far, and said to still be a fascist.

Arriving back in Grand Harbour I found that *Vengeance* was at Kalafrana creek and I made my way there by taxi, to find hardly anybody on board. The other half of the squadron was nearing the end of its seven days at Taormina and the rest were skylarking ashore. Rumour had it that we were preparing to sail within a few days for the Far East.

The following day Cedric told me that I was to report to the captain's quarters. My ill-advised letter had finally caught up with me. I didn't even know where the captain's quarters were. When I arrived Captain Neame was sitting behind his desk with Cedric and Commander Fenwick to one side. He opened the brief proceedings saying that he failed to understand how a junior Lieutenant could have the experience to pass the opinions expressed in my letter. There was a silence and a response was clearly expected. I said that I appreciated that I was only a junior Lieutenant but that I had had more operational experience than most aircrew on the ship and that my views on the Barracuda were justified both by events and the experience of the US Navy in the Pacific. After another silence and a piercing scrutiny by the Captain, Commander Fenwick spoke flatteringly about my past record and current performance. Finally Captain Neame announced that arrangements were being made to send me back to the UK. And that was that.

Was this what I had intended when I wrote that damn fool letter? What had I really expected to happen? I no longer know. I can only remember feeling numb and confused as I packed up my kit. The boys must have thought that I was deserting them at a time when I should have been setting an example. It remains as an episode in my life of which I am ashamed and has been painful to put down in print.

Thank God there were few aboard to see me go. I spent the next few days at a services transit hotel in Valetta. I wasn't even aware that

Vengeance sailed for Australia on 22 May in company with *Venerable* and *Glory*. Nor was I aware that on 1 May the Navy had ceased torpedo training for Barracudas as their Lordships had decided that such few targets as were left afloat in the Far East could now be dealt with by dive-bombing. The squadrons were given permission to operate their aircraft without a TAG and to strip his cockpit of W/T and guns to save weight as I had previously recommended but been scorned.

It is interesting to reflect that only 16 torpedo armed Barracudas ever carried out operational attacks in two missions off the Norwegian coast. This shows how difficult it had become for the Admiralty to adapt its aircraft equipment and training programmes to the rapidly changing scenario.

Thankfully *Vengeance* and the boys on board never saw action. After passing through the Suez Canal they arrived at Ceylon and flew ashore to Katukurunda in monsoon weather early in June where the aircraft were modified to take long range fuel tanks and RATOG (Rocket Assisted Take-off) which was necessary to get a fully loaded Barra into the air in tropical temperatures. With the change in the intended operational use of the Barra six Observers and TAGs were sent back to the UK. It seemed that there was no hurry to get to the war as they were there for a full month, finally sailing for Australia on 7 July and arriving at Jervis Bay, Sydney on the 22nd. The squadron flew ashore and two weeks later the first atomic bomb was dropped on Hiroshima which signalled the end of World War II. Instead of celebrating on VJ Day, 15 August, the ship sailed north spending ten miserable days in the heat of Manus Island, and arriving at Hong Kong on 5 September where the aircrew assisted in alleviating the chaos and misery left behind by the Japanese.

Chapter 17
Finale

At the time 812 Squadron was flying ashore at Trincomalee I was arriving by courtesy of the Merchant Navy at Liverpool docks, having spent most of the voyage suffering from Gyppy tummy. It was many years before my guts recovered from the onslaughts of war and booze.

I was home again and a very happy wife received the news before I made my way down to RNAS Lee-on-Solent (HMS *Daedalus*) where I had instructions to report to the PMO [Principal Medical Officer]. I had already guessed that I was to come before the dreaded 'Twitch' board. Well, I only had myself to blame, and if I was 'twitched', I didn't feel it.

I was put through a lengthy medical, which included what I assumed, by his charm, to be a 'trick cyclist' and was pronounced A1B [Fit for flying duties].

Then came the dodgy bit — the Board — which as far as I recall, comprised a Commander with three or four Lieutenant Commanders. I was lucky that one of these was 'Willy' Wroughton, CO of 800 Squadron on *Indomitable,* who remembered me from those days. It turned out to be a surprisingly friendly affair during which I was asked about my time with 18 Squadron in North Africa and about my views on the Barracuda with which they all seemed to agree. The Commander asked me what I would prefer to do next (not a question I had ever expected in the Navy) and I replied that I would like to be posted to an operational Firefly squadron. By this time I felt much better and they despatched me on leave in good heart. I think I really deserved more 'flak' for my foolishness. I never got a chance to apologise to 'Spike' Regan, who as senior 'O', had to take a lot of 'flak' after my departure from Vengeance.

And so it was back to the comforts of my in-law's house in Newcastle-on-Tyne where my fifteen-month-old son wasn't too keen on the strange man kissing his mother. Although the blackout had gone, rationing was as severe as ever. There was talk of an election and my sympathy with Socialism was ill received.

Most felt that the war with Japan would go on for at least another year, although the desperation of the Japanese was shown by their adoption of suicide attacks on the Allied fleets, which were now closing in on mainland Japan. With a twinge of conscience I sometimes wondered how the boys were getting on in *Vengeance.*

At the end of June I received my final posting to join 703 Squadron at the Naval Air Sea Warfare Development Unit at RAF Thorney Island in Hampshire. This was a trials unit commanded by Lieutenant Commander J. H. 'Jimmy' Dundas RN, in which anti-shipping and anti-submarine tactics were developed using all the latest operational aircraft. All the flying personnel were old hands and none below the rank of Lieutenant. Except for the CO all were RNVR, and most of them married.

The station had the excellent accommodation provided for all the pre-war RAF permanent establishments. I had a comfortable room all to myself and we ate and drank well. For the first week I was given nothing to do so I persuaded one of the RAF Squadron Leaders to take me up in a Mosquito FB VI in order to fulfil a long felt longing to fly in de Havilland's greatest glory. I hadn't been so excited about flying for a long time as I climbed in beside the pilot and strapped myself into the unfamiliar shoulder harness. With the thrust of two 1230 hp Rolls-Royce Merlin 21 engines pressing me into the back of my seat, our take-off felt more like that off a carrier's booster. And what a view. The propellers almost clipped the short nose in front of us. I wondered how one got out of the kite if in a hurry; there was no sliding canopy, so I assumed one attempted to exit through the small door on the starboard side, close to my feet,which we had used to climb into the beast. I kept such macabre thoughts to myself, after all this was just a joyride.

It turned out to be another of those days in which I got more excitement than I had bargained for. After cavorting around the sky at over 300 knots, rolling and looping, he shut down one engine and feathered the propeller before completing a few more dives and rolls.

'How did you like that?' he said with a grin.

'Bloody marvellous!'

'Ready to go back?'

'OK with me!'

He pressed the wrong feathering button and we ended up over Chichester at 2000 feet with no engines and the ground coming up very fast indeed. The engines coughed into life after a windmilling start when we were down to about 500 feet. Dodgy. By any previous standard we came into land very fast — 110 knots over the runway threshold, the cruising speed of a Barracuda.

It came as a surprise to find that most of my flying during the next six months was in Mosquitoes. Mosquitoes on an aircraft carrier? It made the mind boggle. During August we began making trial rocket attacks at varying dive angles on an old wreck off the coast of West Wittering, seeking the best technique for aiming these deadly weapons which suffered considerable gravity drop effect when fired at shallow dive angles.

In mid-August came the almost unbelievable news of the dropping of the atomic bomb on Japan and within days the war was over. Nearly six years of my life. I had made no plans at all for the future, perhaps thinking it would have been tempting fate. I had never really believed that it would ever end and when it came it was disconcerting.

We all went off on a week's leave to celebrate. It was mid-summer and the three of us spent most days on the beach at Whitley Bay making sand castles and retrieving Kenneth Michael from the sea into which he was determined to crawl at a fast rate of knots.

As there had been no sign of the Navy releasing its amateur airmen I decided to look for somewhere for us to live together near Thorney Island. My efforts in this direction were delayed by being sent once more on a course at RNAS Burscough, this time on the ASV 'X' and ANAPS4 'ASH' radars which were now entering service.

ASV 'X' was fitted to the Barracuda III. This was a very effective centimetric wavelength radar with a rotating scanner fitted in a blister below the rear fuselage and giving the sort of all round picture now so familiar on all radar screens. We flew initially in the dear old Anson flying class rooms and then, with little enthusiasm, in the their Barracuda IIIs. With this set I was able to pick up a submarine's snorkel when the sea wasn't too rough and with a responder fitted to a carrier you could easily locate it at over 100 miles. Suddenly navigation had become a whole new ball game.

'ASH' was an American designed centimetric radar fitted to the Firefly, Sea Mosquito, and to various fighter aircraft; the latter for airborne interception. Fully integrated into a unit about the size of a 500 lb bomb, it had a forward scanning aerial which gave a clear picture over a broad arc ahead of the aircraft with individual target discrimination and presented on a small, but very clear, cathode tube with a brown instead of green background. It was sheer delight to fly in a Firefly fitted with ASH. With its four cannons, relatively high speed, good range and bomb load, it seemed to be just what the doctor ordered. On a foggy day, and there were many at Burscough, I could use ASH to navigate up the Ribble estuary and then pick up the airfield runways on the screen.

But now, as far as I was concerned, it was all a bit academic. I wasn't really sure why they wanted to keep us flying — although drawing flying pay at fifteen shillings a day was some incentive for a married man with a family.

No sooner was I back at Thorney Island than I had my final spectacular prang. On the morning of 6 September I went up in our new Barracuda III with Lt 'Gus' Halliday as a pilot to check out the ASV 'X'. Returning to the airfield the engine caught fire, probably due to a broken exhaust stub, and within a few seconds the engine seized. Gus made a valiant attempt to make a dead stick landing on the airfield but we stalled and spun into the shallow water quarter of a mile from the main runway. It flashed through my mind that this was the day the dreaded Barra was finally to get me. I was already standing up, braced against the frontal structure of the cockpit, when we cartwheeled through the water, shearing off both wings and the whole of the rear fuselage behind me. Following the rasping noise of tearing metal came that too well remembered silence. It was only the chill of the water lapping around my neck that convinced me that I was alive and that I ought to be getting out before the kite sank. In fact it was sitting in the mud and I have no recollection of getting out although the photograph of the wreck shows the observer's canopy closed but the observer's windscreen displaced to the port side. We were picked up fairly quickly by a launch and were both able to climb into it. As far as I could tell I was unhurt, Gus had head injuries and was taken to hospital.

Surprisingly the doctor on the launch allowed me to be driven to the Mess after asking me to report to the sick bay for a check-up sometime in the afternoon. I stripped off my wet clothes, had a long hot bath and got into bed, feeling suddenly very tired and shivering uncontrollably. I awoke four hours later. It was tea-time, so I dressed and went down to the mess for some tea. An RAF type asked me if I had heard of the poor buggers who had pranged a Barracuda. I replied that I was one of the poor buggers. He said he was surprised that anyone got out of it alive. I said so was I.

Sick Bay gave me what I thought was a fairly casual check over. It was ten years later that an osteopath put my spine back into shape and restored me to a fully fit person. My medical experiences in the war had not been of the happiest.

On a brighter note I managed to rent a bungalow on the shoreline at Bracklesham Bay. 'Sea Spray' it was called, a wooden building raised some feet off the ground, quite large and comfortable. Joan and our first-born arrived down in the October. I drew our meat ration from the Mess butcher and we ate very well. For the first time I was able to play at being a father. To get to and from the airfield I was mad enough to buy a 1000 cc Matchless motorcycle from Ken Horsefield, a member of the squadron. I had never ridden a motorcycle and this monster should have been attached to a sidecar and not ridden solo. If it fell over on its side it was too heavy for me to pick up and trying to pull it back onto its stand it frequently did so. Driving it through the winter ice was probably more dangerous than flying in a Barracuda.

I went up once more in a Barracuda to carry out a sono-buoy trial just to show the beastly kite that it couldn't beat me. The CO asked me to carry out a dive-bombing trial using the ASV 'X' to come down through cloud.

Feeling thoroughly bolshie I told him he could stuff flying in Barras as far as I was concerned, but would fly in any other aircraft. He didn't think that this was the right attitude for an officer in His Majesty's Navy but he didn't press the matter and I never flew in one again. Not that there wasn't plenty of unsought excitement ahead.

The squadron had now received the first TR37 Sea Mosquitoes fitted with ASH radar in the nose and I took part in extensive dive-bombing tests in which the dive angle was increased stage by stage up to 70 degrees, approaching the target on radar and going into a wing over to enter the dive and then checking the angle on an inclinometer. Diving speed was limited to 380 knots, but we were often close to blacking out during the pull out. My pilot was usually Lt 'Mike' Langman, and on one of these trips Lt 'Jimmy' Harrap in the Mosquito ahead of us got into an almost vertical dive and pulled its wings off. We also lost a Seafire pilot around this time. More funerals, more 'Last Posts'. So this was peace.

Torpedo attack trials using the Nab Tower, or at one time the liner *Queen Mary,* as target, proved equally arduous. During the diving approaches I used the radar to locate and range the target and this involved leaning forward to keep my eyes in the rubber visor of it's display console and holding my hands under my chin to prevent my head sagging as we pulled out of the dive. My back began to feel as though it had been kicked but I felt no desire to have anything more to do with service docs.

My nerves were further frayed when we were forced to land on one engine after a propeller failure and on another occasion we hit a seagull which penetrated the wing as far back as the main spar causing alarming vibration. I began to feel that it was the Mosquito and not the Barracuda which was out to get me, particularly the day we flew up north to RAF Ashington to collect some zero length rocket launchers (which offered less drag than our long launching rails). The Mosquito was prone to swing on take-off if differential throttle was not carefully applied. This day the swing became uncontrollable and we shot off the runway, bouncing and bumping on the rough grass and heading straight towards the substantial hangar buildings. Halfway there we got airborne and cleared the top of the hangars by only a few feet. Perhaps somebody was looking after me although I was now beginning to find it difficult to see the joke. I was enjoying family life.

We arrived at Ashington to find a squadron of Gloster Meteor jets based there. It was exciting to see and hear a jet aircraft for the first time but I was disappointed in the lack of elegance in it's design. It never occurred to me then that I would spend much of my working life on the design of gas turbine engines.

After packing the crates of launchers in the rear hatch I 'phoned my parents and asked them to look out for us on the way back. Only minutes later we were circling the house in a vertical bank and I could see two figures waving in the garden. An hour later we were back at Thorney having our legs pulled about our unorthodox take-off.

I got an urgent call from my wife to get back home as a sea mine had been washed up into the foot of our garden and she had had to evacuate the house when a Navy bomb disposal team came to deal with it. Later we had the team in for tea, just young boys who laughed and joked about it all and who were all killed in a similar operation some weeks later.

In December Lt Cdr 'Dizzy' Womack — ex Senior 'O' in 831 back in my days on *Indomitable* — came down from NA2 SL in London to ask me whether I would be prepared to stay on in the Navy with an appointment as Assistant Operations Officer on the *Magnificent,* the first Canadian aircraft carrier. I have no idea why he chose me, I would have thought that my 'flimsy' showed that I was an awkward character. Even the temptation of a half ring on my sleeve was not enough to persuade me. I told him that I was tired of it all and wanted to be back in Civvy Street as soon as possible. What I really meant was that I wanted to get out before I got killed. I expect I lacked the grace to thank him properly for the offer and for taking the trouble to come and see me.

We spent a cold but happy Christmas at 'Sea Spray' for which I was talked into de-gutting a chicken for the first and last time. Kenneth Michael, now just beginning to string more than two words together, managed to knock back a glass of gin when our backs were turned in the local pub. It seemed a rather early preparation for joining the service but like me, he ended up a sort of engineer.

My last flying assignment was the development of techniques for using anti-submarine 'sonobuoys' from an Avenger II liaising with an RAF team using Wellingtons. The sonobuoys were as yet unreliable and my heart really wasn't in it. In the first week of January 1946, I was climbing down from a Wellington outside our crew room when someone shouted to me that my de-mob papers had come through. I gave the Wellington's big tyre a kick as I passed and thought to Hell with the navy and all aeroplanes.

I didn't mean it. I loved it all.

Bibliography

Sea Flight, Hugh Popham (William Kimber)
Pedestal, Peter C. Smith (William Kimber)
Turns of Fate, Ken Dimbleby (William Kimber)
The Most Dangerous Moment, Michael Tomlinson (William Kimber)
Fighting Admiral, Captain Donald Macintyre (Evans Brothers)
Hurricane, Adrian Stewart (William Kimber)
Wings at Sea, Gerard A. Woods (Conway)
Fairey Barracuda, David Brown (Profile Publications)
The Second World War, Winston S. Churchill (Cassell)
The Squadrons of the Fleet Air Arm, Ray Sturtivant (Air-Britain)
Triumph over Tunisia, Wing Cdr T. H. Wisdom (Allen and Unwin)
Japanese Naval Aces and Fighter Units, Ikuhiko Hata & Yasuho Izawa
    (Airlife)

Appendix 1
831 Squadron (1941-1942)

Pilot	Observer
Lt Cdr P. L. Mortimer, RN (CO)	Lt D. K. Buchanan-Dunlop, RN (SO)
Lt A. S. Kennard, RN	Lt Cdr A. L. O. E. Wilkinson, RANR
Lt B. C. Willoughby, RN *	S/Lt G. T. Shaddick, RN*
Lt R. Hutchinson, RNVR	Lt H. D. H. Womack, RNVR
S/Lt T. W. May, SANR	S/Lt G. C. Marley, RNVR
S/Lt J. L. Fisher, RNVR	S/Lt K. G. Wallace, RNVR
S/Lt M. H. Meredith, RNVR	S/Lt W. L. Protheroe, RNVR**
S/Lt J. D. M. Harris, RNVR	S/Lt V. E. Tucker, RNVR
S/Lt R. J. Colston, RNVR	S/Lt S. G. Green, RNVR
S/Lt D. Brooks, RNVR	S/Lt G. D. Smith, RNVR
S/Lt E. S. Morrell, RNVR	S/Lt D. S. Miller, RNVR
Lt W. E. T. White, RNVR	S/Lt D. Evans, RNVR
S/Lt T. J. Turner, RNVR	S/Lt T. Weston, RNVR
S/Lt J. M. Brigden, RNVR	S/Lt M. E. Radford, RNVR
S/Lt D. P. R. Moore, RNVR	S/Lt E. Hyndman, RNVR
Lt B. P. Hunter, RCNVR	

* Missing, presumed killed, off Java on anti-submarine patrol, 28 January 1942.
** Killed by bomb in wardroom, 12 August 1942

Appendix 2
18 Squadron RAF

Attack on Axis airfield pm — 4 December 1942 (Map 7)

CREW LIST
(* ex 614 Squadron)

Aircraft/Squadron	Aircrew		Awards
'W' BA 875 (18)	W/Cdr H. G. Malcolm	Pilot Killed	VC
	P/O J. Robb	Nav Killed	
	P/O J. Grant	WOP/AG Killed	DFC
'Y' BA 734 (614)	P/O W. H. Irving	Pilot *	
	F/O L. A. Quevatre	Nav *	
	Sgt J. A. Limoges	WOP/AG *	
'D' BA 796 (13)	Sgt W. G. Stott	Pilot Killed	
	F/O W. Gent	Nav Killed	
	Sgt G. A. Booty	WOP/AG Killed	
'D' BA 800 (614)	F/Lt A. Breakey	Pilot Killed	
	F/Sgt A. W. Simpson	Nav Killed	
	F/Sgt S. H. Green	WOP/AG Killed	
'J' BA 325 (614)	P/O G. W. Sims	Pilot	
	F/Sgt S. Litchfield	Nav	
	F/Sgt C. Cosens	WOP/AG	
'H' BA 790 (18)	S/Ldr. R. Eyton-Williams	Pilot Killed	
	F/Lt C. Dent	Nav/Obs Killed	
	F/F/Sgt D. Franklyn	WOP/AG Killed	
'N' BA 795 (18)	P/O E. J. Holloway	Pilot	DFC
	Sub/Lt (A) K. G. Wallace	Obs Injured	
	Sgt H. G. Parsloe	WOP/AG Injured	
'N' BA 869 (614)	F/O C. H. Georges	Pilot * Killed	
	F/Sgt J. Taylor	Nav/B * Killed	
	Sgt W. M. Sorbie	WOP/AG * Killed	

Aircraft/Squadron	Aircrew		Awards
'Q' BA 820 (18)	F/Lt A. W. Eller	Pilot	DFC
	P/O A. F. Harding	Nav Injured	
	P/O N. C. Eckersley	WOP/AG Injured	DFC
'Y' BA 862 (13)	P/O R. D. Hill	Pilot Killed	
	F/Sgt S. F. B. Bryant	Nav/B Killed	
	F/Sgt C. A. Green	WOP/AG Killed	

Appendix 3
812 Squadron (1944-1945)

Pilot	Observer
Lt Cdr C. R. Coxon, RN (CO))	Lt M. F. A. Regan, RN (SO)
Lt P. Poole, RNVR	Lt K. G. Wallace, RNVR
Lt S. F. Bristow, RNVR	Lt R. T. Tobias, RNVR
Lt C. R. Wintringham, RNZNVR	Lt T. S. Dewsnap, RNVR
S/Lt D. Smallwood, RNVR	S/Lt R. W. Roseveare, RNVR
S/Lt P. G. Throssel, RNVR	S/Lt R. Spencer, RNVR
S/Lt L. H. Terry, RNVR	S/Lt J. I. R. Trethowan, RNVR
S/Lt J. Dickson, RNVR	S/Lt D. V. Brook, RNVR
S/Lt R. Burns, RNVR	S/Lt R. H. Hill, RNVR
S/Lt J. B. Cookson, RNVR	S/Lt F. W. Wright, RNVR
S/Lt J. E. Digby, SANF	S/Lt W. A. Broad, RNVR
S/Lt G. R. Pain, RNVR	S/Lt E. M. Fisher, RNVR
S/Lt J. S. Birch, RNVR ***	S/Lt D. Robbins, RNVR ***
S/Lt J. E. Fisher, RNVR	S/Lt P. T. Stansfield, RNVR
S/Lt A. H. F. Muncer, RNVR **	S/Lt H. W. F. Saggs, RNVR
P/O Slater, RNVR	S/Lt D. A. Richards, RNVR
P/O Hunt, RNVR **	S/Lt Crosthwaite, RNVR **
P/O S. Blakey, RNVR *	S/Lt F. W. Alexander, RNVR
S/Lt A. Y. Balfour, RNVR	S/Lt S. T. Onslow, RNVR
S/Lt D.E. Fairweather, RNVR	S/Lt J. J. White, RNVR
S/Lt R. Taylor, RNVR	S/Lt A. D. Brown, RNVR
S/Lt R. F. Panton, RNVR	S/Lt W. F. R. Williams, RNVR
S/Lt S. Marriott, RNVR	S/Lt R. H. F. Wyeth, RNVR
S/Lt G. Hodgkinson, RNVR	S/Lt R. T. Boston, RNVR
S/Lt H. E. Johnson, RNVR	S/Lt D. R. Kennedy, RNVR
S/Lt A. H. Rushbrook, RNZNVR	S/Lt A. G. Cross, RNVR
S/Lt A. Fyles, RNVR	
S/Lt P. R. Collis-Squires, RNVR	
S/Lt R. D. Ashton, RNVR	

* Killed in accident at Crail, 18.7.44
** Killed in accident at Fearn, 25.11.44
*** Missing, presumed killed on exercise at Malta, 6.4.45

Appendix 4
Typical Air Search Plot

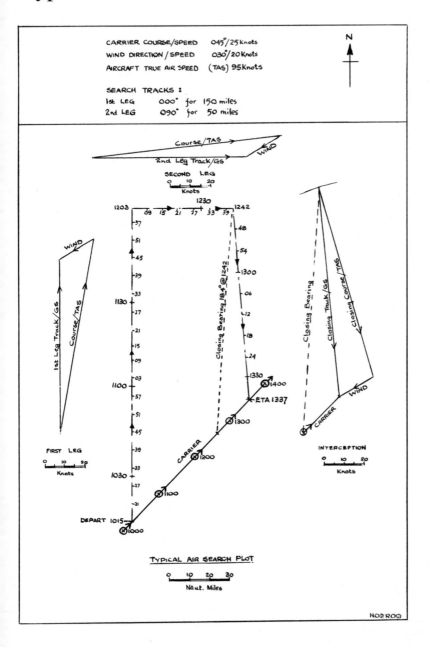

CARRIER COURSE/SPEED   045°/25 knots
WIND DIRECTION/SPEED   030°/20 Knots
AIRCRAFT TRUE AIR SPEED (TAS) 95 Knots

SEARCH TRACKS :
1st LEG   000° for 150 miles
2nd LEG   090° for 50 miles

N

Course/TAS
WIND
2nd Leg Track/GS
SECOND LEG
0   10   20
Knots

1203   09   15   21   27   33   39   1242
-57   1230
-51   -48
-45   -54
-39   1300
-33   -06
1130   -27   -12
-21   -18
-15   -24
-09   1330
-03   1400
1100   -57   ETA 1337
-51   1300
-45
FIRST LEG   -39   CARRIER   1200
0   10   20   -33
Knots   1030   -27
-21
DEPART 1015   1100
1000

WIND
1st Leg Track/GS
Course/TAS

Closing Bearing 184° @ 1242

Closing Bearing
Closing Track/GS
Closing Course/TAS
WIND
CARRIER

INTERCEPTION
0   10   20
Knots

TYPICAL AIR SEARCH PLOT
0   10   20   30
Naut. Miles

NODROG

Index